Volume 2 Topics 9-16

Authors

Randall I. Charles
Professor Emeritus
Department of Mathematics
San Jose State University
San Jose, California

Janet H. Caldwell
Professor of Mathematics
Rowan University
Glassboro, New Jersey

Juanita Copley
Professor Emerita, College of Education
University of Houston
Houston, Texas

Warren Crown
Professor Emeritus of Mathematics
Education
Graduate School of Education
Rutgers University
New Brunswick, New Jersey

Francis (Skip) Fennell
L. Stanley Bowlsbey Professor
of Education and Graduate and
Professional Studies
McDaniel College
Westminster, Maryland

Stuart J. Murphy
Visual Learning Specialist
Boston, Massachusetts

Kay B. Sammons
Coordinator of Elementary Mathematics
Howard County Public Schools
Ellicott City, Maryland

Jane F. Schielack
Professor of Mathematics
Associate Dean for Assessment and
Pre K-12 Education, College of Science
Texas A&M University
College Station, Texas

Mathematicians

Roger Howe
Professor of Mathematics
Yale University
New Haven, Connecticut

Gary Lippman
Professor of Mathematics and Computer
Science
California State University East Bay
Hayward, California

PEARSON

Glenview, Illinois   Boston, Massachusetts   Chandler, Arizona   Upper Saddle River, New Jersey

Contributing Authors

Zachary Champagne
District Facilitator, Duval County Public Schools
Florida Center for Research in Science,
Technology, Engineering, and Mathematics
(FCR-STEM)
Jacksonville, Florida

Jonathan A. Wray
Mathematics Instructional Facilitator
Howard County Public Schools
Ellicott City, Maryland

ELL Consultants

Janice Corona
Retired Administrator
Dallas ISD, Multi-Lingual Department
Dallas, Texas

Jim Cummins
Professor
The University of Toronto
Toronto, Canada

Texas Reviewers

Theresa Bathe
Teacher
Fort Bend ISD

Chrissy Beltran
School Wide Project Coordinator
Ysleta ISD

Renee Cutright
Teacher
Amarillo ISD

Sharon Grimm
Teacher
Houston ISD

Esmeralda Herrera
Teacher
San Antonio ISD

Sherry Johnson
Teacher
Round Rock ISD

Elvia Lopez
Teacher
Denton ISD

Antoinese Pride
Instructional Coach
Dallas ISD

Joanna Ratliff
Teacher
Keller ISD

Courtney Jo Ridehuber
Teacher
Mansfield ISD

Nannie D. Scurlock-McKnight
Mathematics Specialist
A.W. Brown Fellowship-Leadership Academy
Dallas, TX

Brian Sinclair
Math Instructional Specialist
Fort Worth ISD

ISBN-13: 978-0-328-76725-0
ISBN-10: 0-328-76725-5

10 V003 17 16

Look for these digital resources in every lesson!

Digital Resources

 Go to PearsonTexas.com

 Solve
Solve & Share problems plus math tools

 Learn
Visual Learning Animation Plus with animation, interaction, and math tools

A-Z **Glossary**
Animated Glossary in English and Spanish

 Tools
Math Tools to help you understand

 Check
Quick Check for each lesson

 Games
Math Games to help you learn

eText
The pages in your book online

PearsonTexas.com
Everything you need for math anytime, anywhere

Key

Number and Operations

Algebraic Reasoning

Geometry and Measurement

Data Analysis

Personal Financial Literacy

Mathematical Process Standards are found in all lessons.

Digital Resources at PearsonTexas.com

Solve

Learn

A-Z Glossary

Check

Tools

Games

And remember the pages in your book are also online!

Contents

⭐ Topics

Volume I

TOPIC 1 — Numbers 0 to 5

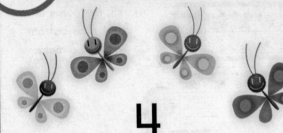

4

Hi, my name is Alex. You can use numbers to show the number of objects.

⭐ TEKS K.1A, K.1B, K.1C, K.1D, K.1E, K.1F, K.1G, K.2, K.2A, K.2B, K.2C, K.2D, K.2I

TOPIC 2 — Comparing Numbers 0 to 5

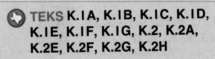

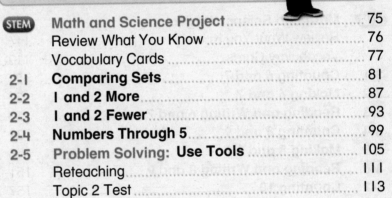

Hi, my name is Marta. There are more forks than plates when you compare.

⭐ TEKS K.1A, K.1B, K.1C, K.1D, K.1E, K.1F, K.1G, K.2, K.2A, K.2E, K.2F, K.2G, K.2H

TOPIC 3

Numbers 6 to 10

Hi, my name is Jackson. You can show the parts that make the whole.

⭐ **TEKS** K.1A, K.1B, K.1C, K.1D, K.1E, K.1F, K.1G, K.2, K.2A, K.2B, K.2C, K.2I

TOPIC 4

Comparing Numbers 0 to 10

6
8

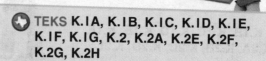

Hi, my name is Emily. The bottom set has 2 more.

⭐ **TEKS** K.1A, K.1B, K.1C, K.1D, K.1E, K.1F, K.1G, K.2, K.2A, K.2E, K.2F, K.2G, K.2H

TOPIC 5 — Numbers to 20

nineteen

Hi, my name is Carlos. I counted 19 objects and wrote 19.

TEKS K.1A, K.1B, K.1C, K.1D, K.1E, K.1F, K.1G, K.2, K.2A, K.2B, K.2C, K.2E, K.2F, K.2G, K.2H

TOPIC 6 — Numbers to 30

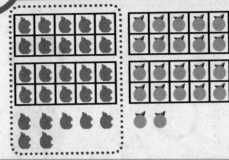

Hi, my name is Jada. There are more apples than oranges.

TEKS K.1A, K.1B, K.1C, K.1D, K.1E, K.1F, K.1G, K.2, K.2A, K.2B, K.2C, K.2F, K.2G

TOPIC 7

Understanding Addition

Hi, my name is Daniel. You can use addition to show joining groups.

★ TEKS **K.IA, K.IB, K.IC, K.ID, K.IE, K.IF, K.IG, K.3, K.3A, K.3B, K.3C**

TOPIC 8

Understanding Subtraction

Hi, it's Marta again. This shows $5 - 2 = 3$.

★ TEKS **K.IA, K.IB, K.IC, K.ID, K.IE, K.IF, K.IG, K.3, K.3A, K.3B, K.3C**

TOPIC 9 Money

Hi, it's Alex again. The coin on the right is a quarter.

● TEKS **K.1A, K.1B, K.1C, K.1D, K.1E, K.1F, K.1G, K.2A, K.2B, K.2C, K.4**

TOPIC 10 More Addition and Subtraction

Hi, it's Jada again. This shows adding. You can use the penguins to show subtracting, too.

● TEKS **K.1, K.1A, K.1B, K.1C, K.1D, K.1E, K.1F, K.1G, K.3A, K.3B, K.3C**

Contents **ix**

Volume 2

TOPIC 11 — Counting to 100

Hi, it's Carlos again. I counted to 34. I can count even higher.

⭐ TEKS **K.1, K.1A, K.1B, K.1C, K.1D, K.1E, K.1F, K.1G, K.5**

TOPIC 12 — Two-Dimensional Shapes

Hi, it's Emily again. This looks like a triangle.

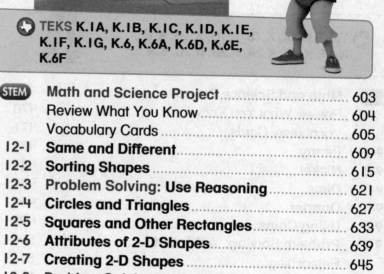

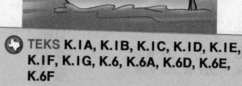

⭐ TEKS **K.1A, K.1B, K.1C, K.1D, K.1E, K.1F, K.1G, K.6, K.6A, K.6D, K.6E, K.6F**

TOPIC 13 Three-Dimensional Solids

Hi, it's Jackson again. You can sort these 3-D figures in different ways.

TEKS K.1A, K.1B, K.1C, K.1D, K.1E, K.1F, K.1G, K.6, K.6A, K.6B, K.6C, K.6D, K.6E

TOPIC 14 Measurement

Hi, it's Marta again. You can compare the sizes of different objects.

TEKS K.1A, K.1B, K.1C, K.1D, K.1E, K.1F, K.1G, K.7, K.7A, K.7B

Contents **xi**

TOPIC 15 — Data

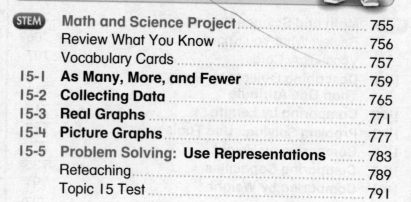

Hi, it's Daniel again. I made a real-object graph.

○ TEKS **K.1, K.1A, K.1B, K.1C, K.1D, K.1E, K.1F, K.1G, K.8, K.8A, K.8B, K.8C**

TOPIC 16 — Personal Financial Literacy

Hi, it's Emily again. You can earn income by walking dogs.

○ TEKS **K.1A, K.1B, K.1C, K.1D, K.1E, K.1F, K.1G, K.9, K.9A, K.9B, K.9C, K.9D**

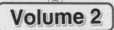

Volume 2

Step Up to Grade 1

These lessons help prepare you for Grade 1.

TEKS 1.1A, 1.1B, 1.1C, 1.1D, 1.1E, 1.1F, 1.1G, 1.2, 1.2B, 1.2C, 1.2E, 1.3B, 1.5B, 1.5C, 1.5D, 1.5E, 1.6, 1.6A, 1.6C, 1.6D, 1.6E

Money

Essential Question: How can we count money?

Math and Science Project: Recycling

Directions Read the character speech bubbles to students. **Find Out!** Have students find out about the impact of littering and how Texas recycles various materials. Say: *Talk to friends and relatives about the items they recycle. Ask them how some people in Texas make money by recycling metal.* **Journal: Make a Poster** Then have students make a poster. Ask them to draw a playground littered with 4 paper, 3 plastic, and 2 metal recyclables. Have them circle the papers in green, the plastics in yellow, and the metals in blue. Finally, have students make up their own price for the metal using coins they have learned and write it below their picture.

Name _____

Review What You Know

★1

5   ⑦

❷2

③   5

❸3

+   ⚪=

♥4

⑤   3   2

✋5

5   15   ⑩

☕6

23   8   ⑬

Directions Have students: ★ circle the number that is greater; ❷ circle the number that is less; ❸ circle the equal sign; ♥–☕ count the counters, and then circle the number that tells how many.

Solve & Share Name ______________________

Lesson 9-1
Penny

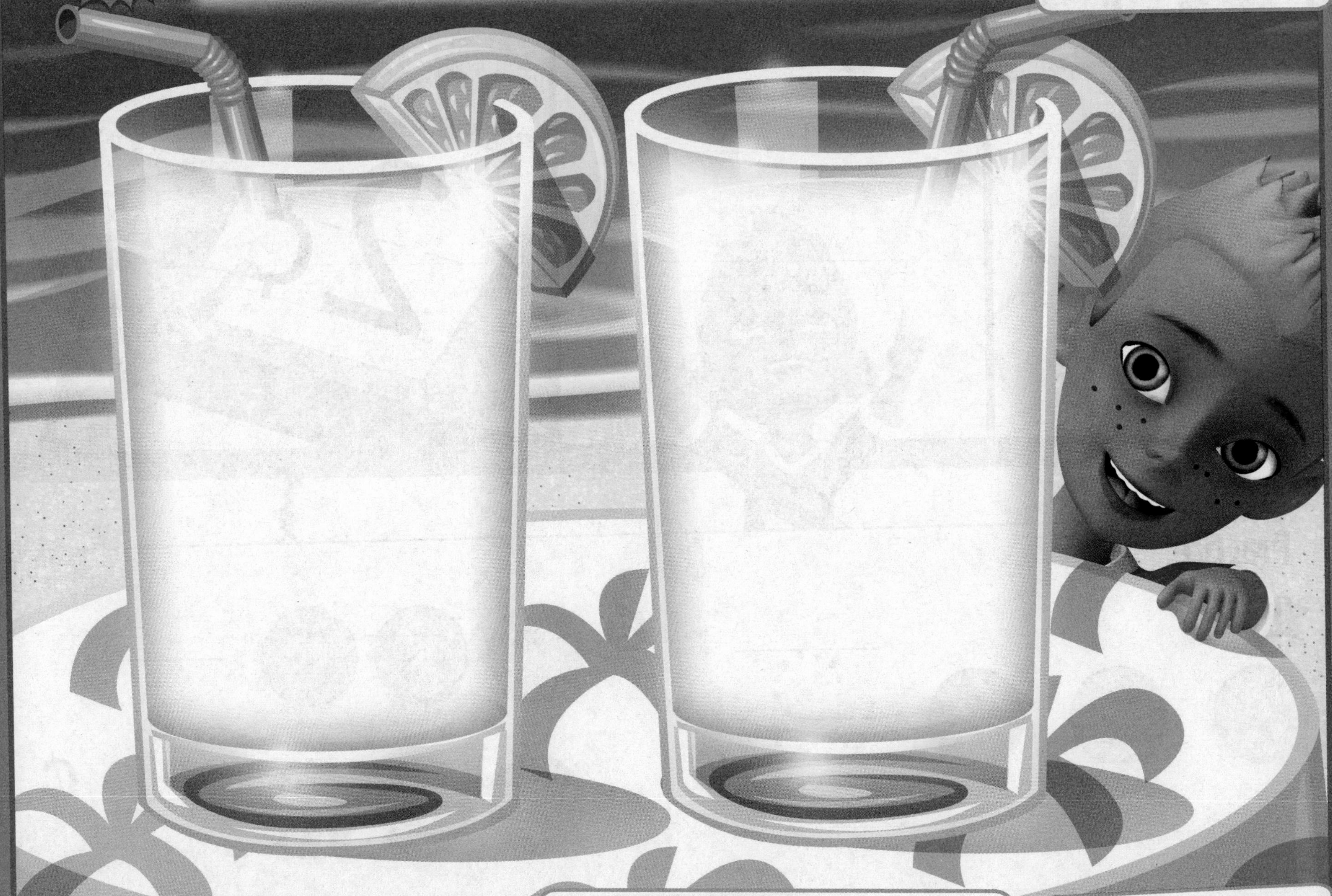

Directions Say: *Alex wants some lemonade from a neighbor's lemonade stand. The lemonade is not free. Draw pictures to show 2 ways Alex can get the lemonade.*

TEKS K.4 Identify coins in order to recognize the need for monetary transactions. Identify U.S. coins by name, including pennies, ... Also, K.2A, K.2B, K.2C. **Mathematical Process Standards** K.1A, K.1C, K.1F.

Digital Resources at PearsonTexas.com
Solve Learn Glossary Check Tools Games

☆ Guided Practice ☆

1 _____ ¢

2 _____ ¢

Directions Have students find the value of the group of pennies, and then write the number of cents.

3 🐟 (5 pennies) _5_ ¢

4 ❤️ (4 pennies) _4_ ¢

5 ✋ (8 pennies) _8_ ¢

6 ☕ (7 pennies) _7_ ¢

7 🌲 (10 pennies) _10_ ¢

Directions Have students find the value of the group of pennies, and then write the number of cents.

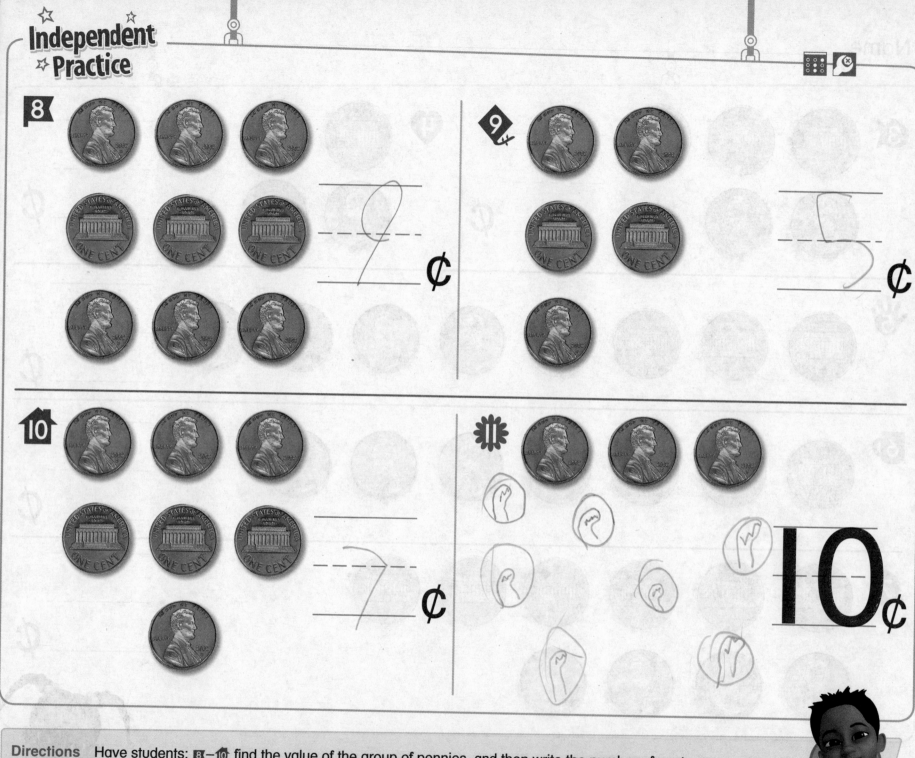

8 _9 ¢_

9 _5 ¢_

10 _7 ¢_

✺ 10¢

Directions Have students: **8–10** find the value of the group of pennies, and then write the number of cents; **✺** draw more pennies to show the number of pennies needed to make 10 cents.

Topic 9 | Lesson 1

Another Look

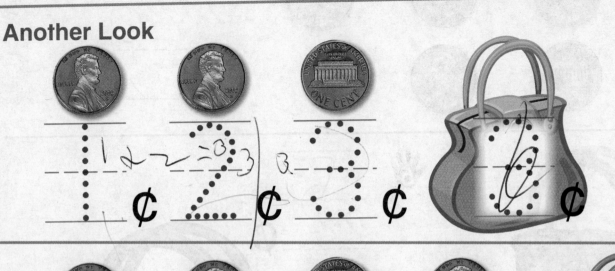

1 ¢   2 ¢   3 ¢   6 ¢

🏠 **HOME CONNECTION**
Your child found the values of groups of pennies.

HOME ACTIVITY Take turns counting out groups of pennies to 10 and saying their value. Be sure to arrange some faceup and some facedown. Count the pennies aloud with your child, and then ask your child to tell how much a penny is worth and give the total value of the pennies.

⭐ 1

_ ¢   2 ¢   3 ¢   9 ¢   10 ¢

🍎 2

_ ¢   2 ¢   3 ¢   9 ¢   5 ¢   5 ¢

Directions Say: *A penny is worth 1 cent. Let's write the numbers as we count on for each penny. Write the total value in the purse.* Then have students: ⭐ and 🍎 write the numbers as they count the value of the group of pennies, and then write the total value in the purse.

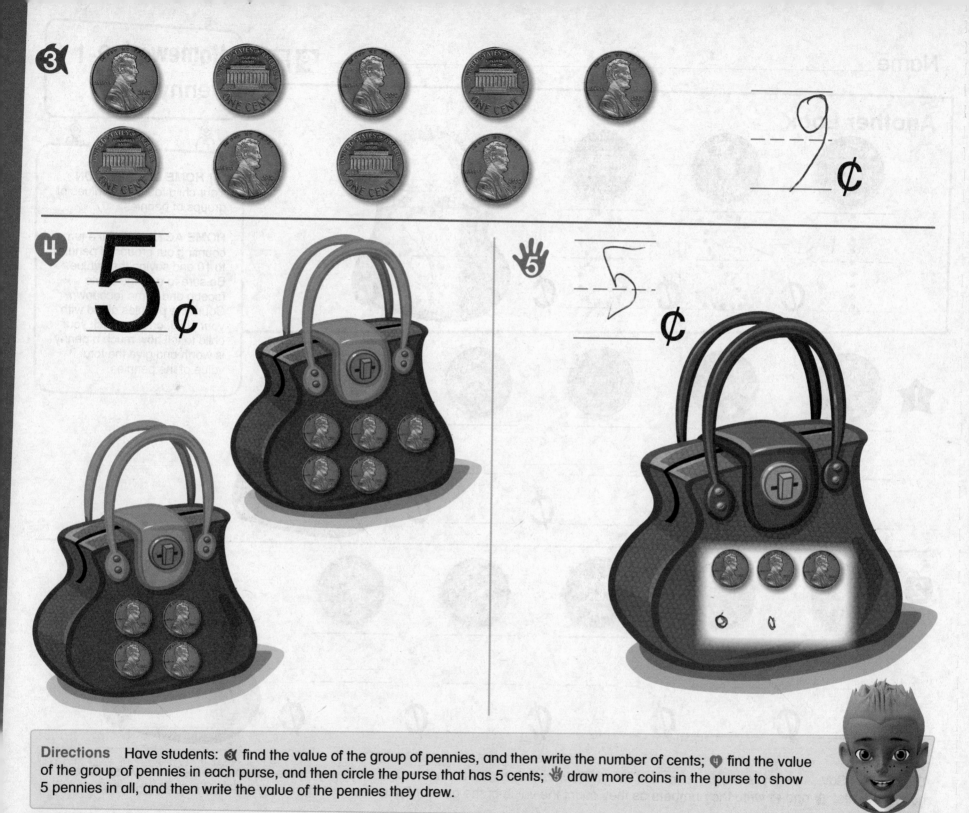

3 ___9___ ¢

4 **5** ¢

5 ___5___ ¢

© Pearson Education, Inc. K

Solve & Share   Name _____

_____
___ ¢

Directions Say: *Alex finds seven cents at the beach. Write how much money he found. Draw the coins he could have found.*

⭐ **TEKS K.4** Identify coins in order to recognize the need for monetary transactions. Identify U.S. coins by name, including pennies, nickels, ... Also, K.2A, K.2B, K.2C. **Mathematical Process Standards** K.1C, K.1D, K.1F, K.1G.

Digital Resources at PearsonTexas.com

Solve   Learn   Glossary   Check   Tools   Games

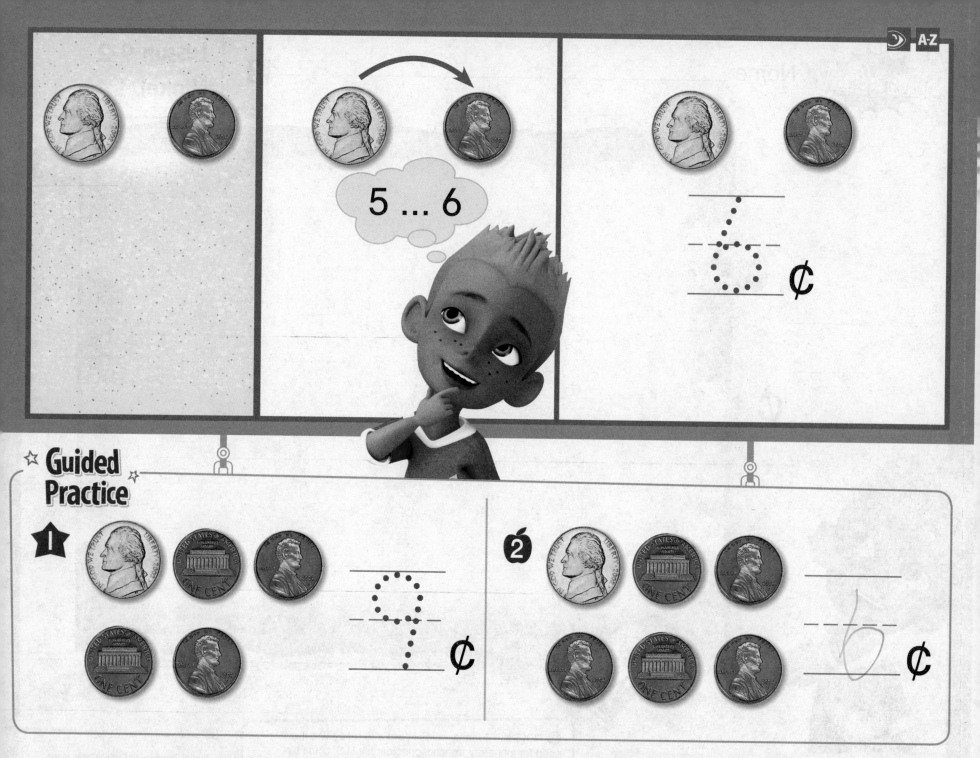

5 ... 6

6 ¢

☆ Guided Practice ☆

1 9 ¢

2 6 ¢

Directions Have students find the value of the group of coins, and then write the number of cents.

© Pearson Education, Inc. K

Topic 9 | Lesson 2

Name _____

❸ ✦

7 ¢

4 ♥

2 ¢

5 ✋

5 ¢

6 ☕

4 ¢

7 🌲

6 ¢

8 🏴

3 ¢

Directions Have students find the value of the group of coins, and then write the number of cents.

Topic 9 | Lesson 2

☆ Independent
☆ Practice

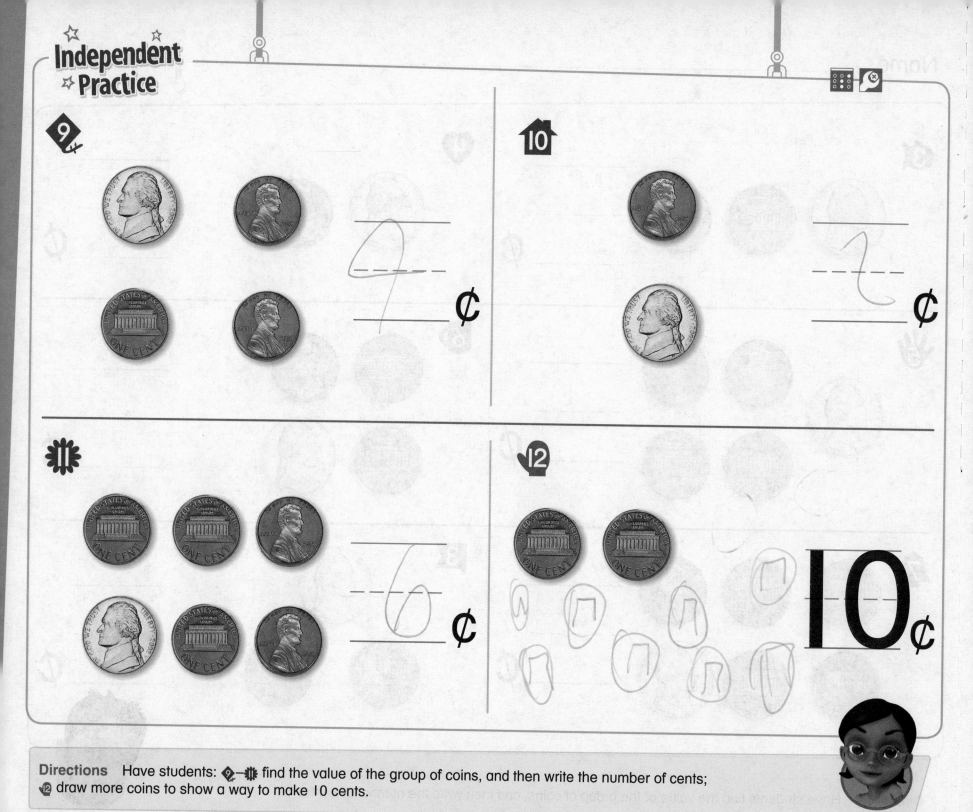

9 _____ 7 _____ ¢

10 _____ 2 _____ ¢

11 _____ 6 _____ ¢

12 **10** ¢

Directions Have students: **9–11** find the value of the group of coins, and then write the number of cents; **12** draw more coins to show a way to make 10 cents.

484 four hundred eighty-four

© Pearson Education, Inc. K

Topic 9 | **Lesson 2**

Another Look

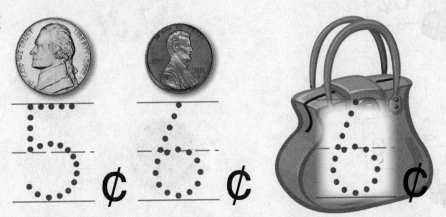

5 ¢   6 ¢   6 ¢

🏠 **HOME CONNECTION**
Your child found the values of groups of coins including nickels and pennies.

HOME ACTIVITY Place 1 nickel and 5 pennies on a table. Say a value from 6 cents to 10 cents. Have your child show that value using the coins and then count aloud from the nickel.

 ★ 1

1 ¢   2 ¢   3 ¢   6 ¢

🍎 2

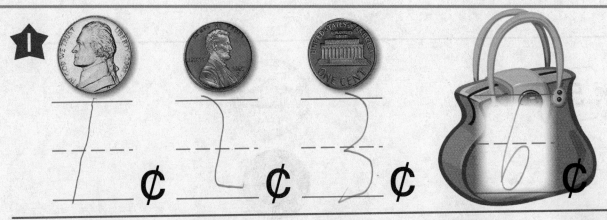

1 ¢   2 ¢   3 ¢   4 ¢   5 ¢   15 ¢

Directions Say: *A nickel is worth 5 cents. Let's write the numbers as we count 5 cents and count on 1 cent. Write the total value in the purse.* Then have students: ★ and 🍎 write the numbers as they count the value of the group of coins, and then write the total value in the purse.

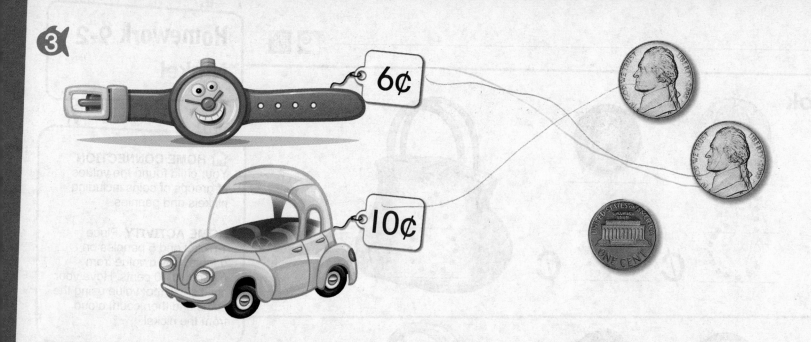

3

6¢

10¢

5¢

7¢

Directions Have students draw a line from each price tag to the coins that are needed to pay for it. Point out that they may use a coin more than once.

Solve & Share

Name _____

_ _ _ _ _ _ ¢

Directions Say: *Alex wants to buy a bag that costs ten cents. Write how much money he needs. Draw the coins he can use. Then use digital tools to solve the problem.*

✪ **TEKS K.4** Identify coins in order to recognize the need for monetary transactions. Identify U.S. coins by name, including pennies, nickels, dimes, ... Also, K.2A, K.2B, K.2C. **Mathematical Process Standards** K.1C, K.1E, K.1F.

Digital Resources at PearsonTexas.com

Solve Learn A-Z Glossary Check Tools Games

5... 6... 7... 8... 9... 10

10 ¢

☆ **Guided Practice** ☆

1

10 ¢

2

10 ¢

Directions Have students find the value of the group of coins, and then write the number of cents.

© Pearson Education, Inc. K

Topic 9 | Lesson 3

Key
Nickel - 5 cents
~~Quarter - 25 cents~~
Dime - 10 cents
penny - 1 cent

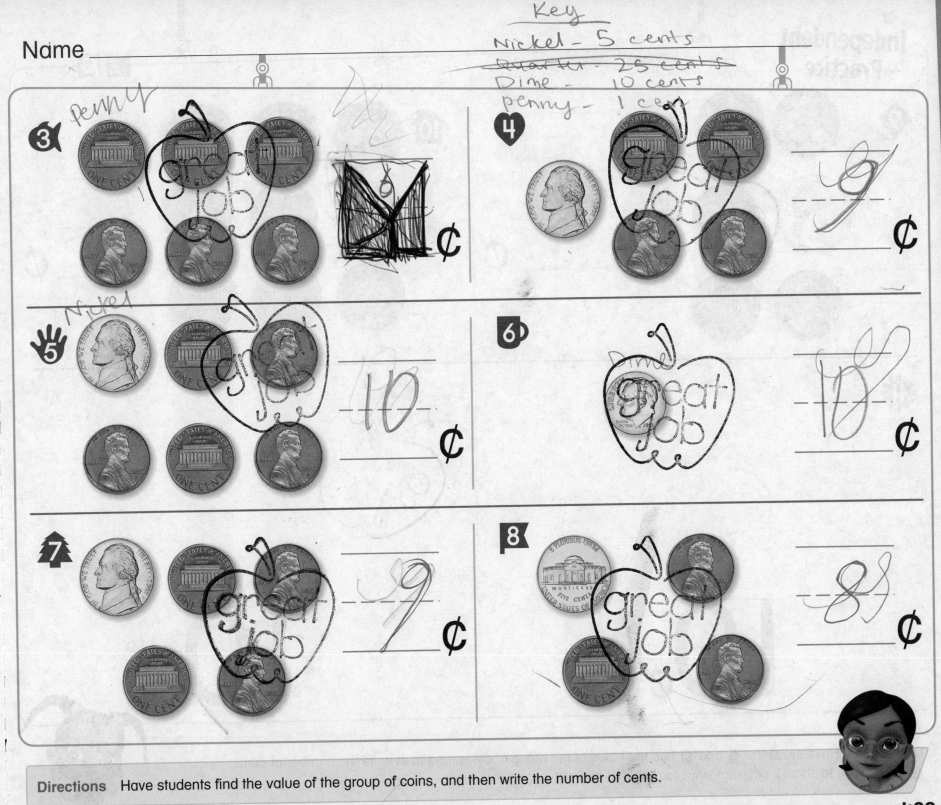

3 penny
¢

4
9 ¢

5 Nickel
10 ¢

6
Dime
¢

7
9 ¢

8
8 ¢

Directions Have students find the value of the group of coins, and then write the number of cents.

9 _____ 10 ¢

10 _____ 9 ¢

Nickel great job

10¢

Quarter, a dime and a nickel = dime

10¢

Directions Have students: ◆ and ⑩ find the value of the group of coins, and then write the number of cents; ⣿ draw coins to show 2 different ways to make 10 cents.

Another Look

 10 ¢

 ¢

🏠 **HOME CONNECTION**
Your child learned the value of a dime in cents. He or she found the values of groups of coins up to 10 cents.

HOME ACTIVITY Set out a group of coins that include dimes, nickels, and pennies, and help your child find the total value of the group.

★ 1 _____ ¢   _____ ¢   _____ ¢    _____ ¢

❷ 2  5 ¢   _____ ¢   _____ ¢   _____ ¢    _____ ¢

Directions Say: *A dime is worth 10 cents. Write the value of the dime. Since there is only a dime, the total value is 10 cents. Write the total value in the purse.* Then have students: ★1 and ❷2 write the numbers as they count the value of the group of coins, and then write the total value in the purse.

3

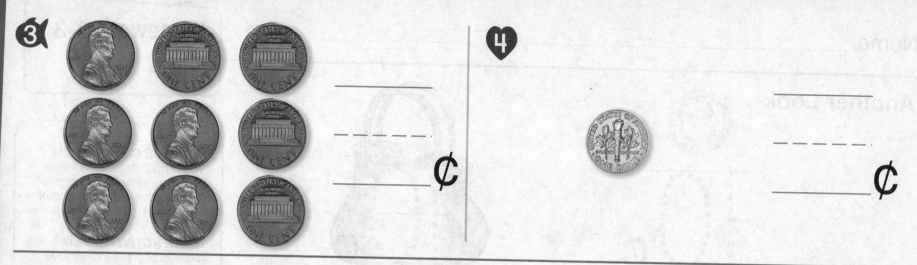

_____

_ _ _ _ _ _ _

_____ ¢

4

_ _ _ _ _ _ _

_____ ¢

5

8¢

 6

10¢

Directions Have students: **3** and **4** find the value of the group of coins, and then write the number of cents; **5** and **6** draw coins to show a way to make the value shown in the purse.

Topic 9 | Lesson 3

Solve & Share   Name _____

Directions Say: *Alex finds a handful of coins at the beach. Circle the coins that are quarters and tell how you know.*

TEKS K.4 Identify coins in order to recognize the need for monetary transactions. Identify U.S. coins by name, including pennies, nickels, dimes, and quarters. **Mathematical Process Standards** K.1A, K.1C, K.1F, K.1G.

Digital Resources at PearsonTexas.com

Solve Learn A-Z Glossary Check Tools Games

Topic 9 | Lesson 4

four hundred ninety-three **493**

☆ Guided Practice ☆

1

2

Directions Have students identify the coins on the left, and then circle the coin on the right that belongs in the group.

© Pearson Education, Inc. K

Name _____

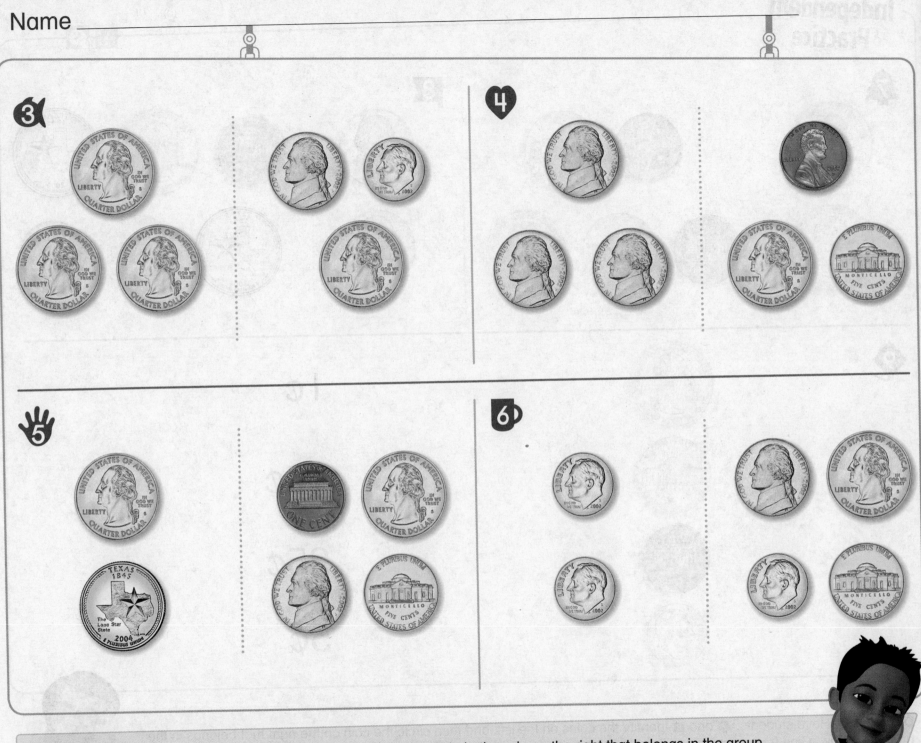

3

4

5

6

Directions Have students identify the coins on the left, and then circle the coin on the right that belongs in the group.

four hundred ninety-five **495**

Topic 9 | Lesson 4

7

8

9

1¢

10¢

25¢

5¢

Directions Have students: **7** and **8** identify the coins on the left, and then circle the coin on the right that belongs in the group; **9** draw a line from each coin to its value.

Name _____

Another Look

🏠 **HOME CONNECTION**
Your child learned to identify quarters.

HOME ACTIVITY Give your child a group of coins and have him or her identify all of the quarters.

★ 1

🍎 2

Directions Say: *A quarter is worth 25 cents. Circle all of the quarters.* Then have students: ★1 and 🍎2 circle the quarters in the group of coins.

3

4

Directions Have students: **3** underline the dime, circle the nickels, draw Xs on the pennies, and leave the quarter unmarked, then find the total value of each type of coin and write the number of cents for each; **4** draw each of the 4 types of coins in the order of their values from highest to lowest.

498 four hundred ninety-eight

© Pearson Education, Inc. K

Topic 9 | Lesson 4

Solve & Share Name _____

10 ¢

⊙ **TEKS K.4** Identify coins in order to recognize the need for monetary transactions. Identify U.S. coins by name, including pennies, nickels, dimes, and quarters. Also, K.2A, K.2B, K.2C. **Mathematical Process Standards** K.1A, K.1C, K.1F, K.1G.

Directions Say: *Alex looks at some toy airplanes. He sees that each plane costs 10 cents. Which coin shows the cost of the airplane?*

Digital Resources at PearsonTexas.com

| Solve | Learn | A-Z Glossary | Check | Tools | Games |

6¢　　6¢　　10¢　　10¢

Guided Practice

1

2

Directions Have students find the cost of each item, and then: **1** circle the item that costs 10 cents; **2** circle the item that costs 8 cents.

© Pearson Education, Inc. K

Name _____

3

4

5 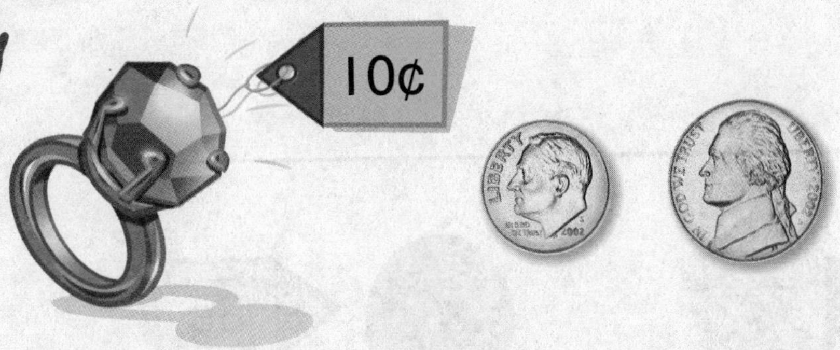 10¢

6 5¢

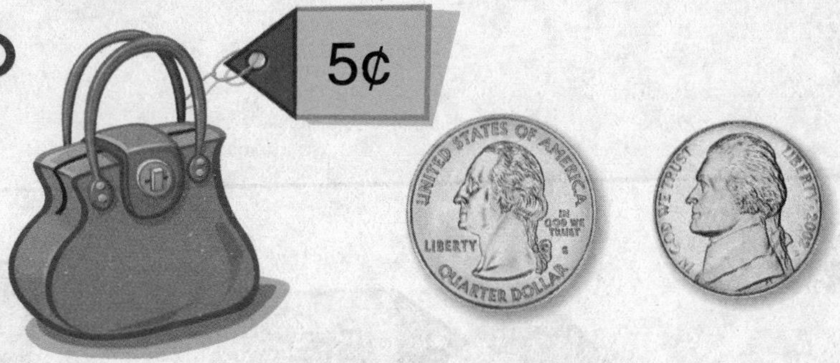

7 25¢

8 1¢

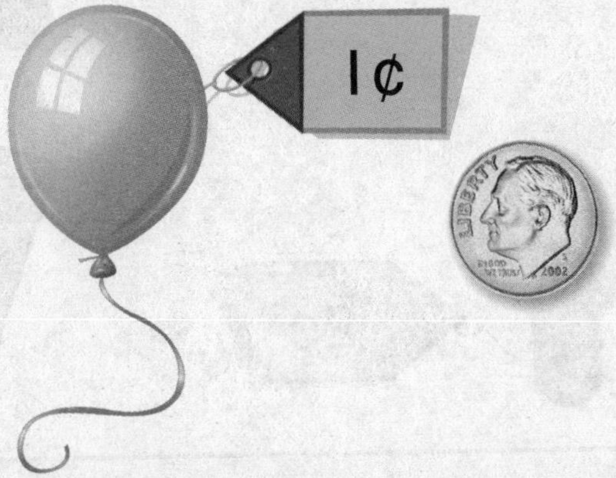

Directions Have students: **3** find the cost of each item, and then circle the item that costs 5 cents; **4** find the cost of each item, and then circle the item that costs 5 cents; **5**–**8** circle the coin that shows the cost of the item.

9

10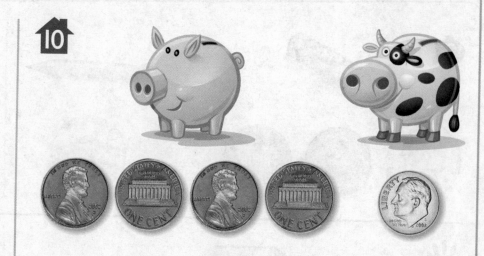

11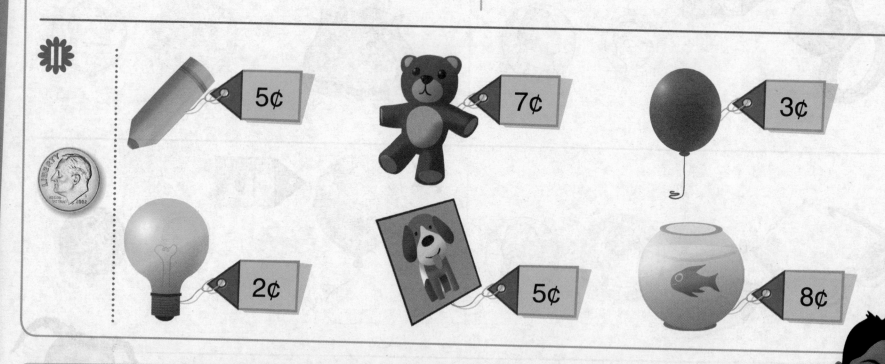

5¢

7¢

3¢

2¢

5¢

8¢

Directions Have students: **9** find the cost of each item, and then circle the item that costs 10 cents; **10** find the cost of each item, and then circle the item that costs 4 cents; **11** circle 2 items they could buy with 10 cents.

Topic 9 | Lesson 5

Name _____

Another Look

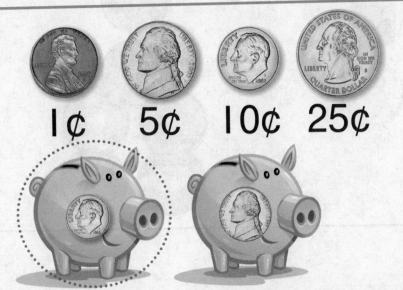

1¢   5¢   10¢   25¢

🏠 **HOME CONNECTION**
Your child identified the values of groups of coins and found coins to show how much each item costs.

HOME ACTIVITY Create a play market with several everyday items or toys. For each item, make a price tag for a value up to 10 cents. Set out several pennies, nickels, dimes, and quarters. Take turns purchasing items by making combinations of coins that add up to the price.

⭐

2

3

Directions Say: *A penny is worth 1 cent, a nickel is worth 5 cents, a dime is worth 10 cents, and a quarter is worth 25 cents. Circle the bank that has 10 cents.* Have students: ⭐ circle the bank that has 25 cents; **2** circle the item that costs 5 cents; **3** circle the item that costs 1 cent.

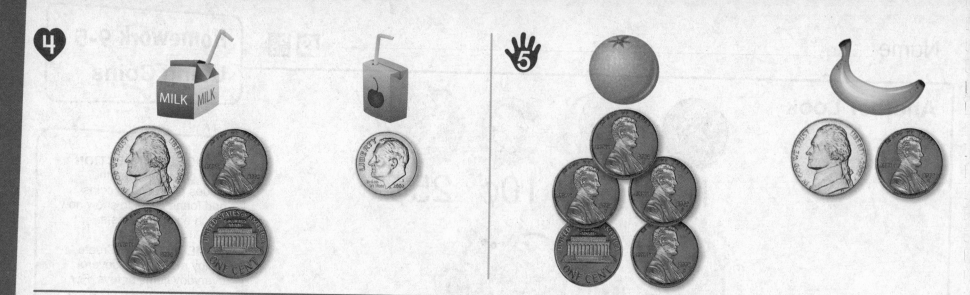

4

6 9¢

4¢

7 5¢ 10¢

Directions Have students: **4** find the cost of each item, and then circle the item that costs 8 cents; **5** find the cost of each item, and then circle the item that costs 6 cents; **6** circle the item that costs nine cents, and then draw coins to show the cost to buy it; **7** circle the item that costs ten cents, and then draw 2 groups of coins that show the cost of the item in 2 different ways.

© Pearson Education, Inc. K

Topic 9 | Lesson 5

10¢

⊕ **K.1C** Select tools, including real objects, manipulatives, ... and techniques, including mental math, estimation, and number sense as appropriate, to solve problems. Also, K.2A, K.2B, K.2C, K.4. **Mathematical Process Standards** K.1A, K.1B.

Directions Say: *The cost of a teddy bear is 10 cents. What are different ways to show the cost of a teddy bear? Draw as many different ways as you can.*

Digital Resources at PearsonTexas.com

Solve   Learn   Glossary   Check   Tools   Games

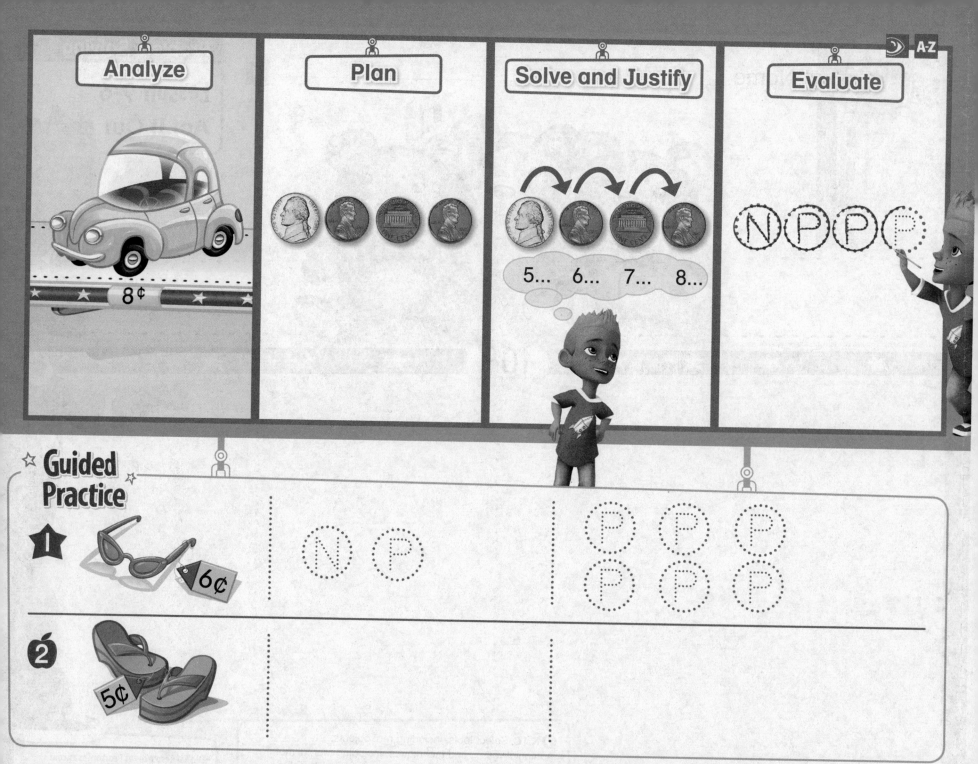

Guided Practice

1. 6¢

2. 5¢

Directions Have students draw coins to show the price of each item in 2 different ways.

© Pearson Education, Inc. K

Name _____

3

🎩 9¢

4

🪭 7¢

✋**5**

👜 10¢

Directions Have students draw coins to show the price of each item in 2 different ways.

Independent Practice

6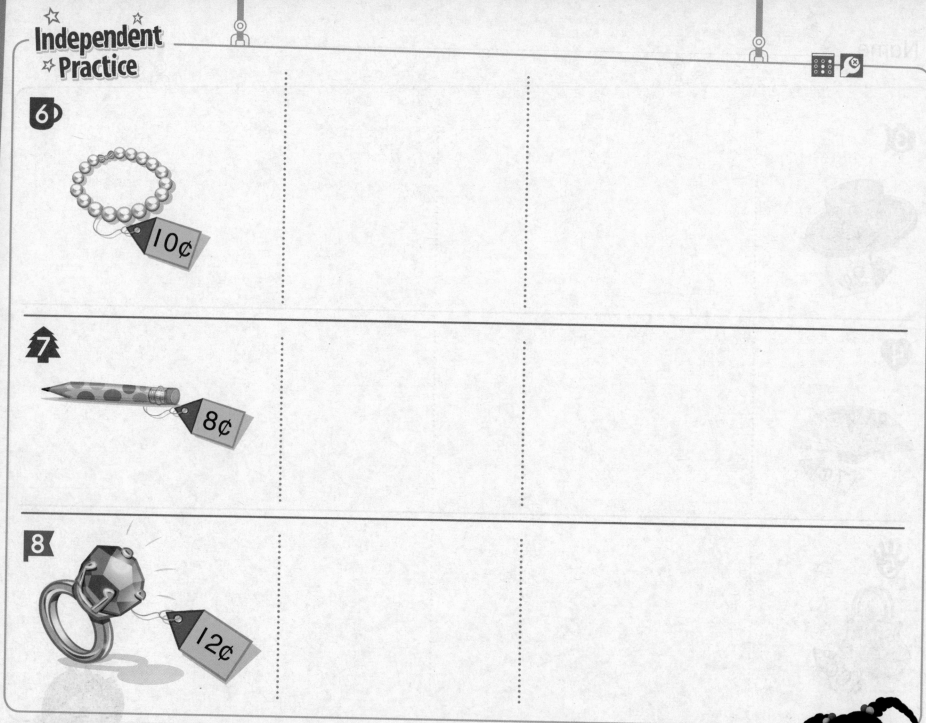

10¢

7

8¢

8

12¢

Directions Have students draw coins to show the price of each item in 2 different ways.

© Pearson Education, Inc. K

Topic 9 | Lesson 6

Name _____

Another Look

8¢

🏠 **HOME CONNECTION**
Your child showed the
cost of items with different
combinations of coins.

HOME ACTIVITY Make a
price tag with a value less
than 10 cents. Set out several
pennies, nickels, dimes, and
quarters. Have your child
show you 2 or 3 different ways
to make different amounts.

1 10¢

2 7¢

3 8¢

Directions Say: *The milk costs 8 cents. Draw a line from the milk to the purse that has the matching amount of money.*
Then have students: **1**–**3** draw a line from each item to the purse that has the matching amount of money.

4

6¢

 **5**

7¢

6

7

Topic 9 | Lesson 6

Name _____

Set A

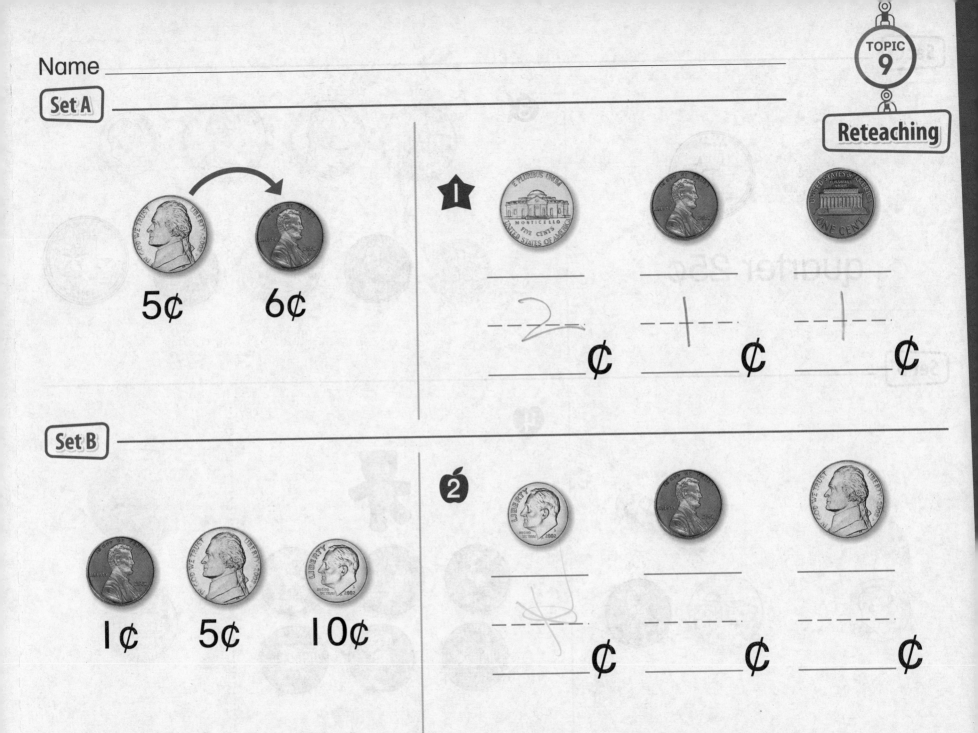

5¢   6¢

⭐ 1

2 ¢   + ¢   + ¢

Set B

❷

1¢   5¢   10¢

¢   ¢   ¢

Directions Have students: ⭐ write the number as they count the value of the group of coins; ❷ show the value of each coin by writing the number of cents.

quarter 25¢

3

4

Directions Have students: **3** circle the quarters and draw Xs on the nickels; **4** find the cost of each item, and then circle the item that costs 6 cents.

Name _____

1 ⭐

O   O   O   O

2 🍎

O 6¢   O 7¢   O 8¢   O 9¢

3 🐟

O   O   O   O

Directions Have students mark the best answer. ⭐ Which coin is worth 10 cents? 🍎 What is the value of the group of coins? 🐟 Which coin is a quarter?

Topic 9

five hundred thirteen **513**

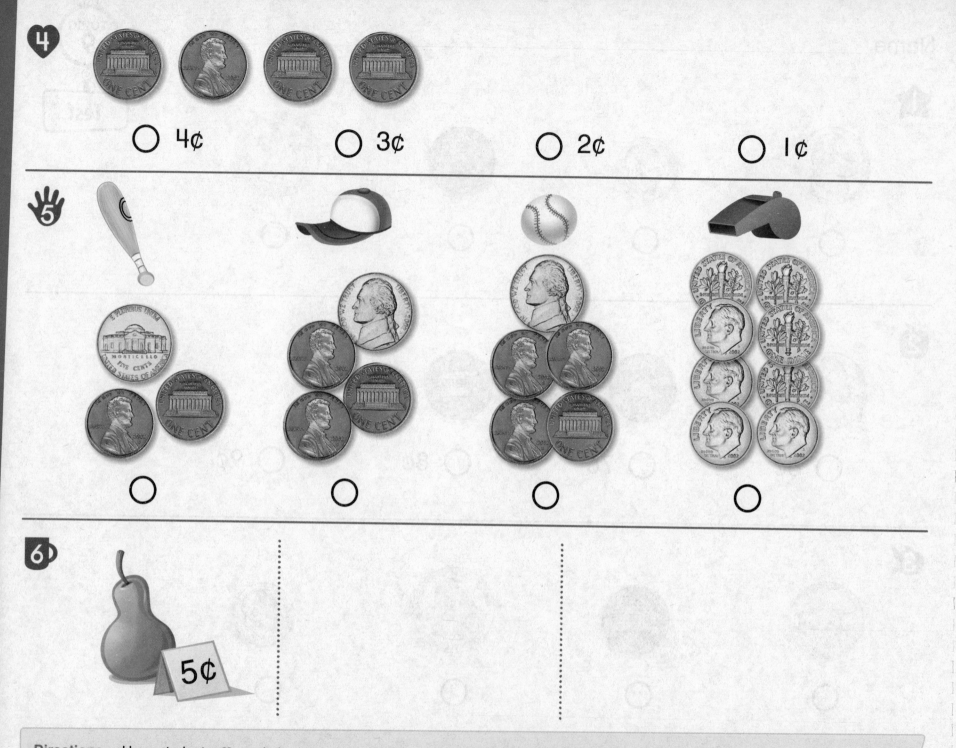

4

○ 4¢   ○ 3¢   ○ 2¢   ○ 1¢

5

○   ○   ○   ○

6

5¢

Directions Have students: **4** mark the best answer. What is the value of the group of coins? **5** mark the best answer. Which shows an item that costs 9 cents? **6** draw coins to show the price of the pear in 2 different ways.

More Addition and Subtraction

Essential Question: What are the different ways to make a number?

Rocks!

Rocks are all different.

Math and Science Project: Sorting Rocks

Directions Read the character speech bubbles to students. **Find Out!** Have students find out about rocks. Say: *Rocks come in all different sizes, shapes, colors, and textures. Talk to friends and relatives about rocks.* **Journal: Make a Poster** Then have students make a poster. Have them write addition and subtraction sentences about the different groups of rocks. Have them draw pictures to go with the rocks they added or subtracted.

Name _____

Review What You Know

1

2

3

4

5

6

Directions Have the students: **1** circle the penny; **2** circle the dime; **3** circle the quarter; **4**–**6** count the pieces of fruit, and then draw counters to show how many.

516 five hundred sixteen

© Pearson Education, Inc. K

Topic 10

Solve & Share

Name _____

$$2 + 2 = 4$$

$$4 - 2 = 2$$

Directions Say: *4 penguins play outside. 2 penguins go in the ice cave. How many penguins are left outside? Circle the number sentence that matches the story. Tell how you know.*

⭐ **TEKS K.3A** Model the action of joining to represent addition and the action of separating to represent subtraction. Also, K.3B. **Mathematical Process Standards** K.1A, K.1C, K.1E, K.1F.

Digital Resources at PearsonTexas.com

  A-Z

Solve Learn Glossary Check Tools Games

Guided Practice

1 

4 + 1 = 5

2 

5 − 1 = 4

Directions Have students listen to each story and use connecting cubes to help act out each story to choose an operation. Then have students complete the addition or subtraction sentence of the related facts. 1 *4 penguins are in a group. 1 penguin joins them. How many penguins are there in all?* 2 *5 penguins are in a group. 1 penguin leaves. How many penguins are there now?*

© Pearson Education, Inc. K

Name _____

3

1 ⊕ 3 = 4

4

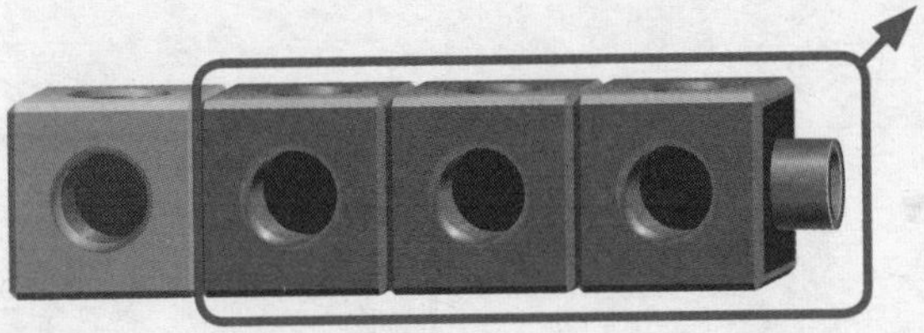

4 ◯ 3 = 1

5

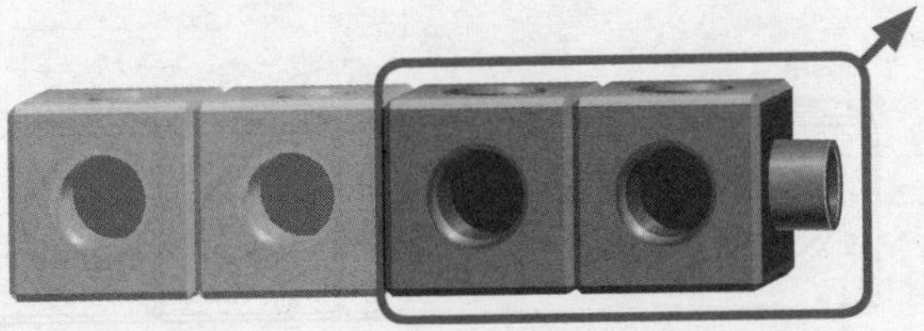

4 ⊖ 2 = 2

6

____ ◯ ____ = ____

Directions Have students use cubes for these facts with 4. Have them decide if the cubes are separating or joining. Encourage them to make up their own stories to match the cubes. Then have them write an addition or subtraction sentence for the related facts in each row.

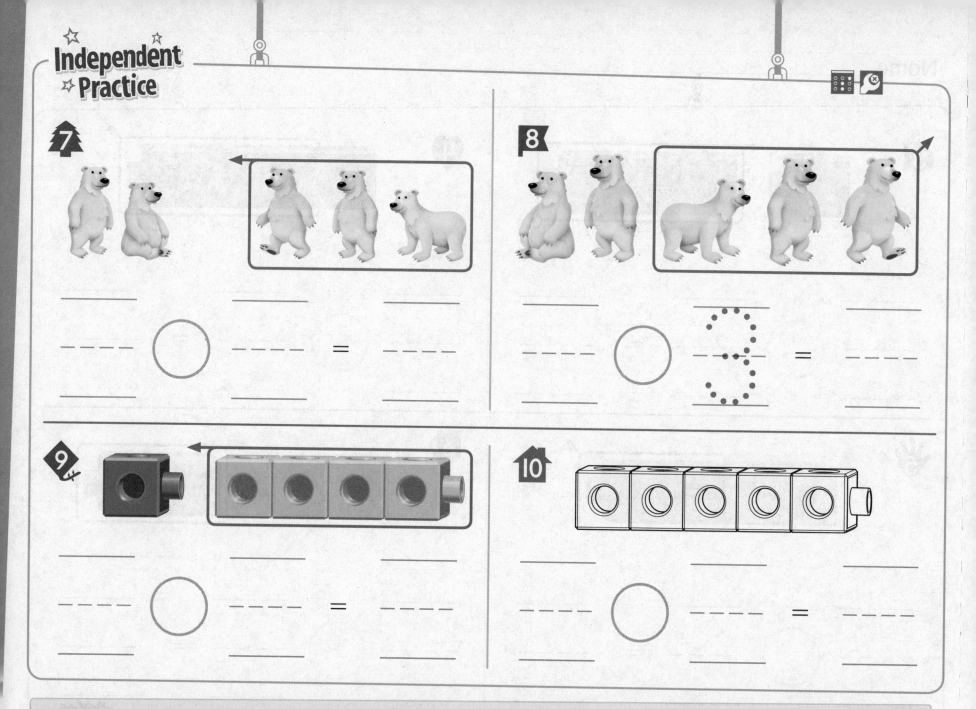

7

_____ ◯ _____ = _____

_____

8

_____ ◯ _____ ● _____ = _____

_____

9

_____ ◯ _____ = _____

_____

10

_____ ◯ _____ = _____

_____

Directions Have students listen to each story, use cubes to help act out each story to choose an operation, and then complete the addition or subtraction sentence of the related facts. 🌲 *2 bears are in a group. 3 bears join them. How many bears are there in all?* 🚩 *5 bears are in a group. 3 bears leave. How many bears are there now?* Then have students: ◆ decide if the cubes show separating or joining, and then write an addition or subtraction sentence to match; 🏠 color the cubes and draw an arrow to show a subtraction story that uses the same numbers as in ◆, and then write a number sentence to match.

Topic 10 | Lesson 1

Name _____

Another Look

$$5 \bigcirc 2 = 3 \qquad 3 \oplus 2 = 5$$

🏠 **HOME CONNECTION**
Your child used cubes to represent related addition and subtraction facts with 4 and 5. Then your child wrote addition or subtraction sentences to represent the cubes.

HOME ACTIVITY Using household objects such as blocks or paper clips, ask your child to make a group of 4 or 5 objects. Then ask your child to break that group into 2 smaller groups and write a number sentence about the groups.

⭐ **1**

_____ _____
_____ ◯ _____ = _____

🍎 **2**

_____ _____
_____ ◯ _____ = _____

Directions   Say: Listen to each story and use counters or other objects to help act out each story to choose an operation. Then complete the addition or subtraction sentence of the related facts. 5 seals are playing. 2 seals leave. How many seals are there now? There are 3 seals playing and 2 seals join them. How many seals are there in all? Then have students listen to each story, use counters or other objects to help act out the story to choose an operation, and then complete the addition or subtraction sentence of the related facts. ⭐ 4 seals are in a group. 1 seal walks away. How many seals are left? 🍎 3 seals are in a group. 1 seal joins them. How many seals are there in all?

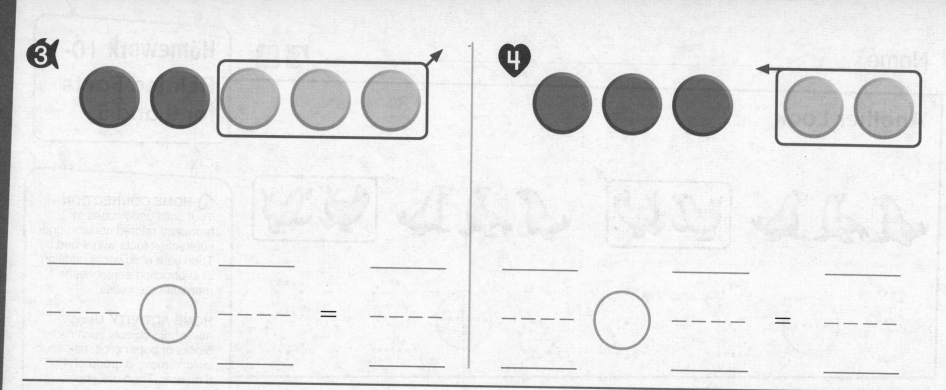

_____   _____   _____   _____   _____   _____

_ _ _ _ ◯ _ _ _ _ = _ _ _ _   _ _ _ _ ◯ _ _ _ _ = _ _ _ _

_____   _____

5

6

$$4 + 1 = 5$$

$$5 - 1 = 4$$

Directions Have students: **3** and **4** decide if the counters show separating or joining, and then write an addition or subtraction sentence to match; **5** draw and color counters to match the addition sentence; **6** draw and color counters to match the subtraction sentence.

Solve & Share Name _____

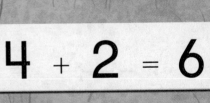

$$4 + 2 = 6$$

$$6 - 2 = 4$$

Directions Say: *4 green ducks eat seeds on the ground. 2 yellow ducks join them. How many ducks are there in all? Circle the number sentence that matches the story. Tell how you know.*

TEKS K.3A Model the action of joining to represent addition and the action of separating to represent subtraction. Also, K.3B. **Mathematical Process Standards** K.1A, K.1C, K.1E.

Digital Resources at PearsonTexas.com

Solve   Learn   Glossary   Check   Tools   Games

Subtract.

$7 - 2 = 5$

Add.

$5 + 2 = 7$

☆ Guided Practice ☆

1    $4 \oplus 3 = 7$

2    $7 - 3 = 4$

Directions Have students listen to each story and use connecting cubes to help them act out each story to choose an operation. Then have students complete the addition or subtraction sentence of the related facts. ❶ *4 ducks are in a group. 3 ducks join them. How many ducks are there in all?* ❷ *7 ducks are in a group. 3 ducks leave. How many ducks are there now?*

Topic 10 | Lesson 2

Name _____

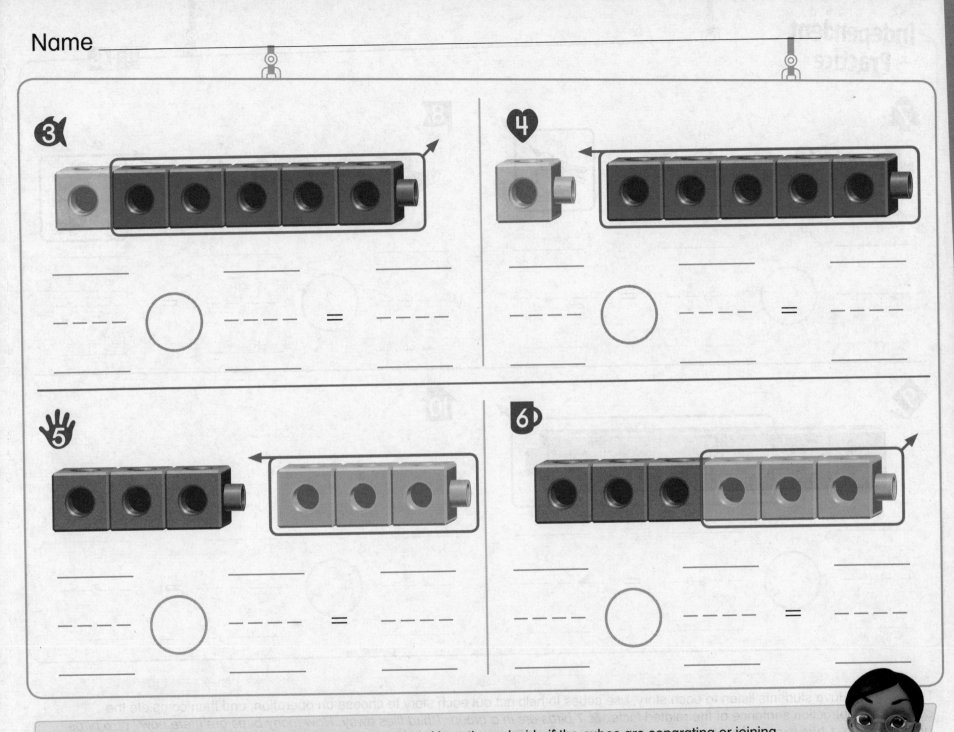

❸

_ _ _ _ _   ◯   _ _ _ _ _   =   _ _ _ _

❹

_ _ _ _ _   ◯   _ _ _ _ _   =   _ _ _ _

❺

_ _ _ _ _   ◯   _ _ _ _ _   =   _ _ _ _

❻

_ _ _ _ _   ◯   _ _ _ _ _   =   _ _ _ _

Directions Have students use cubes for these facts with 6. Have them decide if the cubes are separating or joining. Encourage them to make up their own stories to match the cubes. Then have them write an addition or subtraction sentence for the related facts in each row.

Topic 10 | Lesson 2

five hundred twenty-seven **527**

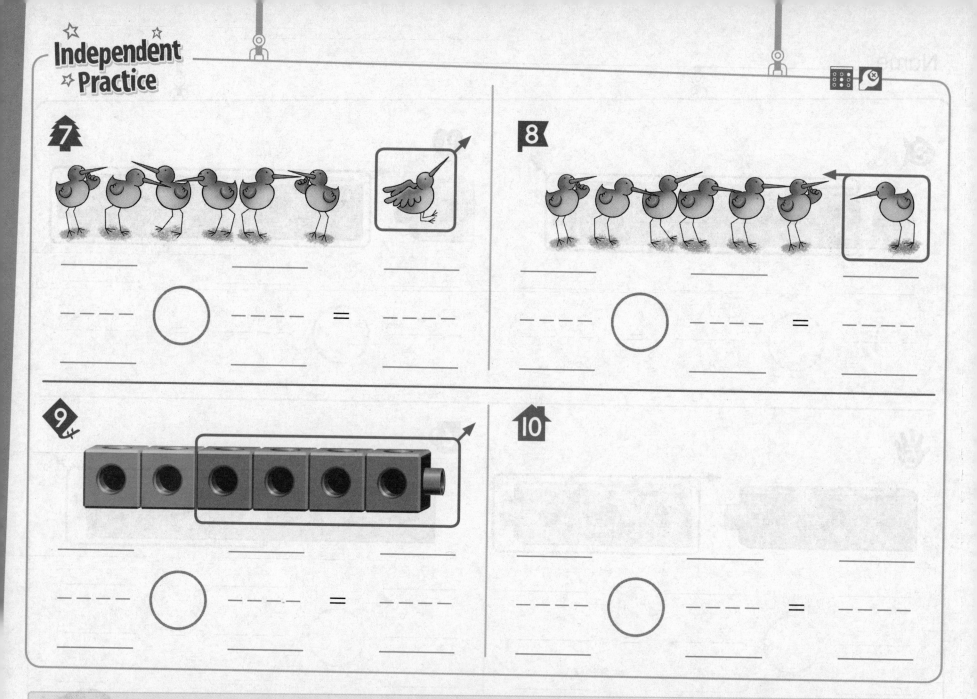

7

◯ ____ = ____

8

◯ ____ = ____

9

◯ ____ = ____

10

◯ ____ = ____

Directions Have students listen to each story, use cubes to help act out each story to choose an operation, and then complete the addition or subtraction sentence of the related facts. **7** *7 birds are in a group. 1 bird flies away. How many birds are there now?* **8** *6 birds are in a group. 1 bird joins them. How many birds are there now?* Then have students: **9** decide if the cubes show separating or joining, and then write an addition or subtraction sentence; **10** draw cubes to show an addition story that uses the same numbers as in **9**, and then write an addition sentence to match.

© Pearson Education, Inc. K

Name _____

Another Look

$5 \oplus 1 = 6$ $6 \odot 1 = 5$

🏠 **HOME CONNECTION**
Your child used cubes to represent related addition and subtraction facts with 6 and 7. Then your child wrote addition or subtraction sentences to represent the cubes.

HOME ACTIVITY Using household objects such as pennies or marbles, ask your child to make a group of 6 or 7. Then have your child break that group into 2 smaller groups and write a number sentence about the groups.

★1

_____ ◯ _____ = _____

🍎2

_____ ◯ _____ = _____

Directions Say: *Listen to each story and use counters or other objects to help act out each story to choose an operation. Then complete the addition or subtraction sentence of the related facts. A group of 5 ducks are quacking and 1 duck joins them. How many ducks are there in all? Then the group of 6 ducks quacks until 1 duck leaves. How many ducks are left?* Then have students listen to each story, use counters or other objects to help act out the story to choose an operation, and then complete the addition or subtraction sentence of the related facts. **★** *3 ducks quack. 4 ducks join them. How many ducks are there in all?* **🍎** *7 ducks quack until 4 ducks leave. How many ducks are left?*

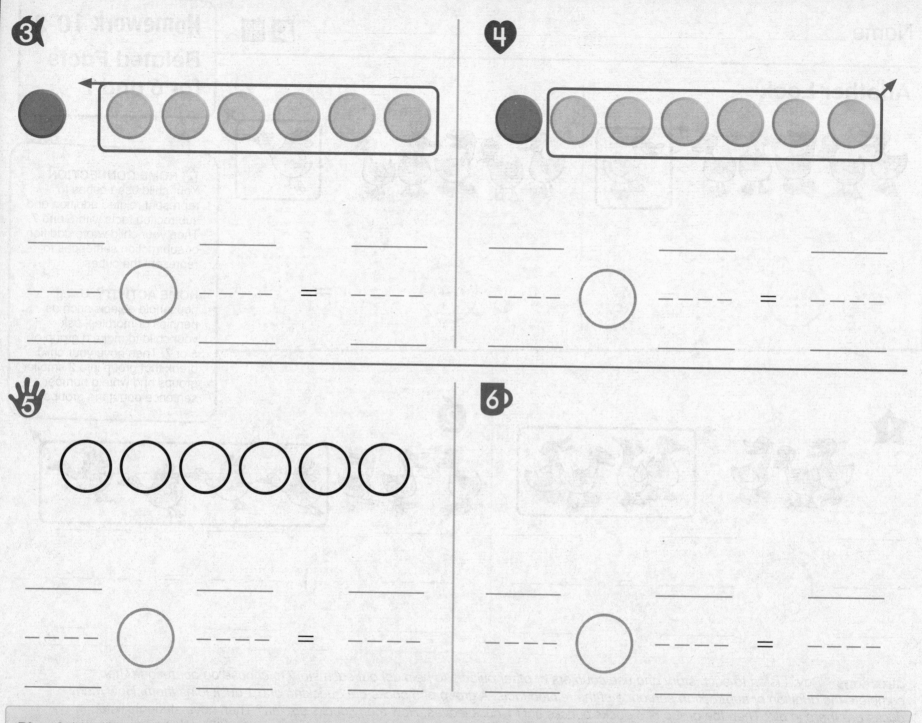

3

_____   _____   _____

– – – – ( ) – – – – = – – – –

_____   _____   _____

4

_____   _____   _____

– – – – ( ) – – – – = – – – –

_____   _____   _____

5

_____   _____   _____

– – – – ( ) – – – – = – – – –

_____   _____   _____

6

_____   _____   _____

– – – – ( ) – – – – = – – – –

_____   _____   _____

Directions Have students: **3** and **4** decide if the counters show separating or joining, and then write an addition or subtraction sentence to match; **5** color the counters to show a subtraction story, and then write a number sentence to match; **6** draw counters to show an addition story that uses the same numbers as in **5**, and then write a number sentence to match.

© Pearson Education, Inc. K

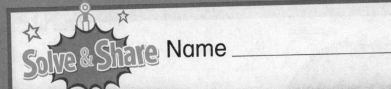

Solve & Share   Name _____

$6 + 3 = 9$

_____ _____ _____

‗ ‗ ‗ ‗ ‗ ‗ = ‗ ‗ ‗ ‗ ‗

_____ _____ _____

Directions Say: *Jada uses cubes for an addition story about 6 + 3 = 9. Think of a subtraction story using these same numbers: 6, 3, and 9. Write your subtraction sentence. Draw a picture and tell a friend your story.*

TEKS K.3A Model the action of joining to represent addition and the action of separating to represent subtraction. Also, **K.3B. Mathematical Process Standards** K.1C, K.1D, K.1E, K.1F.

Digital Resources at **PearsonTexas.com**

 Solve   Learn   Glossary   Check   Tools   Games

6 + 2 = 8

Add.

8 − 2 = 6

Subtract.

☆ Guided Practice ☆

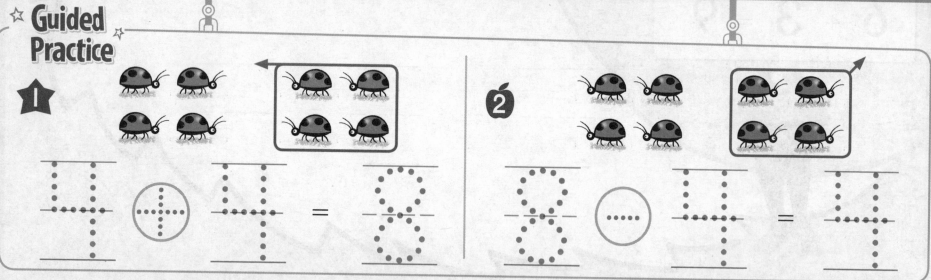

Name _____

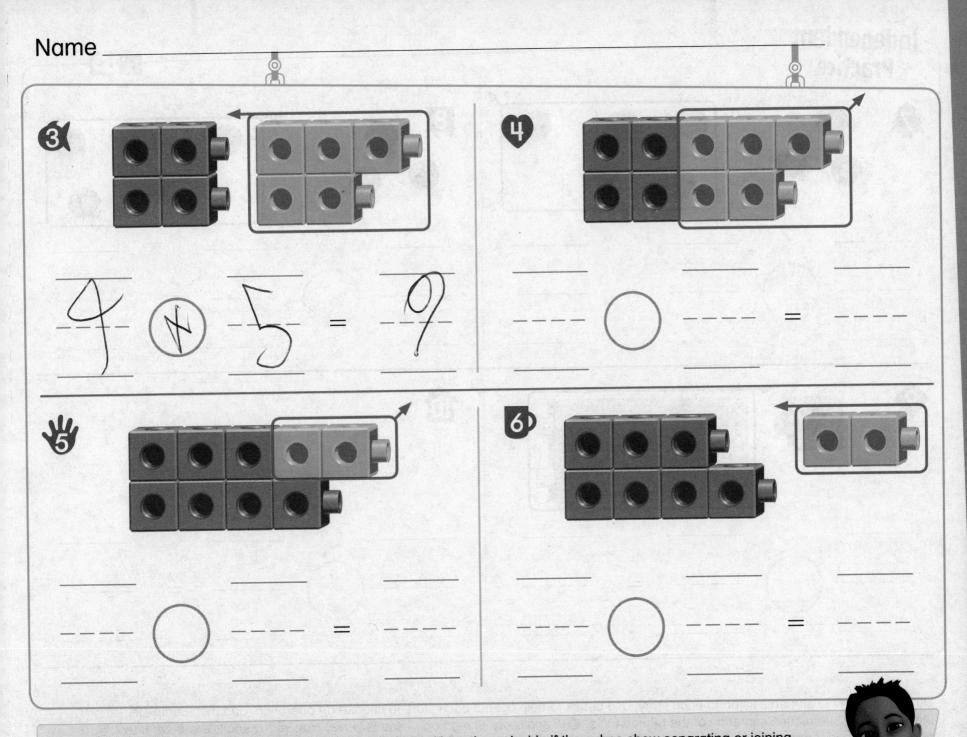

3

$$4 \ \textcircled{4} \ 5 = 9$$

4

_____ ◯ _____ = _____

5

_____ ◯ _____ = _____

6

_____ ◯ _____ = _____

Directions Have students use cubes for these facts with 9. Have them decide if the cubes show separating or joining. Encourage them to make up their own stories to match the cubes. Then have them write an addition or subtraction sentence for the related facts in each row.

Independent ☆Practice

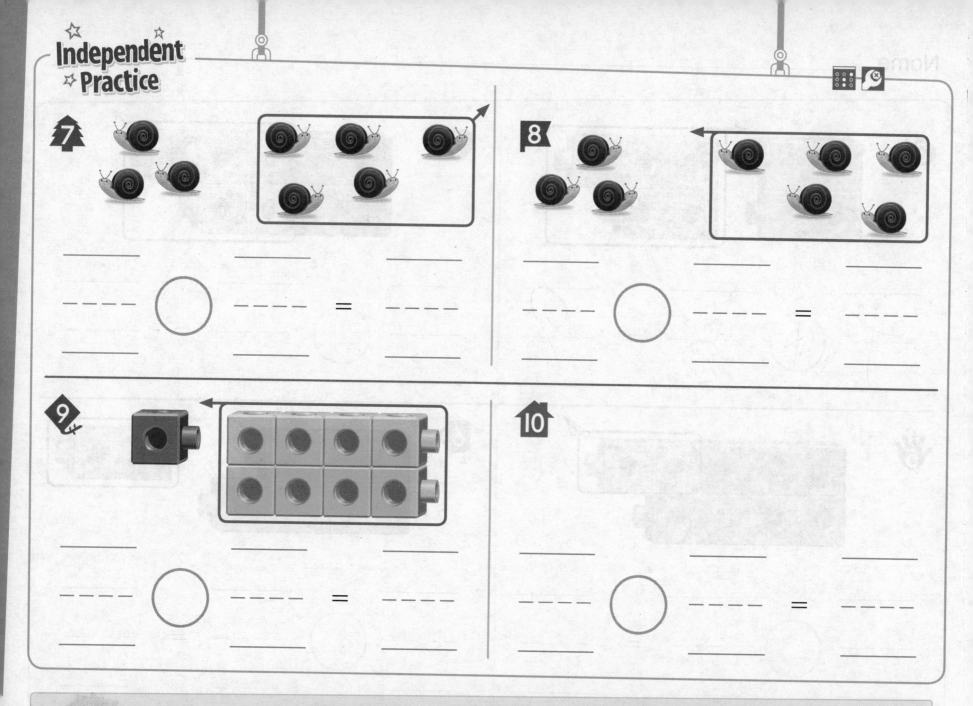

🎄 **7**

_ _ _ _ _ ◯ _ _ _ _ = _ _ _ _ _

🚩 **8**

_ _ _ _ _ ◯ _ _ _ _ = _ _ _ _ _

9

_ _ _ _ _ ◯ _ _ _ _ = _ _ _ _

🏠 **10**

_ _ _ _ _ ◯ _ _ _ _ = _ _ _ _

Directions Have students listen to each story, use cubes to help act out each story to choose an operation, and then complete the addition or subtraction sentence of the related facts. 🎄 *8 snails are in a group. 5 snails leave. How many snails are there now?* 🚩 *3 snails are in a group. 5 snails join them. How many snails are there in all?* Then have students: 🔷 decide if the cubes show separating or joining, and then write an addition or subtraction sentence to match; 🏠 draw cubes to show a subtraction story that uses the same numbers as in 🔷, and then write a subtraction sentence to match.

© Pearson Education, Inc. K

Name _____

Another Look

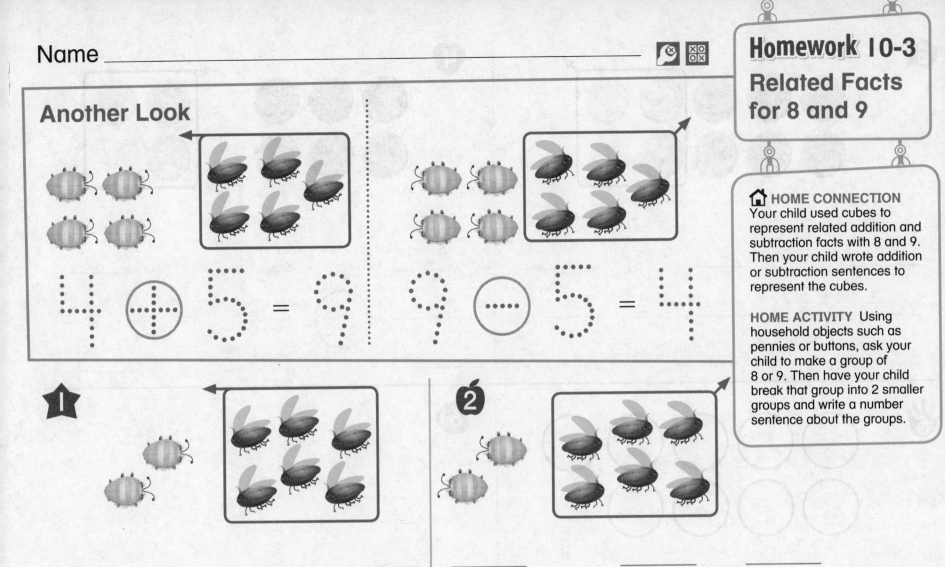

$4 \oplus 5 = 9$ $9 \ominus 5 = 4$

HOME CONNECTION
Your child used cubes to represent related addition and subtraction facts with 8 and 9. Then your child wrote addition or subtraction sentences to represent the cubes.

HOME ACTIVITY Using household objects such as pennies or buttons, ask your child to make a group of 8 or 9. Then have your child break that group into 2 smaller groups and write a number sentence about the groups.

⭐1

❷

____ ◯ ____ = ____   ____ ◯ ____ = ____

Directions Say: *Listen to each story and use counters or other objects to help act out each story to choose an operation. Then complete the addition or subtraction sentence of the related facts. A group of 4 bugs crawl and 5 bugs join them. How many bugs are there in all? Then the group of 9 bugs buzz until 5 bugs leave. How many bugs are left?* Then have students listen to each story, use counters or other objects to help act out the story to choose an operation, and then complete the addition or subtraction sentence of the related facts. ⭐ *A group of 2 bugs crawl and 6 bugs join them. How many bugs are there in all?* ❷ *The group of 8 bugs buzz until 6 bugs leave. How many bugs are left?*

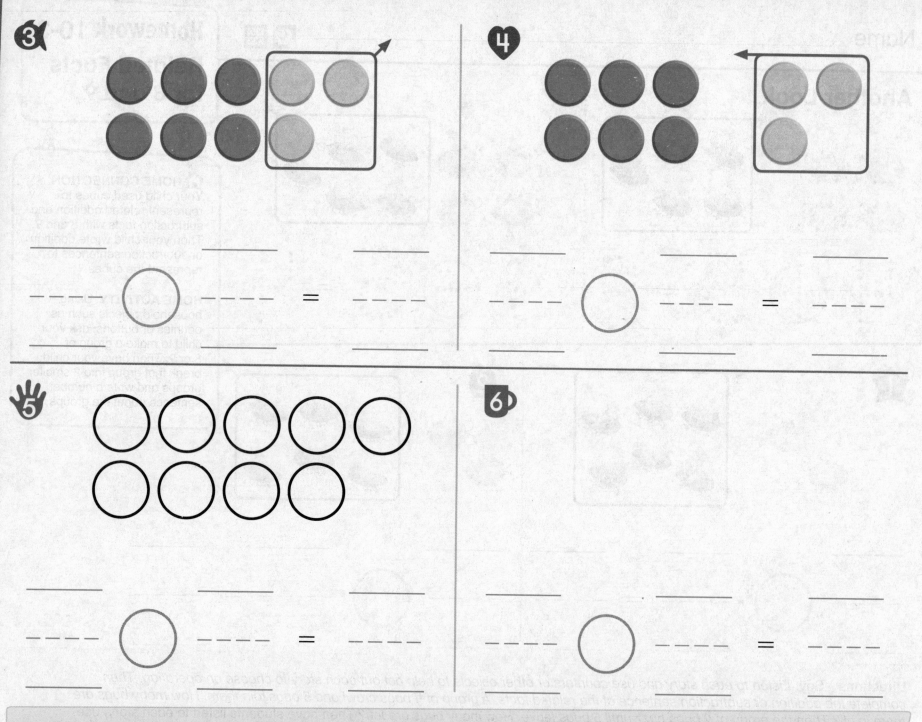

3

____ ____ ◯ ____ = ____

____   ____   ____

4

____ ____ ◯ ____ = ____

____   ____   ____

5

____ ____ ◯ ____ = ____

____   ____   ____

6

____ ____ ◯ ____ = ____

____   ____   ____

Directions Have students: **3** and **4** decide if the counters show separating or joining, and then write an addition or subtraction sentence to match; **5** color the counters to show a subtraction story, and then write a number sentence to match; **6** draw counters to show an addition story that uses the same numbers as in **5**, and then write an addition sentence to match.

Solve & Share Name _____

10 − 2 = 8

_____ _____

_ _ _ _ + _ _ _ _ = _ _ _ _

_____ _____ _____

Directions Say: *Jada uses cubes for a subtraction story about 10 − 2 = 8. Think of an addition story using these same numbers: 10, 2, and 8. Write your addition sentence. Draw a picture and tell a friend your story.*

TEKS K.3A Model the action of joining to represent addition and the action of separating to represent subtraction. Also, K.3B. **Mathematical Process Standards** K.1C, K.1E, K.1F.

Digital Resources at PearsonTexas.com

Solve Learn Glossary Check Tools Games

$6 + 4 = 10$

$10 - 4 = 6$

☆ Guided Practice ☆

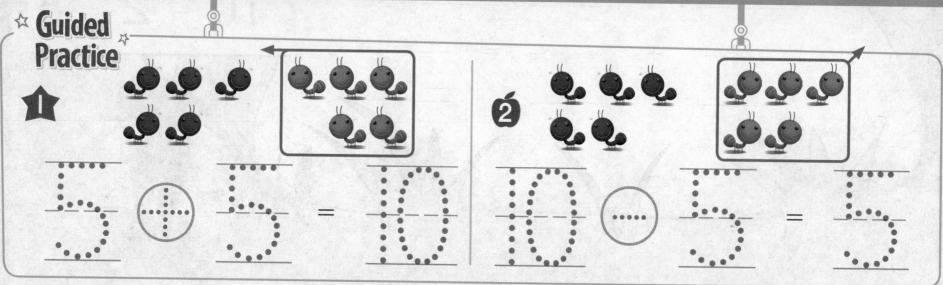

1 5 ⊕ 5 = 10

2 10 ⊖ 5 = 5

Directions Have students listen to each story and use connecting cubes to help act out the story to choose an operation. Then have students complete the addition or subtraction sentence of the related facts. ⭐ *5 ants are in a group. 5 ants join them. How many ants are there in all?* ❷ *10 ants are in a group. 5 ants turn and walk away. How many ants are left?*

© Pearson Education, Inc. K

Topic 10 | Lesson 4

Name _____

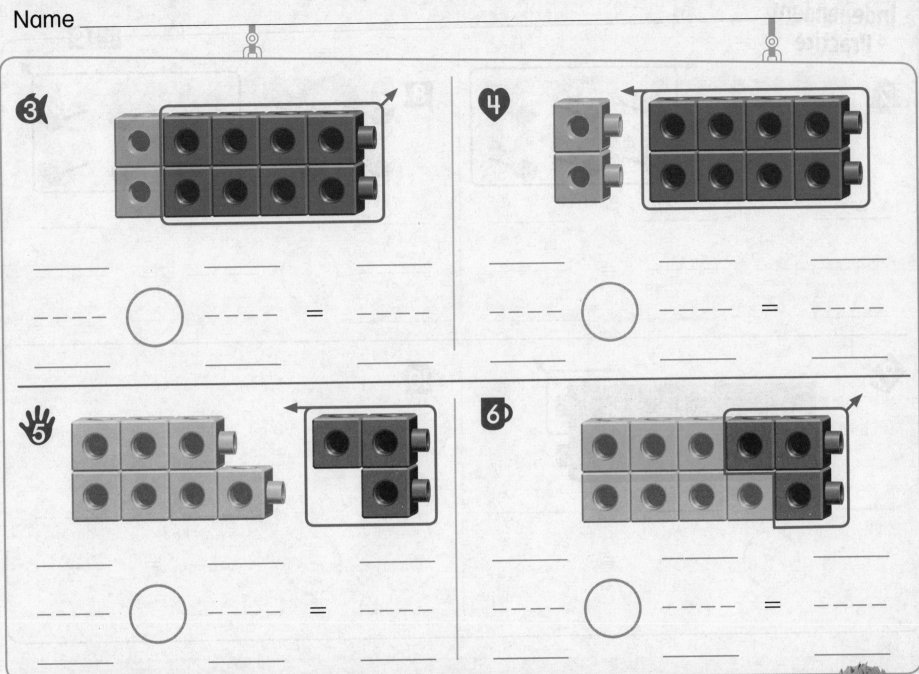

3

_ _ _ _ _ ◯ _ _ _ _ _ = _ _ _ _ _

4

_ _ _ _ _ ◯ _ _ _ _ _ = _ _ _ _ _

5

_ _ _ _ _ ◯ _ _ _ _ _ = _ _ _ _ _

6

_ _ _ _ _ ◯ _ _ _ _ _ = _ _ _ _ _

Directions Have students use cubes for these facts with 10. Have them decide if the cubes are separating or joining. Encourage them to make up their own stories to match the cubes. Then have them write an addition or subtraction sentence for the related facts in each row.

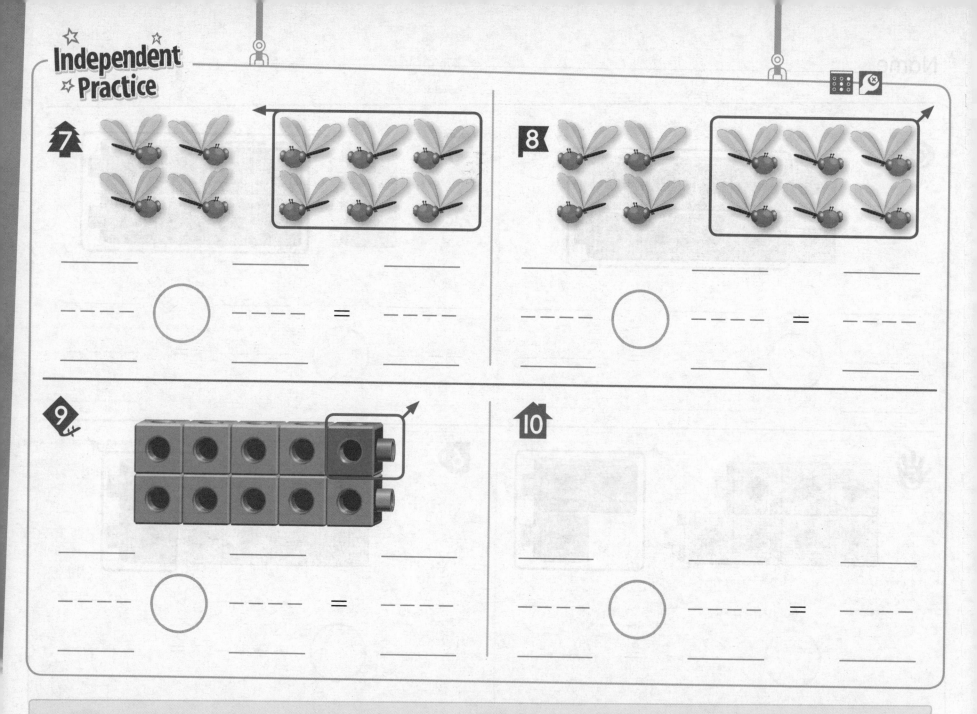

🎄 **7**

_____ ◯ _____ = _____

_____

🚩 **8**

_____ ◯ _____ = _____

_____

◆ **9**

_____ ◯ _____ = _____

_____

⌂ **10**

_____ ◯ _____ = _____

_____

Directions Have students listen to each story, use cubes to help act out each story to choose an operation, and then complete the addition or subtraction sentence of the related facts. 🎄 *4 dragonflies are in a group. 6 dragonflies join them. How many dragonflies are there in all?* 🚩 *10 dragonflies are in a group. 6 dragonflies turn and leave. How many dragonflies are there now?* Then have students: ◆ decide if the cubes show separating or joining, and then write an addition or subtraction sentence to match; ⌂ draw cubes to show an addition story that uses the same numbers as in ◆, and then write an addition sentence to match.

© Pearson Education, Inc. K

Name _____

Another Look

$$3 \bigoplus 7 = 10$$

$$10 \bigodot 7 = 3$$

🏠 **HOME CONNECTION**
Your child used cubes to represent related addition and subtraction facts with 10. Then your child wrote addition or subtraction sentences to represent the cubes.

HOME ACTIVITY Draw 10 large circles on a piece of paper. Have your child count the number of circles. Then have your child put household objects, like pennies or paper clips, on some of the circles. Have your child write a number sentence that shows the number of empty circles plus the number of circles with objects. The number sentence should equal 10.

⭐1

___ ___

___ ◯ ___ = ___

②2

___ ___

___ ◯ ___ = ___

Directions Say: *Listen to each story and use counters or other objects to help act out each story to choose an operation. Then complete the addition or subtraction sentence of the related facts. There are 3 bees in a group. 7 bees join them. How many bees are there in all? Then there are 10 bees in the group. 7 bees fly away. How many bees are left?* Then have students listen to each story, use counters or other objects to help act out the story to choose an operation, and then complete the addition or subtraction sentence of the related facts. ⭐ *10 bees are in a group. 4 bees fly away. How many bees are left?* ② *6 bees are in a group. 4 bees join them. How many bees are there in all?*

Topic 10 | Lesson 4
Digital Resources at PearsonTexas.com
five hundred forty-one **541**

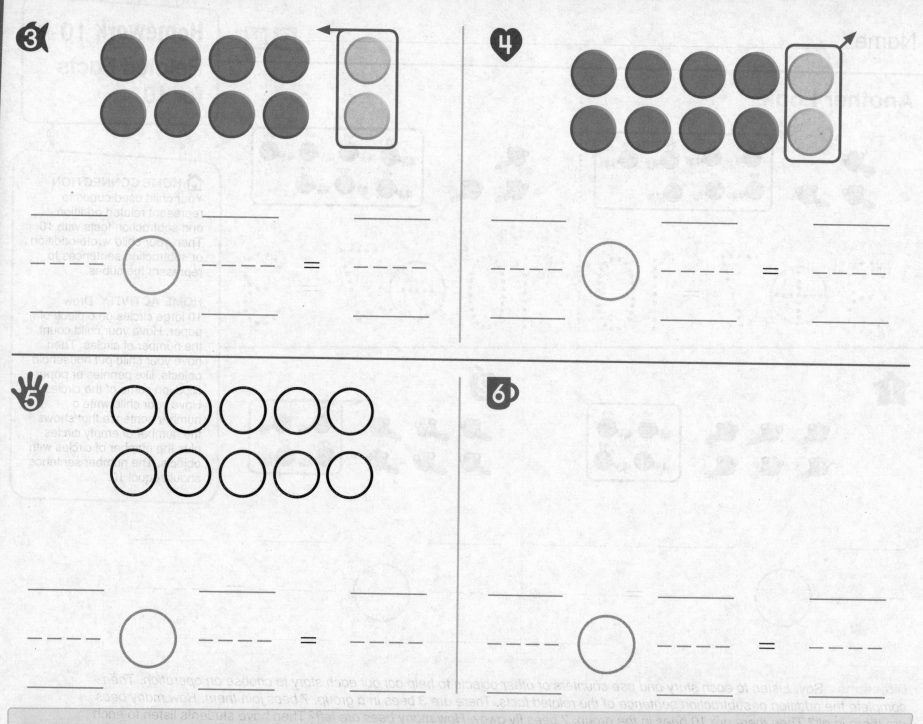

3

_____ _____ _____

◯ - - - - - = - - - - - _____

4

_____ _____ _____

◯ - - - - - = - - - - - _____

5

_____ _____ _____

- - - - - ◯ - - - - - = - - - - -

6

_____ _____ _____

- - - - - ◯ - - - - - = - - - - -

Directions Have students: **3** and **4** decide if the counters show separating or joining, and then write an addition or subtraction sentence to match; **5** color the counters to show a subtraction story, and write a number sentence to match; **6** draw counters to show an addition story that uses the same numbers as in **5**, and then write an addition sentence to match.

© Pearson Education, Inc. K

Directions Say: *Jada sees 9 fish at the pet store. She buys 2 of the fish. How many fish are left in the tank? Explain how you solved the problem. Use objects, pictures, or a number sentence to help explain.*

TEKS K.3C Explain the strategies used to solve problems involving adding and subtracting within 10 using spoken words, concrete and pictorial models, and number sentences. Also, K.3A, K.3B. **Mathematical Process Standards** K.1A, K.1B, K.1D, K.1G.

Digital Resources at PearsonTexas.com

Solve   Learn   Glossary   Check   Tools   Games

☆ Guided Practice ☆

1

Directions Have students use connecting cubes to solve the problem. Then have them draw the cubes and explain their work. Say: *Carlos brings 7 apples to share with his class at the zoo. He drops 5 apples and they roll away. How many apples are left?*

© Pearson Education, Inc. K

Topic 10 | Lesson 5

2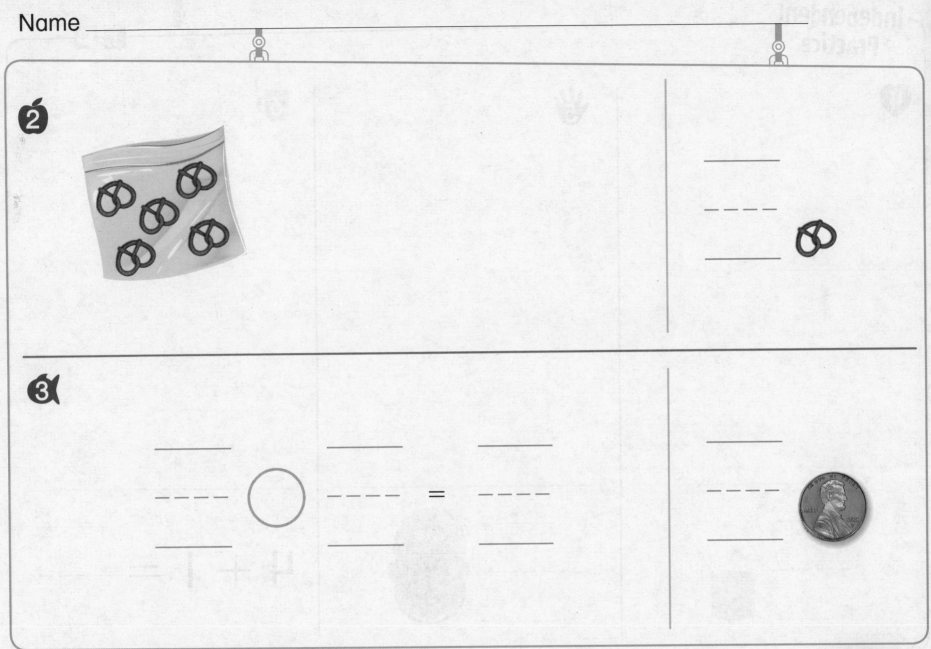

3

_____ ◯ _____ = _____

_____ _____ _____

Directions Have students: **2** listen to the story, complete the picture to solve the problem, and then explain their work. Say: *Marta packs 5 pretzels for the school trip. Her friend gives her 3 more pretzels. How many pretzels does Marta have in all?* **3** complete the number sentence to solve the problem, and then explain their work. Say: *On the school trip, Marta finds 6 pennies on the ground. She gives 2 pennies to a friend. How many pennies does Marta have left?*

—————

_ _ _ _

—————

_ _ _ _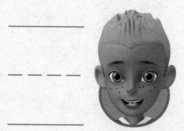

$$4 + 1 = \text{\_ \_ \_}$$

_ _ _ _

Directions Have students listen to each story, use objects, drawings, or a number sentence to solve the problem, and then explain their work. ♥ *The zoo has 10 cans of paint. They use 7 cans to paint the zoo fence. How many cans of paint do they have left?* ✋ *On Monday, 5 students sign up to go to the zoo for a class trip. On Tuesday, 4 more students sign up. How many students sign up in all?* Then have students: ☕ draw objects or pictures to show a story for 4 + 1, and then solve and explain their story.

Topic 10 | Lesson 5

Name _____

Another Look

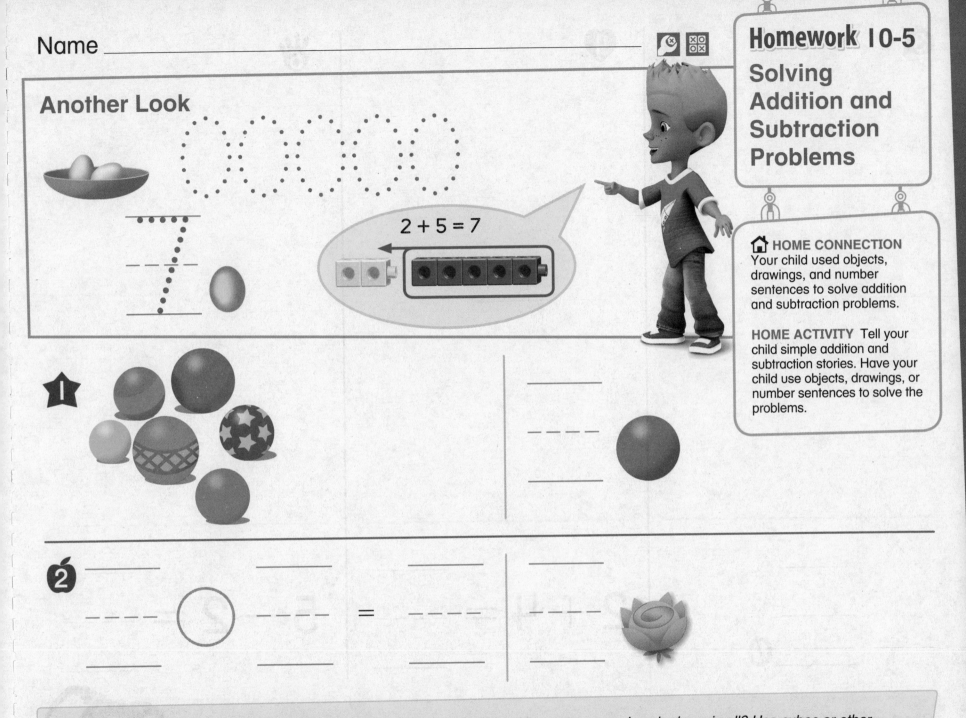

2 + 5 = 7

🏠 **HOME CONNECTION** Your child used objects, drawings, and number sentences to solve addition and subtraction problems.

HOME ACTIVITY Tell your child simple addition and subtraction stories. Have your child use objects, drawings, or number sentences to solve the problems.

⭐1

2 ___ ___ ___ ◯ ___ ___ = ___ ___ ___

Directions Say: *Alex has 2 eggs in a bowl and 5 eggs in an egg carton. How many eggs does he have in all? Use cubes or other objects to act out the story and then write the number that tells how many eggs he has in all.* Then have students listen to the story, complete the picture to solve the problem, and then explain their work. ⭐ *The playground has 6 balls. 4 students each take a ball. How many balls are left?* 2 *Jada puts 4 flowers on a shelf. Alex puts 4 more flowers on the shelf. How many flowers are there in all?*

Homework 10-5

Solving
Addition and
Subtraction
Problems

5

_____

_ _ _ _
¢

$2 + 4 =$ _ _ _ _

_____

$5 - 2 =$ _ _ _ _

_____

Directions Have students: **3** listen to the story, use objects, drawings, or a number sentence to solve the problem, and then explain their work. Say: *Jada has 4 cents for a ball. Her dad gives her 5 more cents. How many cents does Jada have in all?* **4** and **5** draw objects or pictures to show a story for each number sentence, and then solve and explain their story.

548 five hundred forty-eight

Topic 10 | Lesson 5

Solve & Share

Name _____

8 Zebras

Directions Say: *Jada sees 3 zebras. Some more zebras join the group. Now Jada sees 8 zebras. How many zebras joined the group? Use objects, pictures, or a number sentence to help explain.*

★ **TEKS K.3C** Explain the strategies used to solve problems involving adding and subtracting within 10 using spoken words, concrete and pictorial models, and number sentences. Also, K.3A, K.3B. **Mathematical Process Standards** K.1B, K.1D, K.1E, K.1F.

Digital Resources at PearsonTexas.com

Solve   Learn   Glossary   Check   Tools   Games

9 Alligators

9 − 7 = 2

7 walked away.

☆ Guided Practice ☆

★1

5¢

¢

Directions Have students use connecting cubes to solve the problem. Then have them draw the cubes and explain their work.
Say: *You have 2 cents. A ball at the zoo costs 5 cents. How many more cents do you need?*

Name _____

②

_____
- - - - -
_____

③

_____   _____   _____
- - - - (+) - - - - = - - - -
_____   _____   _____

Directions Have students: **②** listen to the story, complete the picture to solve the problem, and then explain their work.
Say: *6 turtles walk on a zoo walking path. Some turtles leave the path for a pond. Now 4 turtles walk on the path. How many
turtles left for the pond?* **③** complete the number sentence to solve the problem, and then explain their work. Say: *3 frogs
play in the pond. Some more frogs hop in the pond. Now there are 7 frogs in the pond. How many frogs hopped in the pond?*

❤ 4

✋ 5

☕ 6

_____

____ 😊

____

____ ¢

____

$2 + $ ____ $= 7$

Directions Have students listen to each story, use objects, drawings, or a number sentence to solve the problem, and then explain their work. ❤ *4 students want to play a game. The game needs 10 students. How many more students are needed for the game?* ✋ *Your friend has 7 cents. He gives you some money. Now he has 2 cents. How much money did your friend give you?* Then have students: ☕ complete the number sentence, draw a picture to match the number sentence, and then tell a friend a story to go with their picture.

© Pearson Education, Inc. K

Name _____

Another Look

8 Lions

$4 + 4 = 8$

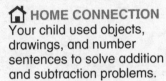

🏠 **HOME CONNECTION**
Your child used objects, drawings, and number sentences to solve addition and subtraction problems.

HOME ACTIVITY Tell your child addition and subtraction stories. Have your child use objects, drawings, or number sentences to solve the problems.

⭐1

_____

- - - - - - - - - - - -

_____

Directions Have students listen to the story, use cubes or other objects to act out the story, and then write the number that tells how many lions are hiding. Say: *4 lions roar outside. Some more lions hide. The zoo has 8 lions. How many lions are hiding?* Then have students: ⭐ listen to the story, and then use objects, drawings, or a number sentence to solve the problem. Say: *There were 7 birds sitting on the elephant's back. Now there are 2 birds. How many birds flew away?*

2

 3

 4

_____

$\underline{\quad\quad}$ ¢

3 + ----- = 9

4 − ----- = 1

© Pearson Education, Inc. K

Solve & Share Name _____

5 Snakes

7 snakes swim away.

3 snakes swim away.

Directions Say: *The zoo lake has 5 snakes. 2 snakes are behind the rocks. The rest swam away. Carlos says 7 snakes swam away. Jada says 3 snakes swam away. Circle the person that is correct. Show how you know with a picture, objects, or a number sentence.*

TEKS K.1D Communicate mathematical ideas, reasoning, and their implications using multiple representations, including symbols, diagrams, graphs, and language as appropriate. Also, K.3A, K.3B, K.3C. **Mathematical Process Standards** K.1, K.1A, K.1B, K.1E, K.1G.

Digital Resources at PearsonTexas.com

Solve   Learn   Glossary   Check   Tools   Games

Analyze

Plan

3

?

Solve and Justify

3

Evaluate

3 – 2 = 1

1 monkey is left!

☆ **Guided Practice** ☆

1

5 + 4 = 9

Directions Have students listen to the story and solve the problem. Say: *Carlos eats 5 crackers for lunch. He eats 4 crackers for a snack. How many crackers does he eat in all?* Have students write the total in the speech bubble. Have them draw counters to show each part of the story. Then re-read the problem and ask them to write the number sentence that matches the story.

Name _____

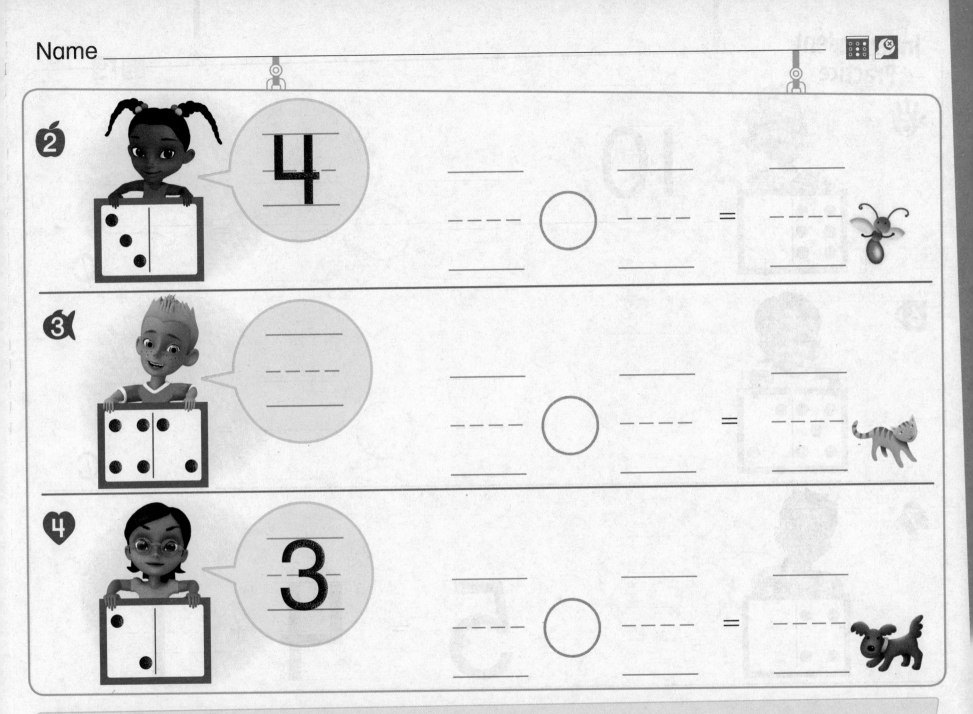

2 4 ___ ⟋ ◯ ⟋ = ___

3 = ◯ = =

4 3 ⟋ ◯ ⟋ = ___

5 10

_____ ◯ - - - - = - - - - ¢

6

_____ ◯ - - - - = - - - - ¢

7

5 = 4 + 1

Topic 10 | Lesson 7

Name _____

Another Look

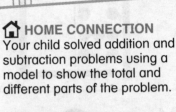

 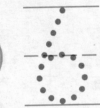 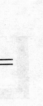 

Directions Have students listen to the story, draw counters to complete the model, and then write a number sentence to solve the problem. Say: *4 cats play. 6 dogs join them. How many cats and dogs play in all?* Then have students: ⭐ listen to the story, complete the model, and then write a number sentence to solve the problem. Say: *10 cats play. 4 cats leave. How many cats are left?*

2

$\_\_\_ \bigcirc \_\_\_ = \_\_\_$

$\_\_\_ ¢$

3

$\_\_\_$

$6 = 4 + 2$

4

$\_\_\_$

$2 = 6 - 4$

Directions Have students: **2** listen to the story, draw counters to complete the model, and then write a number sentence to solve the problem. Say: *Alex has a dime. He spends 7 cents on a pencil. How much money does Alex have now?* **3** draw counters to complete the model for 6 = 4 + 2, and then tell an addition story for the model; **4** draw counters and write the total in the speech bubble to complete the model for 2 = 6 − 4, and then tell a subtraction story for the model.

560 five hundred sixty

Topic 10 | Lesson 7

Name _____

Set A

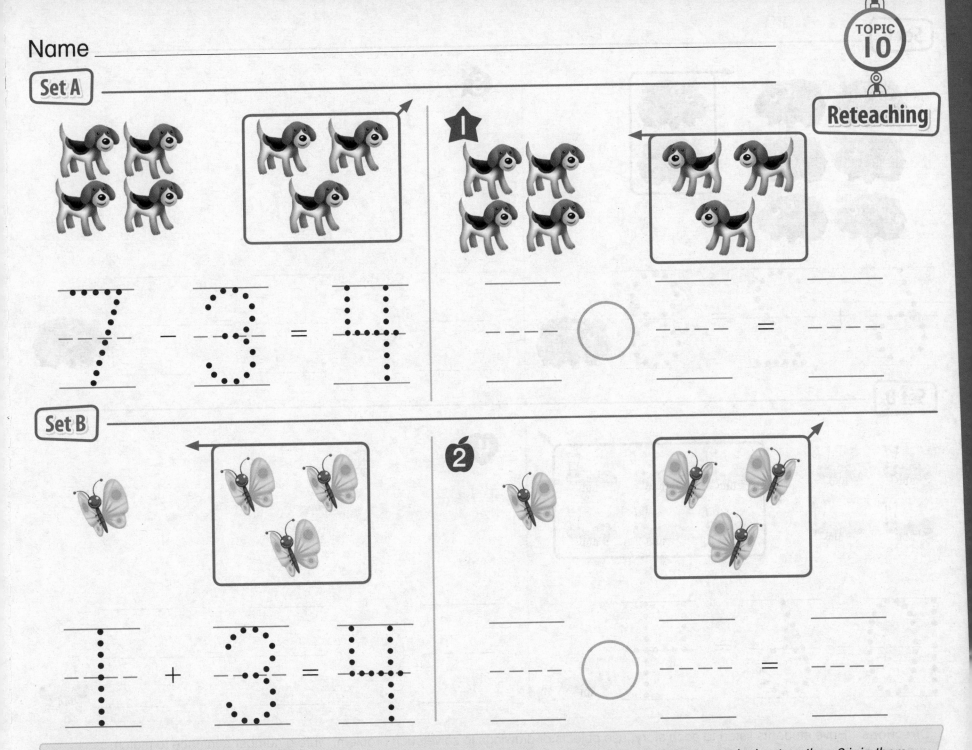

1

7 − 3 = 4

____ ◯ ____ = ____

Set B

2

1 + 3 = 4

____ ◯ ____ = ____

Directions Have students listen to each story, and then write a number sentence to match. **1** 4 dogs are playing together. 3 join them. How many are there in all? **2** 4 butterflies are in a field. 3 fly away. How many are there now?

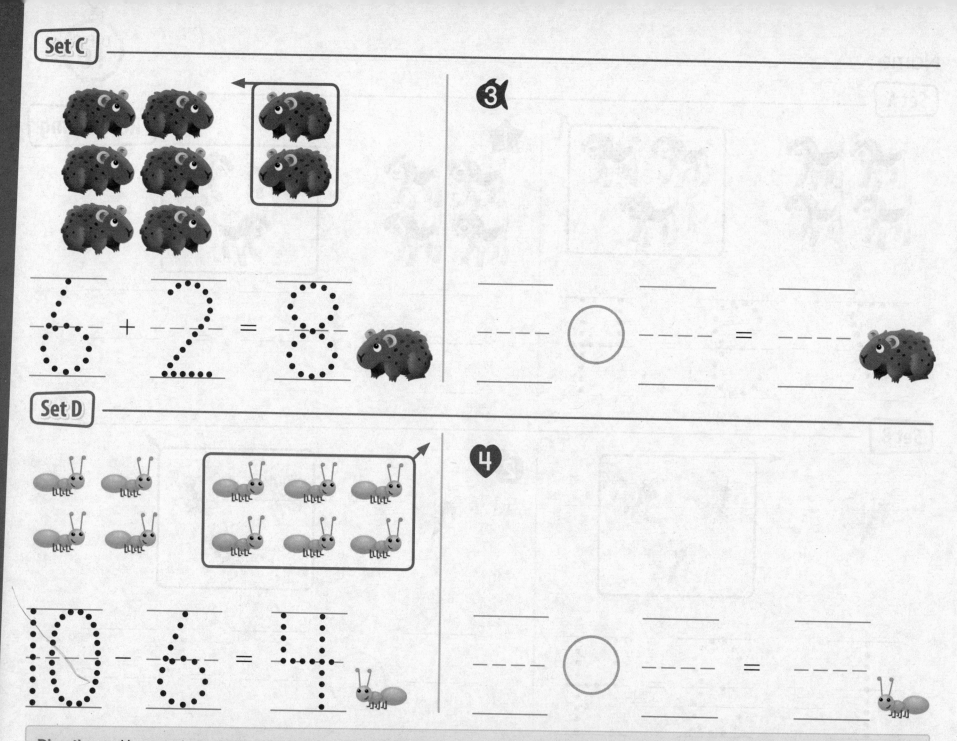

6 + 2 = 8

3

10 - 6 = 4

4

Directions Have students listen to each story, use objects or drawings to solve each problem, write a number sentence to match, and then explain their work. ③ *8 guinea pigs are in a cage at the pet store. Someone buys 2 of them. How many are left?* ④ *Roger has 4 ants. He needs 10 ants for his ant farm. How many more does he need?*

© Pearson Education, Inc. K

Name _____

1

○ $3 - 2 = 1$

○ $5 - 2 = 3$

○ $3 + 2 = 5$

○ $3 + 3 = 6$

2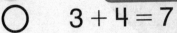

○ $3 + 4 = 7$

○ $3 + 3 = 6$

○ $6 - 3 = 3$

○ $3 - 3 = 0$

3

○ $5 - 4 = 1$

○ $9 - 4 = 5$

○ $4 + 4 = 8$

○ $5 + 4 = 9$

4

○ $3 - 2 = 1$

○ $5 - 2 = 3$

○ $3 + 7 = 10$

○ $3 + 3 = 6$

Directions Have students mark the best answer. ★ 3 cats are in a group. 2 cats join them. How many cats are there in all? Which number sentence matches this story? ❷ 6 birds are in a group. 3 birds leave. How many birds are there now? Which number sentence matches this story? ❸ 9 dogs are in a group. 4 dogs leave. How many dogs are there now? Which number sentence matches this story? ❹ 3 snails are in a group. 7 snails join them. How many snails are there in all? Which number sentence matches this story?

3   4   5   6

○   ○   ○   ○

8   6   3   2

○   ○   ○   ○

_____

- - - - -

_____

- - - - ○ - - - - = - - - -

_____

Directions Have students: mark the best answer. Say: *There are 4 apples in a bowl. To make an apple pie, Jada needs 8 apples in all. How many more apples does Jada need?* mark the best answer. Say: *There are 8 birds on a branch. Some of the birds fly away. Now there are 6 birds on the branch. How many birds flew away?* listen to the story, write a number sentence to solve the problem, and then write the total in the speech bubble to complete the model. Say: *Carlos sees 4 caterpillars in a tree and 2 caterpillars in the grass. How many caterpillars does Carlos see in all?*

564 five hundred sixty-four   © Pearson Education, Inc. K   **Topic 10**

Counting to 100

Essential Question: How can numbers to 100 be counted using a hundred chart?

Ants!

Ants live in colonies.

Math and Science Project: Ant Colonies

Directions Read the character speech bubbles to students. **Find Out!** Have students find out about ant colonies. Say: *Talk to friends and relatives about ant colonies. Ask about the different jobs ants in a colony might have.* **Journal: Make a Poster** Then have students make a poster. Have them draw an ant colony with 5 groups of ants, and 10 ants in each group. Then have them use a hundred chart to count by 10 to 50 and tell how many ants there are in all.

Name _____

Review What You Know

1

$5 + 4 = 9$

$5 - 4 = 1$

2

$6 - 3 = 3$

3

$7 - 4 = 3$

4

5   3   2

5

5   15   10

6

23   8   13

Directions Have students: **1** circle the subtraction sentence; **2** circle the minus sign; **3** circle the difference; **4–6** circle the correct number of counters shown in each set.

hundred chart

pattern

My Word Cards

10 20 30 40 50

Point to the numbers.
Say: *When you count by 10s you are using a number **pattern**.*

1	2	3	4	5	6	7	8	9	10
11	12	13	14	15	16	17	18	19	20
21	22	23	24	25	26	27	28	29	30
31	32	33	34	35	36	37	38	39	40
41	42	43	44	45	46	47	48	49	50
51	52	53	54	55	56	57	58	59	60
61	62	63	64	65	66	67	68	69	70
71	72	73	74	75	76	77	78	79	80
81	82	83	84	85	86	87	88	89	90
91	92	93	94	95	96	97	98	99	100

column

row

Point to the hundred chart.
Say: *A **hundred chart** helps us count larger numbers and find number patterns.*

Solve & Share Name _____

1	2	3	4	5	6	7	8	9	10
11	12	13	14	15	16	17	18	19	20
21	22	23	24	25	26	27	28	29	30
31	32	33	34	35	36	37	38	39	40
41	42	43	44	45	46	47	48	49	50
51	52	53	54	55	56	57	58	59	60
61	62	63	64	65	66	67	68	69	70
71	72	73	74	75	76	77	78	79	80
81	82	83	84	85	86	87	88	89	90
91	92	93	94	95	96	97	98	99	100

Directions Say: *Carlos looks at the chart. He knows 21 comes after 20. What number comes after 30? How do you know?*

★ **TEKS K.5** Identify the pattern in the number word list. Recite numbers up to at least 100 by ones and tens beginning with any given number. **Mathematical Process Standards** K.1C, K.1D, K.1F, K.1G.

Digital Resources at PearsonTexas.com

Solve   Learn   Glossary   Check   Tools   Games

Topic 11 | Lesson 1

41	42	43	44	45	46	47	48	49	50
51	52	53	54	55	56	57	58	59	60
61	62	63	64	65	66	67	68	69	70
71	72	73	74	75	76	77	78	79	80
81	82	83	84	85	86	87	88	89	90
91	92	93	94	95	96	97	98	99	100

61	62	63	64	65	66	67	68	69	70
71	72	73	74	75	76	77	78	79	80
81	82	83	84	85	86	87	88	89	90
91	92	93	94	95	96	97	98	99	100

☆ Guided Practice ☆

1

1	2	3	4	5	6	7	8	9	10
11	12	13	14	15	16	17	18	19	20
21	22	23	24	25	26	27	28	29	30
31	32	33	34	35	36	37	38	39	40

2

61		63	64	65	66		68		70
	72	73	74	75	76	77		79	80
81	82	83	84	85	86	87	88	89	
91	92	93	94	95	96	97	98	99	

Directions Have students count by 1s to write the missing numbers.

© Pearson Education, Inc. K

Topic 11 | Lesson 1

Name _____

1	2	3	4	5	6	7	8	9
11	12	13	14	15	16	17	18	19
21	22	23	24	25	26	27	28	29
31	32	33	34	35	36	37	38	39
41	42	43	44	45	46	47	48	49
51	52	53	54	55	56	57	58	59
61	62	63	64	65	66	67	68	69
71	72	73	74	75	76	77	78	79
81	82	83	84	85	86	87	88	89
91	92	93	94	95	96	97	98	99

1	2	3	4		6	7	8	9	10
11	12	13	14	15		17	18		20
21	22				26	27	28	29	30
31	32	33	34	35	36	37		39	
	42	43	44	45		47	48	49	50
51	52	53	54	55		57		59	60
		63	64	65	66	67	68	69	70
71	72	73	74		76	77	78		80
81		83	84	85	86	87		89	
91	92	93	94	95	96	97	98		

Directions Have students count by 1s to write the missing numbers.

Independent Practice

1	2	3	4		6	7	8	9	10
11	12	13	14		16	17	18	19	20
21	22	23	24		26	27	28	29	30
31	32	33	34		36	37	38	39	40
41	42	43	44		46	47	48	49	50
51	52	53	54		56	57	58	59	60
61	62	63	64		66	67	68	69	70
71	72	73	74		76	77	78	79	80
81	82	83	84		86	87	88	89	90
91	92	93	94		96	97	98	99	100

1	2		4	5	6	7	8	9	10
11	12	13			16	17	18	19	20
21	22	23	24	25			28	29	30
31	32	33		35	36	37	38		
41	42		44	45	46	47	48	49	50
51			54	55	56	57	58	59	60
61	62	63	64	65	66		68	69	
71	72	73	74	75	76	77		79	
81		83	84		86	87	88	89	90
91	92	93	94	95	96	97	98		

Directions Have students: count by 1s to write the missing numbers; count by 1s to write the missing numbers, and then circle the column that has numbers ending in 3.

Topic 11 | Lesson 1

Name _____

Another Look

1	2	3	4	5	6	7	8	9	10
11	12	13	14	15	16	17	18	19	20
21	22	23	24	25	26	27	28	29	30
31	32	33	34	35	36	37	38	39	40
41	42	43	44	45	46	47	48	49	50

🏠 **HOME CONNECTION**
Your child counted to 100 and wrote numbers on a hundred chart. Your child also identified missing numbers on a hundred chart.

HOME ACTIVITY Point to a hundred chart from this lesson. Take turns making up riddles and guessing the answers. For example, ask your child: *What number comes just after 31 and just before 33?* [32] *What number is in the 4th column and the 6th row?* [54]

 1

1	2	3	4	5	6	7	8		10
11	12	13	14	15	16	17	18		20
21	22	23	24	25	26	27	28		30
31	32	33	34	35	36	37	38		40
41	42	43	44	45	46	47	48		50

 2

1	2	3	4	5	6	7	8	9	10
11	12	13	14	15	16	17	18	19	20
21	22	23	24	25	26	27	28	29	30
41	42	43	44	45	46	47	48	49	50
51	52	53	54	55	56	57	58	59	60

Directions Say: *What number comes just after 6? You can count by 1s to write all the missing numbers.* Then have students: 🌟 and ② count by 1s to write the missing numbers.

1			4	5	6	7		9	10
11		13	14	15	16		18	19	20
21	22	23	24	25			28	29	30
	32	33	34	35	36	37	38		
41		43	44	45	46	47	48	49	50

	42	43	44	45	46	47	48		50
51	52	52	54	55			58	59	
61	62		64	65	66	67	68		70
71	72	73	74	75	76	77			80
81	82	83	84		86	87	88	89	
91	92	93	94	95	96	97	98		

11		13		15	16	17	18	19	20
	22	23	24	25	26	27	28		30
	32		34	35	36	37	38		40
41	42	43		45	46	47	48		
51		53	54	55	56	57		59	60

51	52	53	54	55	56	57	58	59	60
61	62	63	64	65	66	67	68	69	70
71	72	73	74	75	76	77	78	79	80
81	82	83	84	85	86	87	88	89	90
91	92	93	94	95	96	97	98	99	100

Directions Have students: ❸ and ❹ count by 1s to write the missing numbers; ✋ count by 1s to write the missing numbers, and then circle the column that has numbers ending in 4; ☕ circle the number that is 1 more than 72, and then draw an X on the number that is 1 less than 90.

Solve & Share   Name _____

1	2	3	4	5	6	7	8	9	10
11	12	13	14	15	16	17	18	19	20
21	22	23	24	25	26	27	28	29	30
31	32	33	34	35	36	37	38	39	40
41	42	43	44	45	46	47	48	49	50
51	52	53	54	55	56	57	58	59	60
61	62	63	64	65	66	67	68	69	70
71	72	73	74	75	76	77	78	79	80
81	82	83	84	85	86	87	88	89	90
91	92	93	94	95	96	97	98	99	100

Directions Say: *Numbers can form patterns, too. What pattern do you see if you count by 10s on a hundred chart?*

⭐ **TEKS K.5** Identify the pattern in the number word list. Recite numbers up to at least 100 by ones and tens beginning with any given number. **Mathematical Process Standards** K.1B, K.1C, K.1D, K.1G.

Digital Resources at PearsonTexas.com

 Solve   Learn   A-Z Glossary   Check   Tools   Games

☆ Guided Practice

1

21	22	23	24	25	26	27	28	29	30
31	32	33	34	35	36	37	38	39	40
41	42	43	44	45	46	47	48	49	50
51	52	53	54	55	56	57	58	59	60

2

1	2	3	4	5	6	7	8	9	10
11	12	13	14	15	16	17	18	19	20
21	22	23	24	25	26	27	28	29	30
31	32	33	34	35	36	37	38	39	40

Directions Have students: **1** count by 10s beginning with 30, and then circle the numbers to show the pattern; **2** count by 10s beginning with 2, and then color the boxes yellow to show the pattern.

576 five hundred seventy-six

Topic 11 | Lesson 2

Name _____

 3

1	2	3	4	5	6	7	8	9	⑩
11	12	13	14	15	16	17	18	19	20
21	22	23	24	25	26	27	28	29	30
31	32	33	34	35	36	37	38	39	40
41	42	43	44	45	46	47	48	49	50
51	52	53	54	55	56	57	58	59	60
61	62	63	64	65	66	67	68	69	70
71	72	73	74	75	76	77	78	79	80
81	82	83	84	85	86	87	88	89	90
91	92	93	94	95	96	97	98	99	100

 4

1	2	③	4	5	6	7	8	9	10
11	12	13	14	15	16	17	18	19	20
21	22	23	24	25	26	27	28	29	30
31	32	33	34	35	36	37	38	39	40
41	42	43	44	45	46	47	48	49	50
51	52	53	54	55	56	57	58	59	60
61	62	63	64	65	66	67	68	69	70
71	72	73	74	75	76	77	78	79	80
81	82	83	84	85	86	87	88	89	90
91	92	93	94	95	96	97	98	99	100

 5

1	2	3	4	⑤	6	7	8	9	10
11	12	13	14	15	16	17	18	19	20
21	22	23	24	25	26	27	28	29	30
31	32	33	34	35	36	37	38	39	40
41	42	43	44	45	46	47	48	49	50
51	52	53	54	55	56	57	58	59	60
61	62	63	64	65	66	67	68	69	70
71	72	73	74	75	76	77	78	79	80
81	82	83	84	85	86	87	88	89	90
91	92	93	94	95	96	97	98	99	100

 6

1	2	3	4	5	6	7	⑧	9	10
11	12	13	14	15	16	17	18	19	20
21	22	23	24	25	26	27	28	29	30
31	32	33	34	35	36	37	38	39	40
41	42	43	44	45	46	47	48	49	50
51	52	53	54	55	56	57	58	59	60
61	62	63	64	65	66	67	68	69	70
71	72	73	74	75	76	77	78	79	80
81	82	83	84	85	86	87	88	89	90
91	92	93	94	95	96	97	98	99	100

Directions Have students count aloud by 10s beginning with the circled number, and then circle each number as they count.

Independent Practice

 7

1	2	3	④	5	6	7	8	9	10
11	12	13	14	15	16	17	18	19	20
21	22	23	24	25	26	27	28	29	30
31	32	33	34	35	36	37	38	39	40
41	42	43	44	45	46	47	48	49	50
51	52	53	54	55	56	57	58	59	60
61	62	63	64	65	66	67	68	69	70
71	72	73	74	75	76	77	78	79	80
81	82	83	84	85	86	87	88	89	90
91	92	93	94	95	96	97	98	99	100

8

1	2	3	4	5	6	⑦	8	9	10
11	12	13	14	15	16	17	18	19	20
21	22	23	24	25	26	27	28	29	30
31	32	33	34	35	36	37	38	39	40
41	42	43	44	45	46	47	48	49	50
51	52	53	54	55	56	57	58	59	60
61	62	63	64	65	66	67	68	69	70
71	72	73	74	75	76	77	78	79	80
81	82	83	84	85	86	87	88	89	90
91	92	93	94	95	96	97	98	99	100

 9

1	2	3	4	5	6	7	8	⑨	10
11	12	13	14	15	16	17	18	19	20
21	22	23	24	25	26	27	28	29	30
31	32	33	34	35	36	37	38	39	40
41	42	43	44	45	46	47	48	49	50
51	52	53	54	55	56	57	58	59	60
61	62	63	64	65	66	67	68	69	70
71	72	73	74	75	76	77	78	79	80
81	82	83	84	85	86	87	88	89	90
91	92	93	94	95	96	97	98	99	100

10

51	52	53	54	55	56	57	58	59	
61	62	63	64	65	66	67	68	69	
71	72	73	74	75	76	77	78	79	
81	82	83	84	85	86	87	88	89	
91	92	93	94	95	96	97	98	99	

Directions Have students: **7**–**9** count by 10s beginning with the circled number, and then color the boxes yellow to show the pattern; **10** write the missing number after 59, count by 10s beginning with that number, write the missing numbers, and then color the boxes yellow to show the pattern.

Topic 11 | Lesson 2

Another Look

1	2	3	4	5	6	7	8	9	10
11	12	13	14	15	16	17	18	19	20
21	22	23	24	25	26	27	28	29	30
31	32	33	34	35	36	37	38	39	40
41	42	43	44	45	46	47	48	49	50
51	52	53	54	55	56	57	58	59	60
61	62	63	64	65	66	67	68	69	70
71	72	73	74	75	76	77	78	79	80
81	82	83	84	85	86	87	88	89	90
91	92	93	94	95	96	97	98	99	100

HOME CONNECTION
Your child counted by 10s from a given number and determined the pattern on a hundred chart.

HOME ACTIVITY Point to a number on a hundred chart, such as 27. Have your child count by 10s from that number. Then ask your child to describe the pattern. For example, all the numbers end with 7. Repeat with other numbers.

 1

1	2	3	4	5	6	7	8	9	10
11	12	13	14	15	16	17	18	19	20
21	22	23	24	25	26	27	28	29	30
31	32	33	34	35	36	37	38	39	40
41	42	43	44	45	46	47	48	49	50
51	52	53	54	55	56	57	58	59	60
61	62	63	64	65	66	67	68	69	70
71	72	73	74	75	76	77	78	79	80
81	82	83	84	85	86	87	88	89	90
91	92	93	94	95	96	97	98	99	100

 2

1	2	3	4	5	6	7	8	9	10
11	12	13	14	15	16	17	18	19	20
21	22	23	24	25	26	27	28	29	30
31	32	33	34	35	36	37	38	39	40
41	42	43	44	45	46	47	48	49	50
51	52	53	54	55	56	57	58	59	60
61	62	63	64	65	66	67	68	69	70
71	72	73	74	75	76	77	78	79	80
81	82	83	84	85	86	87	88	89	90
91	92	93	94	95	96	97	98	99	100

Directions Say: *You can count by 10s beginning at any number. Let's count by 10s beginning with 1 and circle each number. What pattern do you see?* Then have students: **1** count by 10s beginning with 2, and then circle the numbers to show the pattern; **2** count by 10s beginning with 5, and then circle the numbers to show the pattern.

3

1	2	3	4	5	6	7	8	9	10
11	12	13	14	15	16	17	18	19	20
21	22	23	24	25	26	27	28	29	30
31	32	33	34	35	36	37	38	39	40
41	42	43	44	45	46	47	48	49	50
51	52	53	54	55	56	57	58	59	60
61	62	63	64	65	66	67	68	69	70
71	72	73	74	75	76	77	78	79	80
81	82	83	84	85	86	87	88	89	90
91	92	93	94	95	96	97	98	99	100

 4

1	2	3	4	5	6	7	8	9	10
11	12	13	14	15	16	17	18	19	20
21	22	23	24	25	26	27	28	29	30
31	32	33	34	35	36	37	38	39	40
41	42	43	44	45	46	47	48	49	50
51	52	53	54	55	56	57	58	59	60
61	62	63	64	65	66	67	68	69	70
71	72	73	74	75	76	77	78	79	80
81	82	83	84	85	86	87	88	89	90
91	92	93	94	95	96	97	98	99	100

 5

1	2	3		5	6		8	9	10
11	12	13		15	16		18	19	20
21	22	23		25	26		28	29	30
31	32	33		35	36		38	39	40
41	42	43		45	46		48	49	50
51	52	53		55	56		58	59	60
61	62	63		65	66		68	69	70
71	72	73		75	76		78	79	80
81	82	83		85	86		88	89	90
91	92	93		95	96		98	99	100

 6

1	2	3	4	5	6	7	8	9	
11	12	13	14	15	16	17	18	19	
21	22	23	24	25	26	27	28	29	
31	32	33	34	35	36	37	38	39	
41	42	43	44	45	46	47	48	49	
51	52	53	54	55	56	57	58	59	
61	62	63	64	65	66	67	68	69	
71	72	73	74	75	76	77	78	79	
81	82	83	84	85	86	87	88	89	
91	92	93	94	95	96	97	98	99	100

Directions Have students: **3** count by 10s beginning with 6, and then color the boxes yellow to show the pattern; **4** count by 10s beginning with 5, and then color the boxes yellow to show the pattern; **5** count by 10s beginning with 4, write the missing numbers, and then repeat beginning with 7; **6** count by 10s backward beginning with 100, and then write the missing numbers.

© Pearson Education, Inc. K

Topic 11 | Lesson 2

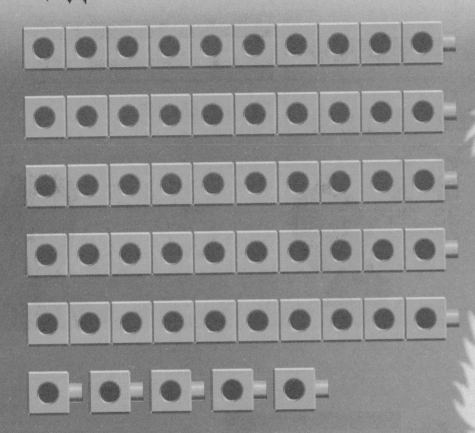

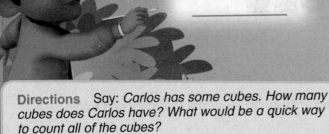

Directions Say: *Carlos has some cubes. How many cubes does Carlos have? What would be a quick way to count all of the cubes?*

⭐**TEKS K.5** Identify the pattern in the number word list. Recite numbers up to at least 100 by ones and tens beginning with any given number. **Mathematical Process Standards** K.1C, K.1D, K.1F, K.1G.

Digital Resources at PearsonTexas.com

  A-Z
Solve   Learn   Glossary   Check   Tools   Games

10
20
30

31 32 33 34

Guided Practice

⭐ 1

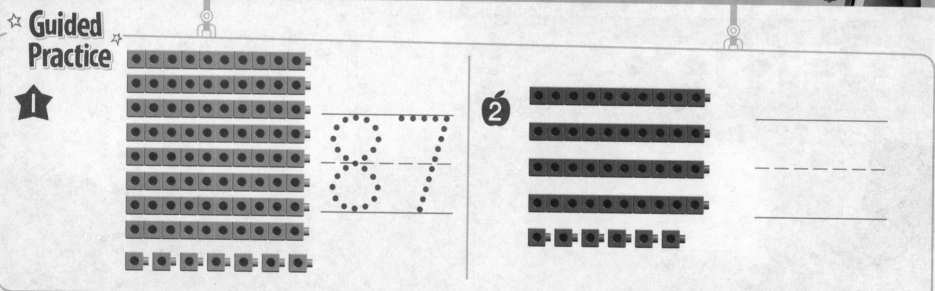

2

Directions Have students count by 10s and then by 1s to write the number that tells how many. Remind students that they can use a hundred chart to count by 10s and then count on by 1s.

© Pearson Education, Inc. K

Name _____

3
_____

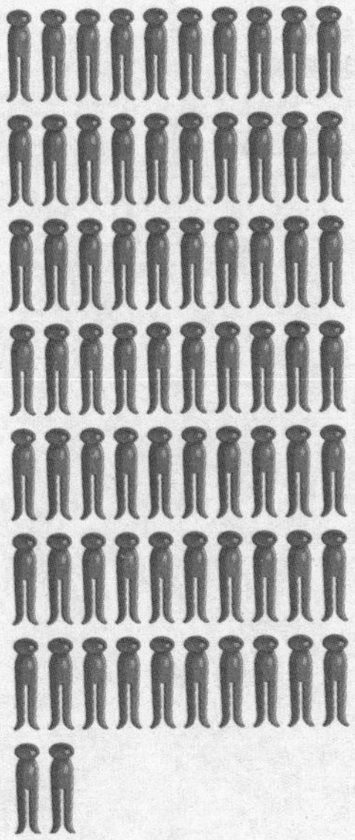

- - - - - - - - -

4
_____

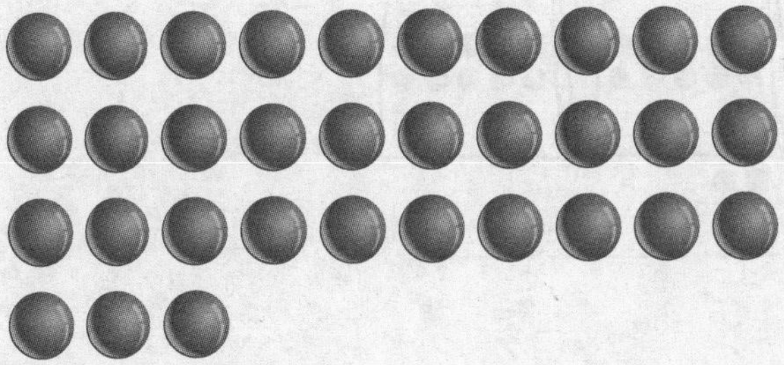

- - - - - - - - -

_____

5
_____

- - - - - - - - -

_____

6
_____

- - - - - - - - -

_____

Directions Have students count by 10s and then by 1s to write the number that tells how many. If needed, allow students to use a hundred chart.

Topic 11 | Lesson 3

five hundred eighty-three **583**

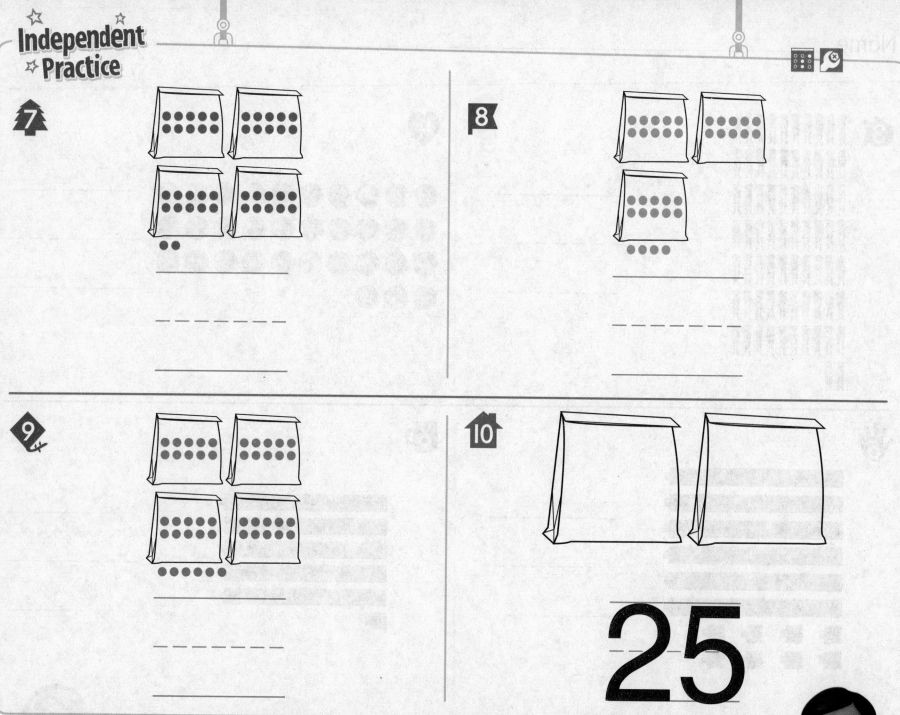

Independent Practice

7

_____

_ _ _ _ _ _ _ _

_____

8

_ _ _ _ _ _ _ _

9

_____

_ _ _ _ _ _ _ _

10

25

Directions Have students: **7–9** count by 10s and then by 1s to write the number that tells how many; **10** draw dots to show how to arrange the number 25 for fast counting.

© Pearson Education, Inc. K

Another Look

31

🏠 **HOME CONNECTION**
Your child counted objects by 10s and 1s to find how many.

HOME ACTIVITY Set out a large number of pennies, beads, or other small objects. Have your child arrange the objects in groups of 10 for fast counting. Then have your child count by 10s and 1s to find how many.

⭐ 1

_____

- - - - - - - - - -

_____

🍎 2

_____

- - - - - - - - - -

_____

Directions Say: *Alex arranged his counting beads into groups of 10 for fast counting. Count the beads by 10s and then by 1s. How many beads are there? Write the number that tells how many.* Then have students: ⭐ and 🍎 count the beads by 10s and then by 1s to write the number that tells how many.

3

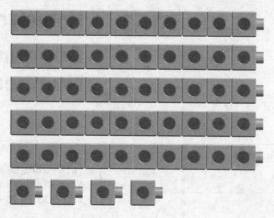

_____

_ _ _ _ _ _ _ _ _ _ _

_____

4

_ _ _ _ _ _ _ _ _ _ _

 5

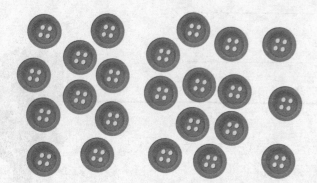

_____

_ _ _ _ _ _ _ _ _ _ _

_____

6

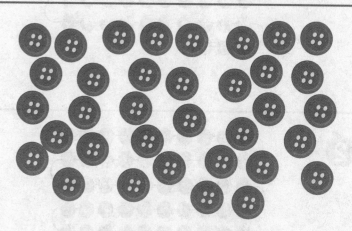

_____

_ _ _ _ _ _ _ _ _ _ _

_____

Directions Have students count by 10s and then by 1s to write the number that tells how many; ✋ and ☕ circle groups of buttons for fast counting, and then count by 10s and 1s to write the number that tells how many.

586 five hundred eighty-six   © Pearson Education, Inc. K   **Topic 11** | Lesson 3

 **Name** _____

1	2	3	4	5	6	7	8	9	10
11	12	13	14	15	16	17	18	19	20
21	22	23	24	25	26	27	28	29	30
31	32	33	34	35	36	37	38	39	40
41	42	43	44	45	46	47	48	49	50
51	52	53	54	55	56	57	58	59	60
61	62	63	64	65	66	67	68	69	70
71	72	73	74	75	76	77	78	79	80
81	82	83	84	85	86	87	88	89	90
91	92	93	94	95	96	97	98	99	100

six

sixteen

twenty-six

Directions Say: *Carlos wants to say the number words for all the numbers in the yellow column. He knows that the number 6 is said as six, 16 is said as sixteen, and 26 is said as twenty-six. How can he say the other numbers in this column?*

⭐ **TEKS K.5** Identify the pattern in the number word list. Recite numbers up to at least 100 by ones and tens beginning with any given number. **Mathematical Process Standards** K.1D, K.1E, K.1F.

Digital Resources at PearsonTexas.com

Solve   Learn   Glossary   Check   Tools   Games

Topic 11 | Lesson 4

five hundred eighty-seven **587**

31	32	33	34	35	36	37	38	39	40
41	42	43	44	45	46	47	48	49	50
51	52	53	54	55	56	57	58	59	60

51	52	53	54	55	56	57	58	59	60
61	62	63	64	65	66	67	68	69	70
71	72	73	74	75	76	77	78	79	80
81	82	83	84	85	86	87	88	89	90
91	92	93	94	95	96	97	98	99	100

forty,
forty-**one**, forty-**two**,
forty-**three**, forty-**four**,
forty-**five**, forty-**six**,
forty-**seven**, forty-**eight**,
forty-**nine**

fifty-five, **sixty**-five,
seventy-five, **eighty**-five,
ninety-five

☆ Guided Practice ☆

1

twenty-**six**,
twenty-**seven**,
twenty-**eight**,
twenty-**nine**

20
(30)

2

thirty-**seven**,
forty-**seven**,
fifty-**seven**,
sixty-**seven**

68

77

Directions Read each list of number words aloud. Have students listen for each pattern, and then circle the number that comes next.

Topic 11 | Lesson 4

Name _____

3 🐟
eighty-**six**,
eighty-**seven**,
eighty-**eight**,
eighty-**nine**

90
99

4 ❤
ninety-**five**,
ninety-**six**,
ninety-**seven**,
ninety-**eight**

99
88

5 ✋
twenty-two,
thirty-two,
forty-two,
fifty-two

53
62

6 ☕
fifty-eight,
sixty-eight,
seventy-eight,
eighty-eight

89
98

7 🌲
forty-**six**,
forty-**seven**,
forty-**eight**,
forty-**nine**

50
59

8 🚩
fifty-two,
sixty-two,
seventy-two,
eighty-two

92
83

Directions Recite the number words together. Have students circle the number that comes next in the pattern.

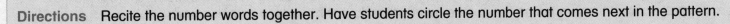

_____

fifty-nine, sixty-nine, _____, eighty-nine, ninety-nine

_____

thirty-seven, thirty-eight, thirty-nine, _____, forty-one

_____

seventy-six, _____, seventy-eight, seventy-nine, eighty

ten, eleven, twelve, _____, fourteen, _____, sixteen, seventeen

Directions Recite the number words together. Have students: — write the number that is missing from the pattern; write the numbers that are missing from the pattern, and then underline the number words that do **not** have *teen* in their names.

© Pearson Education, Inc. K

Name _____

Another Look

eighty 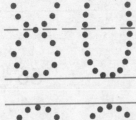 80

eighty-one 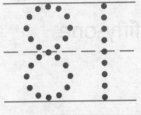 81

eighty-two  82

eighty-three 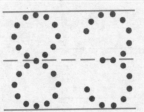 83

🏠 HOME CONNECTION
Your child recited and identified the patterns in the names of numbers up to 100.

HOME ACTIVITY Make cards with numerals on one side and matching number names on the other side. Use the number names to make patterns counting by 1s and 10s omitting some numbers. Recite the number names together. Have your child put the missing number card in the correct place and then turn it over to check the pattern.

 1

twenty-seven _____

twenty-eight _____

twenty-nine _____

thirty _____

Directions Say: *Look at the pattern in the number words. Let's say each number word together. Write the numbers that match the number words.* Then have students: ⭐ say each number word in the pattern, and then write the matching numbers.

Topic 11 | Lesson 4   Digital Resources at **PearsonTexas.com**   five hundred ninety-one **591**

2

51

fifty-three

fifty-one

52

_____

fifty-two

- - - - - - - - - - -

3

_____

- - - - - - - - - - -

fifty-five

_____

56

55

fifty-seven   fifty-six

4

_____   _____

- - - - - - - - - -   - - - - - - - -

thirty-seven, _____, thirty-nine, _____

1s

10s

5

_____   _____

- - - - - - - - - -   - - - - - - - -

two, twelve, _____, _____, forty-two

1s

10s

Directions Have students: **2** and **3** draw lines to match the numbers with their number names, and then write the missing number; **4** and **5** recite the number words together, write the missing numbers in the pattern, and then circle the number that describes the pattern.

20 21 22

40 50 60

Directions Say: *Carlos sees 2 rows of baseball jerseys. The first, second, and third jerseys have a number. But the other jerseys have no number. What number goes on each jersey? How can Carlos solve this problem?*

TEKS K.1F Analyze mathematical relationships to connect and communicate mathematical ideas. Also, K.5. **Mathematical Process Standards** K.1, K.1A, K.1B, K.1D.

Analyze

Plan

Solve, Justify, and Evaluate

Count by 10s.

Guided Practice

1

 53  54  55  56  57

Directions Have students look at the row, find the pattern, and then write the missing numbers.

© Pearson Education, Inc. K

Topic 11 | Lesson 5

Name ______________________________

2	70	____	50	40	____	20
3	50	____	70	____	90	100
4	____	41	42	____	44	45
5	55	54	____	____	51	____

Directions Have students look at each row, find the pattern, and then write the missing numbers.

6

22   32   42   52   ___   ___

7

34   33   32   31   ___   ___

8

50   60   70   ___   ___   ___

9

100   ___   ___   ___   ___   ___   ___   ___

Directions Have students: **6–8** look at each row, find the pattern, and then write the missing numbers; **9** start with 100, make up a pattern, and then write numbers to show the pattern.

© Pearson Education, Inc. K
Topic 11 | Lesson 5

Name _____

Another Look

30   40   50   (60 70 80 traced)

   trucks

🏠 **HOME CONNECTION**
Your child looked at a number pattern, identified the pattern, and wrote missing numbers.

HOME ACTIVITY Choose a number pattern on this page and have your child continue the pattern by adding four more numbers. Repeat by choosing a different pattern.

⭐ 6   7   8   _____ _____ _____

    trucks

❷ 10   20   30   _____ _____ _____

 trucks ...

Directions Say: *How can Alex find what numbers come next in the pattern? Look at the numbers. What is the pattern? Since the pattern is counting by 10s, what numbers come after 50?* Write the numbers. Then have students: ⭐ and ❷ look at each row, find the pattern, and then write the missing numbers.

3 60 50 40 ___ ___ ___

4 ___ ___ ___ ___ ___ ___   1s 10s

5 ___ ___ ___ ___ ___ ___   1s 10s

Directions Have students: **3** look at the row, find the pattern, and then write the missing numbers; **4** write numbers to make a pattern that counts backward by 1s; **5** write numbers to make a pattern that counts backward by 10s.

© Pearson Education, Inc. K

Topic 11 | Lesson 5

Set A

1	2	3	4	5	6	7	8	9	10
11	12	13	14	15	16	17	18	19	20
21	22	23	24	25	26	27	28	29	30
31	32	33	34	35	36	37	38	39	40
41	42	43	44	45	46	47	48	49	50
51	52	53	54	55	56	57	58	59	60
61	62	63	64	65	66	67	68	69	70
71	72	73	74	75	76	77	78	79	80
81	82	83	84	85	86	87	88	89	90
91	92	93	94	95	96	97	98	99	100

41	42	43	44	45	46	47	48		50
51	52	53	54		56	57	58	59	
61	62	63	64	65	66	67	68	69	70
	72	73	74	75		77	78	79	80
81	82		84	85	86	87	88		90
91	92	93	94	95	96	97	98	99	

Set B

❷

forty-five,

forty-six,

forty-seven,

forty-eight

39

(49)

fifty-one,

fifty-two,

fifty-three,

fifty-four

55

50

Directions Have students: ⭐ count by 1s to write the missing numbers; ❷ recite the number words together, and then circle the number that comes next in the pattern.

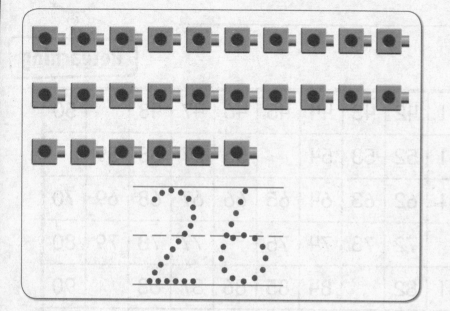

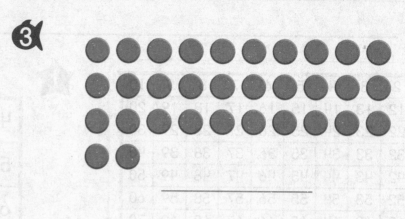

3

4

1	2	3	4	5	6	7	8	9	⑩
11	12	13	14	15	16	17	18	19	20
21	22	23	24	25	26	27	28	29	30
31	32	33	34	35	36	37	38	39	40
41	42	43	44	45	46	47	48	49	50

51	52	53	54	㊵	56	57	58	59	60
61	62	63	64	65	66	67	68	69	70
71	72	73	74	75	76	77	78	79	80
81	82	83	84	85	86	87	88	89	90
91	92	93	94	95	96	97	98	99	100

Directions Have students: **3** count by 10s and then by 1s to write the number that tells how many; **4** count by 10s beginning with 55, and then color the boxes yellow to show the pattern.

Test

1

41	42	43	44	45	46	47	48	49	50
51		53	54	55	56	57	58	59	60
61	62	63	64	65	66	67	68	69	70

2

61	62	63	64	65	66	67	68	69	70
71	72	73	74	75	76	77	78	79	80
81	82	83	84	85	86	87	88	89	90
91	92	93	94	95	96	97	98	99	100

- ○ 49
- ○ 51
- ○ 52
- ○ 53

- ○ 64, 74, 84, 94
- ○ 70, 71, 72, 73
- ○ 70, 75, 80, 85
- ○ 70, 80, 90, 100

3

 80 70 60   40

 59   55
○   ○

 50   35
○   ○

Directions Have students mark the best answer. **1** Which number is missing? **2** Which group of numbers shows counting by 10s starting with 70? **3** Which number is missing?

4

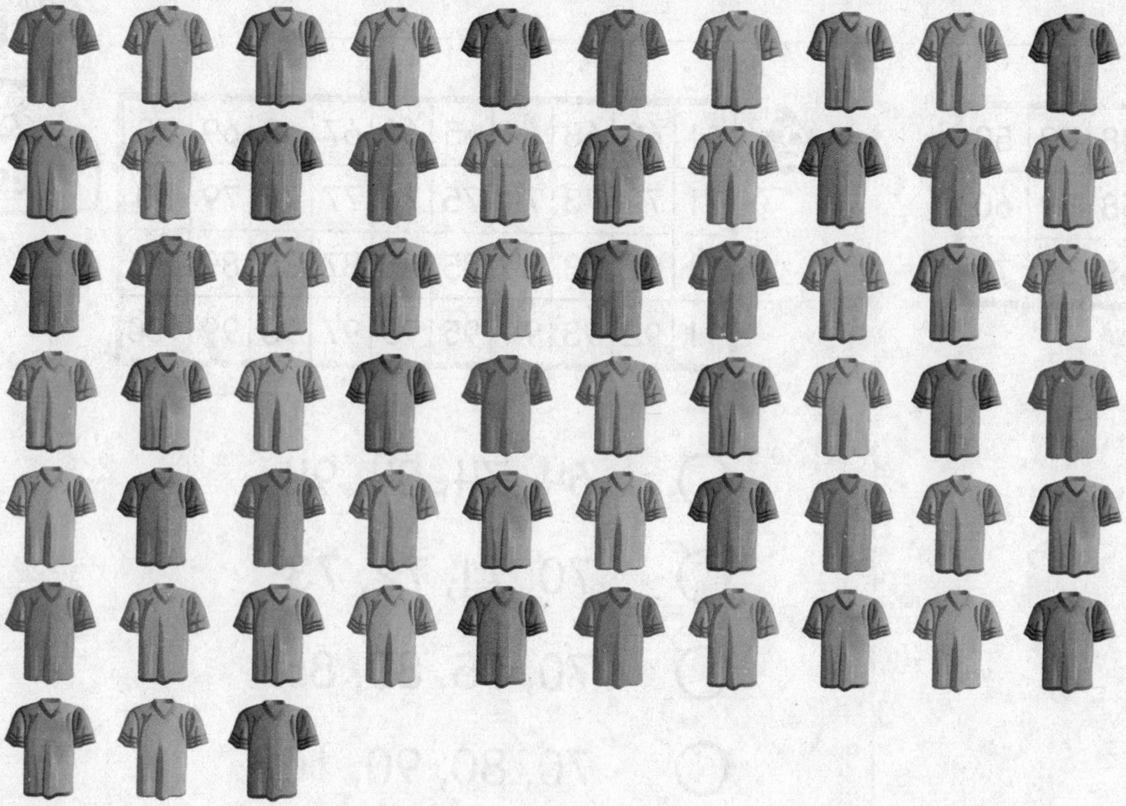

83 ○   73 ○   70 ○   63 ○

5

_____

_ _ _ _ _ _ _ _ _

seventy-five, seventy-six, _____ , seventy-eight, seventy-nine

© Pearson Education, Inc. K

Math and Science Project: Shapes Are Everywhere

Directions Read the character speech bubbles to students. **Find Out!** Have students observe the properties of objects using the description words *bigger, smaller, heavier, lighter, shape, color,* and *texture.* Say: *Shapes are everywhere and they come in various sizes and colors. Talk to your friends and relatives about squares, circles, triangles, and rectangles you see around you.* **Journal: Make a Poster** Then have students make a poster. Have them draw everyday objects in different sizes and colors that are squares, circles, triangles, and rectangles.

Name _____

Review What You Know

1

10 20 30 40 50

10 12 15 21 30

2

1	2	3	4	5	6	7	8	9	10
11	12	13	14	15	16	17	18	19	20
21	22	23	24	25	26	27	28	29	30
31	32	33	34	35	36	37	38	39	40
41	42	43	44	45	46	47	48	49	50
51	52	53	54	55	56	57	58	59	60
61	62	63	64	65	66	67	68	69	70
71	72	73	74	75	76	77	78	79	80
81	82	83	84	85	86	87	88	89	90
91	92	93	94	95	96	97	98	99	100

3

4

_____   _____

5

_____

6

23   8   13

Directions Have students: **1** circle the list of numbers that show a pattern counting by 10s; **2** circle the hundred chart; **3** circle the penny and draw an X on the nickel; **4** count the objects, write the numbers, and circle the group that has more; **5** count the objects and write the number; **6** circle the number that tells how many counters.

My Word Cards

Directions Have students cut out the vocabulary cards. Read the front of the card, and then ask them to explain what the word or phrase means.

same (alike)

different

sort

does not belong

circle

triangle

Directions Review the definitions and have students study the cards. Extend learning by having students draw pictures for each word on a separate piece of paper.

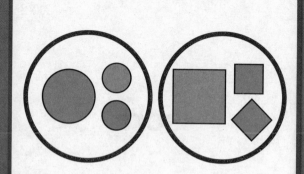

Point to the groups.
Say: *You can **sort** objects by shape.*

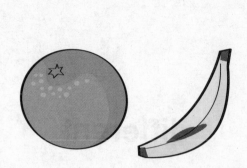

Point to the fruit.
Say: *These items are **different**. One is an orange and one is a banana.*

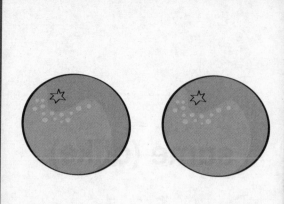

Point to the fruit.
Say: *These items are the **same**, or **alike**. Both are oranges.*

Point to the shape.
Say: *This shape is a **triangle**.*

Point to the shape.
Say: *This shape is a **circle**.*

Point to the bee.
Say: *The bee **does not belong** in this group of dogs.*

My Word Cards

Directions Have students cut out the vocabulary cards. Read the front of the card, and then ask them to explain what the word or phrase means.

A-Z

side

corner

vertex (vertices)

rectangle

square

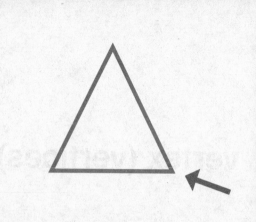

Point to the vertex of the triangle.
Say: *Another word for corner is **vertex**. This triangle has 3 **vertices**.*

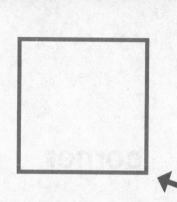

Point to the corner of the square.
Say: *The point where sides come together is called the **corner**. This square has 4 corners.*

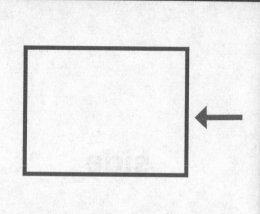

Point to the side of the rectangle.
Say: *This is one **side** of the rectangle. It has 4 sides in all.*

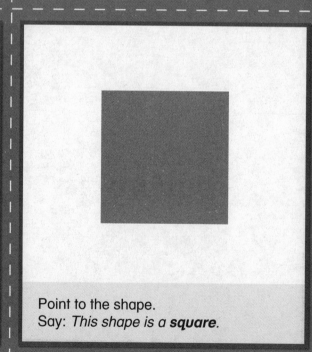

Point to the shape.
Say: *This shape is a **square**.*

Point to the shape.
Say: *This shape is a **rectangle**.*

Solve & Share Name _____

Directions Say: *Emily is playing with some shape blocks. Which shape is the same as the blocks she is holding? Let's color the shape that is the same as the blocks.*

⭐ **TEKS K.6E** Classify and sort a variety of regular and irregular two- and three-dimensional figures regardless of orientation or size. Also, K.6. **Mathematical Process Standards** K.1A, K.1B, K.1D, K.1F, K.1G.

Digital Resources at PearsonTexas.com

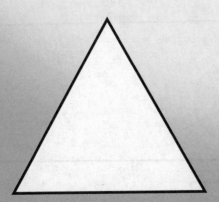 Solve   Learn   A-Z Glossary   Check   Tools   Games

Topic 12 | Lesson 1

☆ Guided Practice ☆

1

2

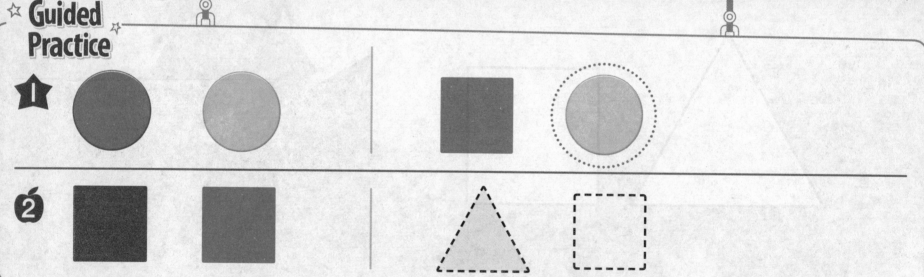

Directions Have students: **1** circle the shape on the right that is the same as the shapes on the left; **2** trace and color the shape on the right that is different from the shapes on the left.

Name _____

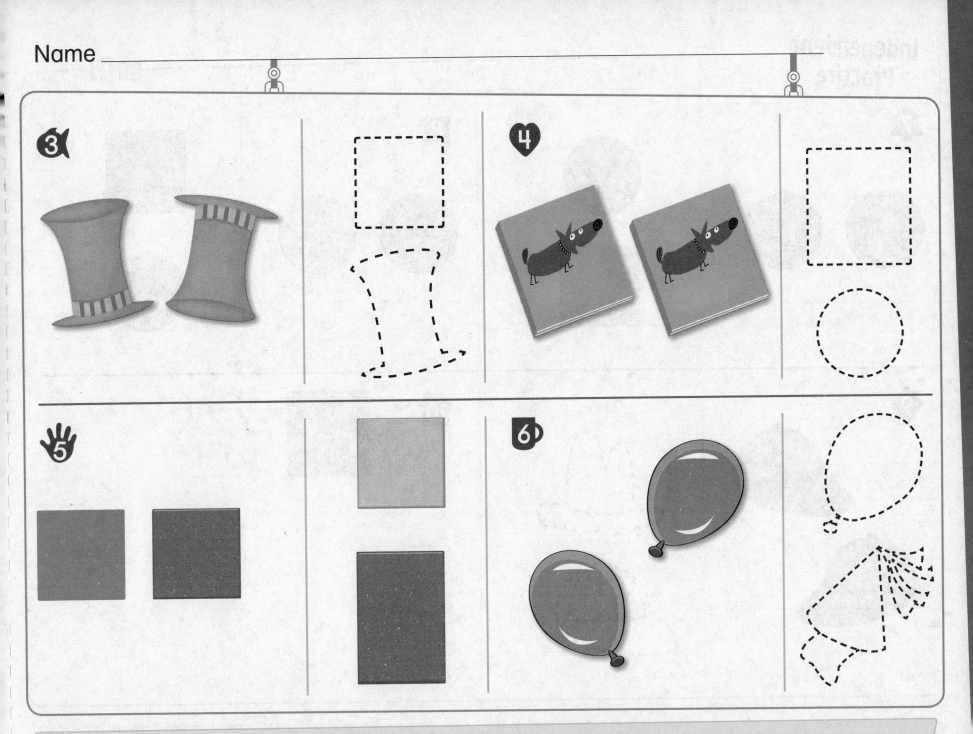

Directions Have students: ❸ trace and color the object on the right that is the same as the objects on the left; ❹ trace and color the object on the right that is different from the objects on the left; ✋ circle the shape on the right that is different from the shapes on the left; ❻ trace and color the object on the right that is the same as the objects on the left.

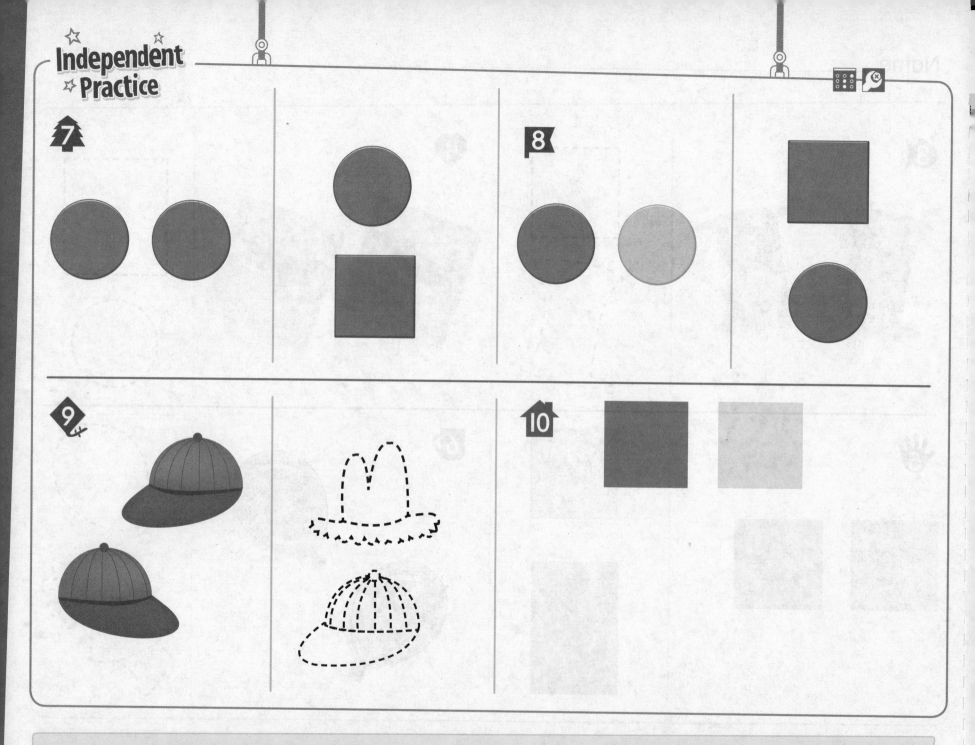

7

8

9

10

Directions Have students: **7** circle the shape on the right that is the same as the shapes on the left; **8** circle the shape on the right that is different from the shapes on the left; **9** trace and color the object on the right that is the same as the objects on the left; **10** draw and color any shape that is different from these shapes.

© Pearson Education, Inc. K

Name _____

Another Look

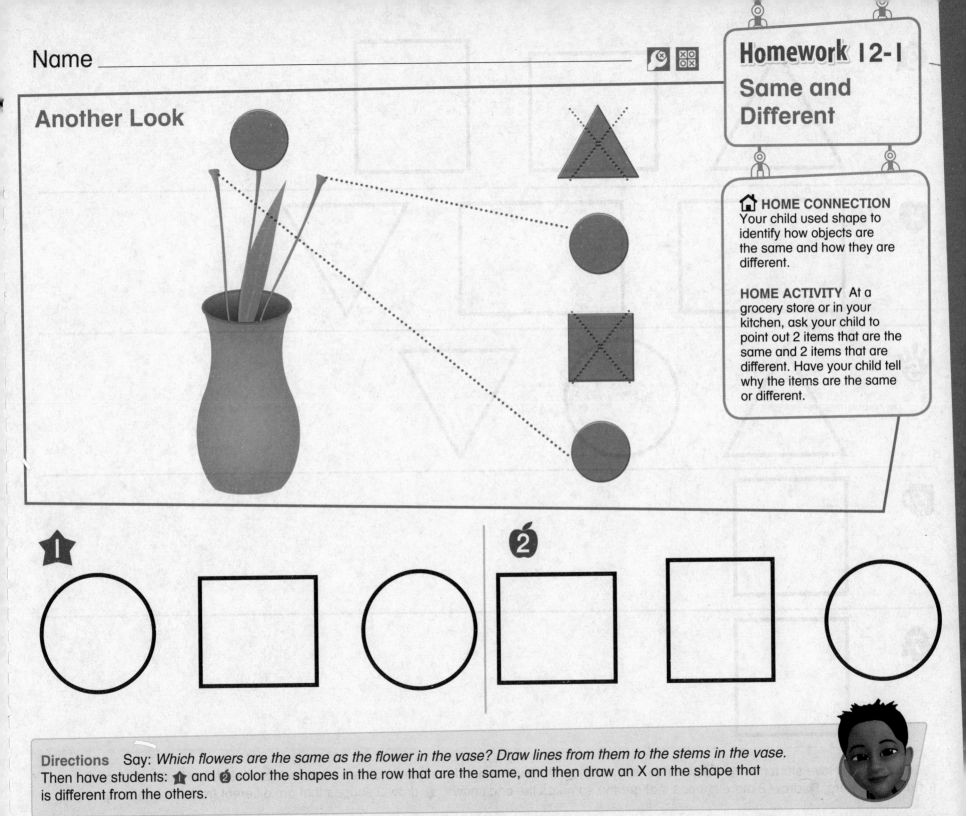

🏠 **HOME CONNECTION**
Your child used shape to identify how objects are the same and how they are different.

HOME ACTIVITY At a grocery store or in your kitchen, ask your child to point out 2 items that are the same and 2 items that are different. Have your child tell why the items are the same or different.

⭐1

②

Directions Say: *Which flowers are the same as the flower in the vase? Draw lines from them to the stems in the vase.* Then have students: ⭐ and ② color the shapes in the row that are the same, and then draw an X on the shape that is different from the others.

Directions Have students: ❸–✋ color the shapes in each row that are the same, and then draw an X on the shape that is different from the others; ☕ draw 2 more shapes that are the same as the one shown; 🌲 draw 2 shapes that are different from the one shown.

© Pearson Education, Inc. K

Topic 12 | Lesson 1

Solve & Share Name _____

Directions Say: *Emily is holding a handful of objects. She looks at them and puts the ones that are alike in some way in her purse. How can you find out which objects she put into her purse? Draw these objects in the purse.*

TEKS K.6E Classify and sort a variety of regular and irregular two- and three- dimensional figures regardless of orientation or size. Also, K.6. Mathematical Process Standards K.1B, K.1D, K.1F, K.1G.

Digital Resources at PearsonTexas.com

 Solve Learn **A-Z** Glossary Check Tools Games

☆ Guided Practice ☆

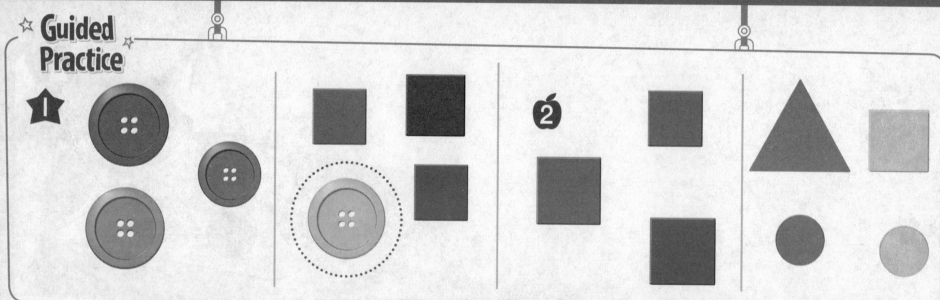

Directions Have students identify how the objects in each group are sorted, and then circle the object on the right that belongs in that group.

© Pearson Education, Inc. K

Name _____

Directions Have students circle the objects that would be in the same group if they were sorted by shape.

Topic 12 | Lesson 2

six hundred seventeen 617

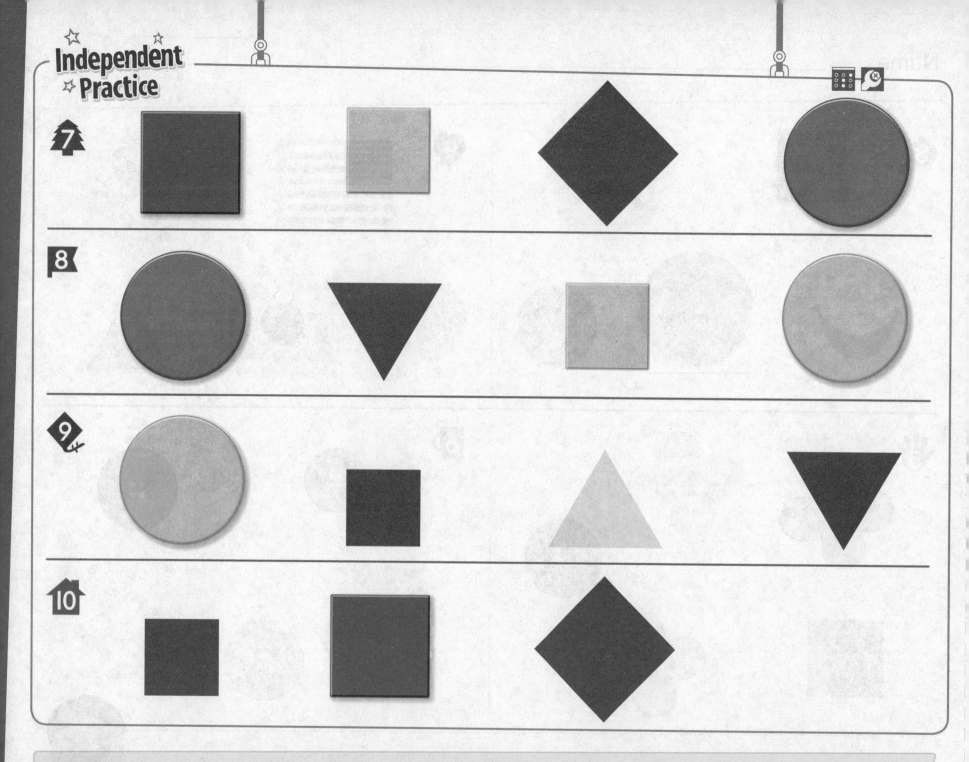

7

8

9

10

Directions Have students: **7**—**9** circle the objects that have the same shape; **10** draw an object that has the same shape as the others.

© Pearson Education, Inc. K

Topic 12 | Lesson 2

Name _____

Another Look

🏠 **HOME CONNECTION** Your child sorted objects by shape. He or she also identified which shapes belong in a group.

HOME ACTIVITY Place objects in the shape of 3 squares, a circle, and a triangle on a table in a random order. Ask your child to sort the objects by shape. Your child should put the 3 squares in a group.

Directions Say: *Look at these objects. Circle the objects that have the same shape.* Then have students: ⭐ and ② circle the objects that have the same shape.

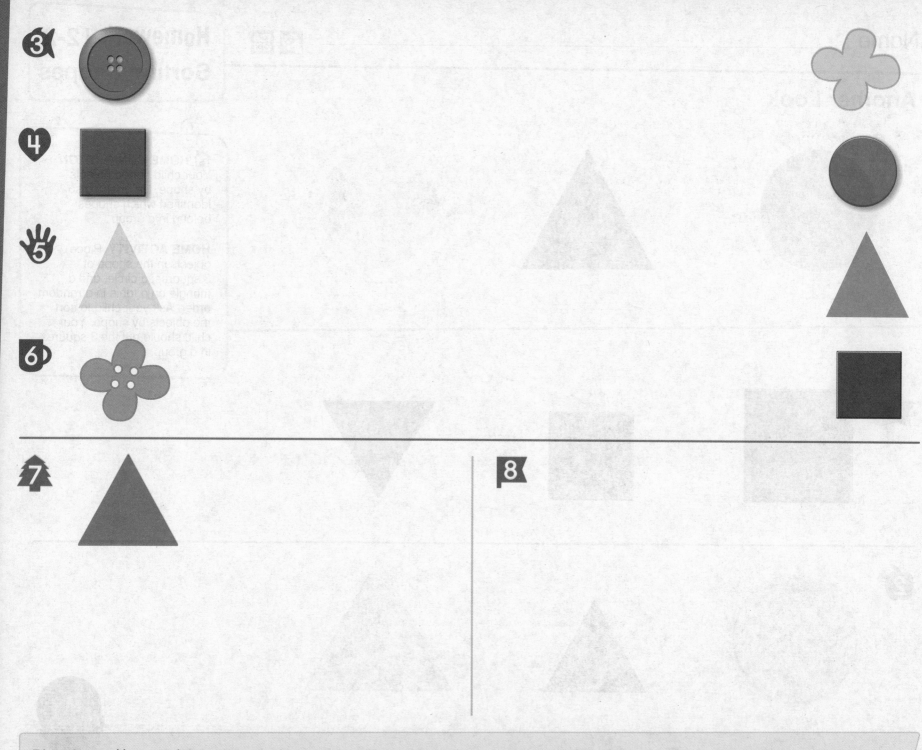

3

4

5

6

7

8

Directions Have students: **3–6** draw a line from each object on the left to the matching shape on the right; **7** draw an object that has the same shape as the one shown; **8** draw 2 objects that have the same shape and I object that does not belong.

620 six hundred twenty

© Pearson Education, Inc. K

Topic 12 | Lesson 2

Directions Say: *Emily is looking at a row of 4 shapes. How are the 2 shapes on the left alike? Which other shape is like these 2 shapes? Circle this shape and explain your thinking.*

⊕ **TEKS K.1D** Communicate mathematical ideas, reasoning, and their implications using multiple representations, including symbols, diagrams, graphs, and language as appropriate. Also, **K.6, K.6E. Mathematical Process Standards K.1B, K.1F.**

Digital Resources at PearsonTexas.com

Solve Learn Glossary Check

Guided Practice

1

2

Directions Say: *How are the shapes sorted? How can you find out?* Have students look at the group of shapes on the left, decide how they are sorted, and then circle the shape on the right that belongs in the group.

six hundred twenty-two

Topic 12 | **Lesson 3**

Name _____

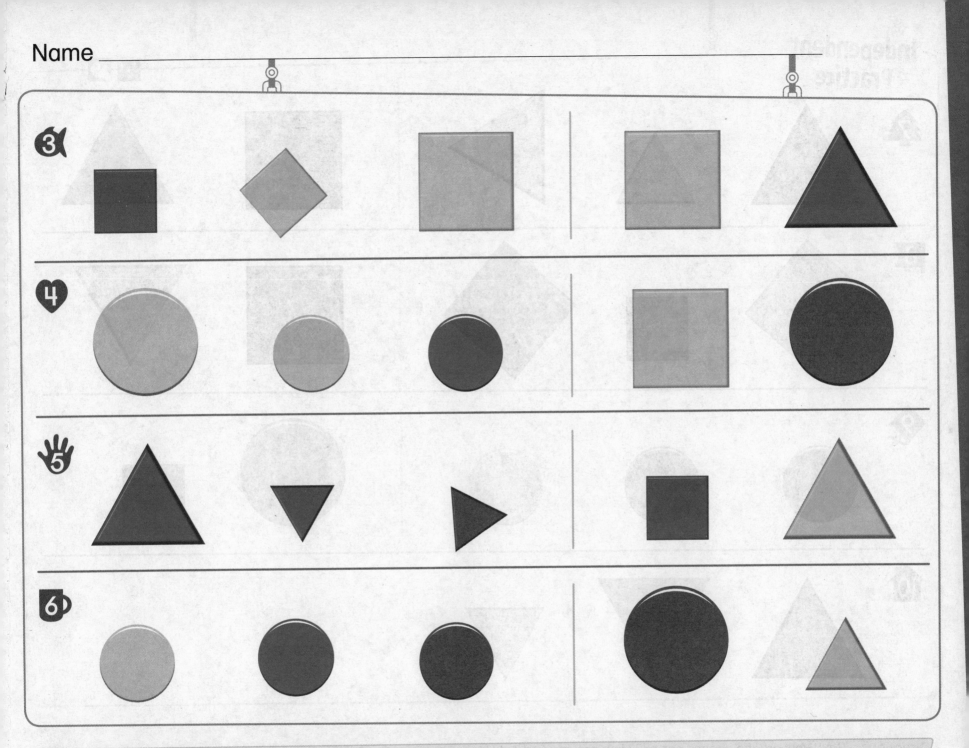

Directions Say: *How are the shapes sorted? How can you find out?* Have students look at the group of shapes on the left, decide how they are sorted, and then circle the shape on the right that belongs in the group.

Topic 12 | Lesson 3

six hundred twenty-three **623**

Independent Practice

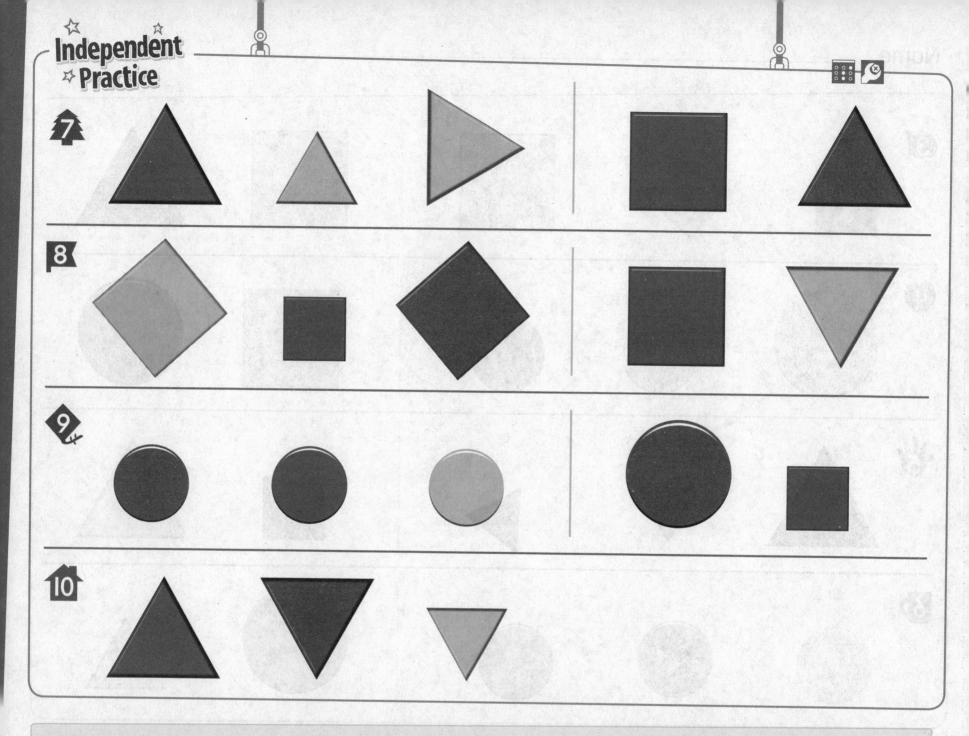

7

8

9

10

Directions Say: *How are the shapes sorted? How can you find out?* Have students: **7–9** look at the group of shapes on the left, decide how they are sorted, and then circle the shape that belongs in the group; **10** look at the group of shapes, and then draw a shape that belongs in the group.

Topic 12 | Lesson 3

Name _____

Another Look

🏠 **HOME CONNECTION**
Your child used the attribute of shape to decide how shapes can be sorted. Your child looked at a set of shapes and identified how the shapes were alike. Then your child looked at 2 other shapes and circled the one that belonged with that set.

HOME ACTIVITY Open a drawer in your kitchen or in a bedroom and ask your child to tell you ways the objects could be put into different groups by shape.

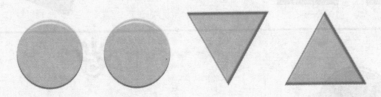

Directions Say: *How can these shapes be sorted? Circle the group that shows sorting by shape.* Have students:
⭐ circle the group that is sorted by shape.

Topic 12 | Lesson 3   Digital Resources at PearsonTexas.com   six hundred twenty-five **625**

2

3

4

5

Directions Have students: **2**—**3** circle the row that is sorted by shape; **4** draw an X on the shape that does not belong if this group were sorted by shape, and then draw an object that belongs in the group; **5** draw 3 objects that belong together in a group sorted by shape.

626 six hundred twenty-six

© Pearson Education, Inc. K

Topic 12 | Lesson 3

Solve & Share

Name _____

Directions Say: *The zoo has a polar animals exhibit. There are polar bears and penguins. Place the shapes in the animal pens that are the same shape. Tell how the shapes in the pens are different.*

⭐ **TEKS K.6A** Identify two-dimensional shapes, including circles, triangles, rectangles, and squares as special rectangles. Also, K.6, K.6D, K.6E, K.6F. **Mathematical Process Standards** K.1A, K.1D, K.1F.

Digital Resources at PearsonTexas.com

  A-Z
Solve   Learn   Glossary   Check   Tools   Games

☆ **Guided Practice** ☆

1

2

Directions Remind students that circles and triangles can be any size. Have students color the circle in each row, and then draw an X on each triangle.

© Pearson Education, Inc. K

Name _____

3

4

5

Directions Have students: **3** and **4** color the circle in each row, and then draw an X on each triangle; **5** draw an X on the objects that are shaped like a circle, and then circle the objects that are shaped like a triangle.

Topic 12 | Lesson 4

six hundred twenty-nine **629**

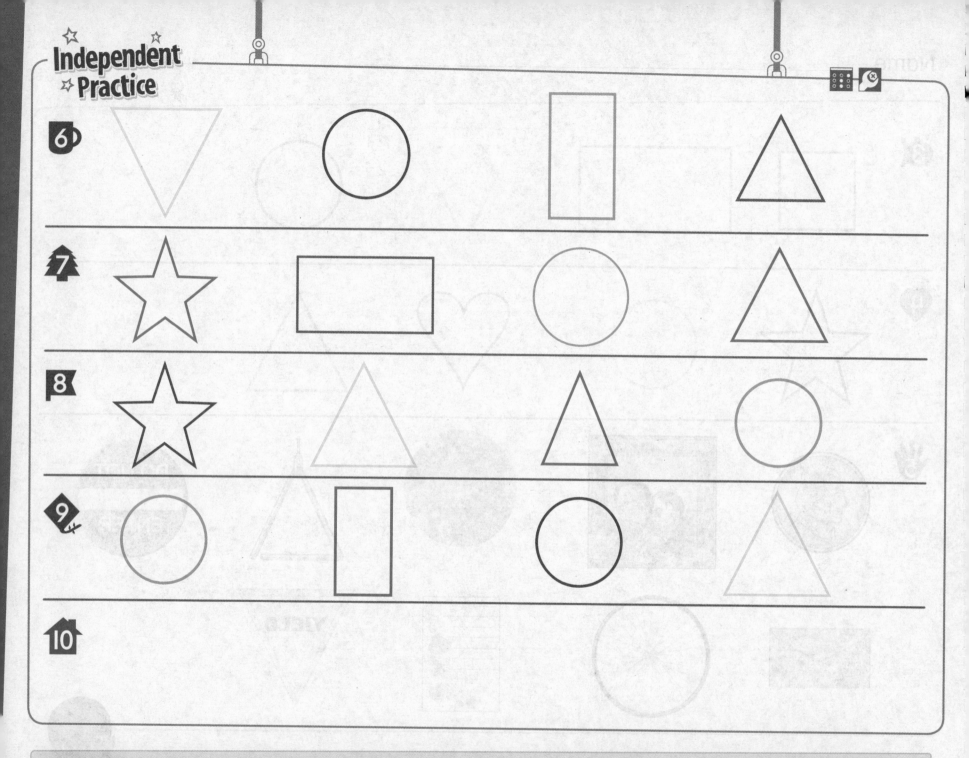

6

7

8

9

10

Directions Have students: 6–9 color the circles in each row, and then draw an X on each triangle; 10 draw a small red circle and a large blue triangle.

© Pearson Education, Inc. K

Name _____

Another Look

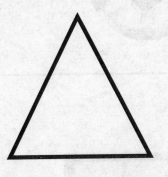

🏠 **HOME CONNECTION**
Your child identified circles and triangles.

HOME ACTIVITY Look through a magazine with your child. Ask him or her to find pictures of things shaped like a circle or a triangle.

1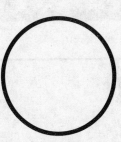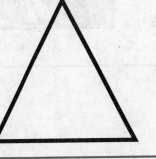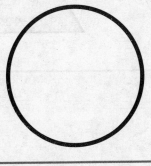

2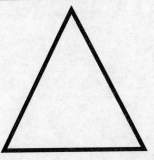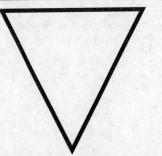

Directions Say: *Look at the shape on the left. Color the shape on the right that matches it. What is the name of this shape?* Then have students: **1** and **2** look at the shape on the left, and then color the shapes on the right that match it.

3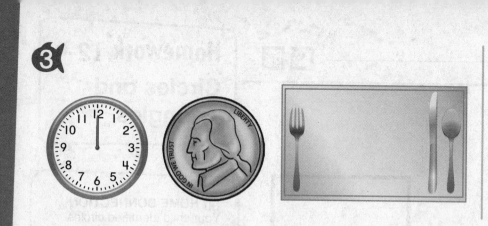

4

5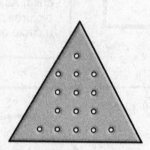

6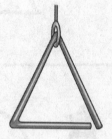

7

8

Directions Have students: **3** and **4** draw an X on the objects that are shaped like a circle; **5** and **6** circle the objects that are shaped like a triangle; **7** draw a large red circle and a small blue triangle; **8** draw a picture using at least 2 circles and 1 triangle.

632 six hundred thirty-two   © Pearson Education, Inc. K   **Topic 12** | Lesson 4

Solve & Share

Name _____

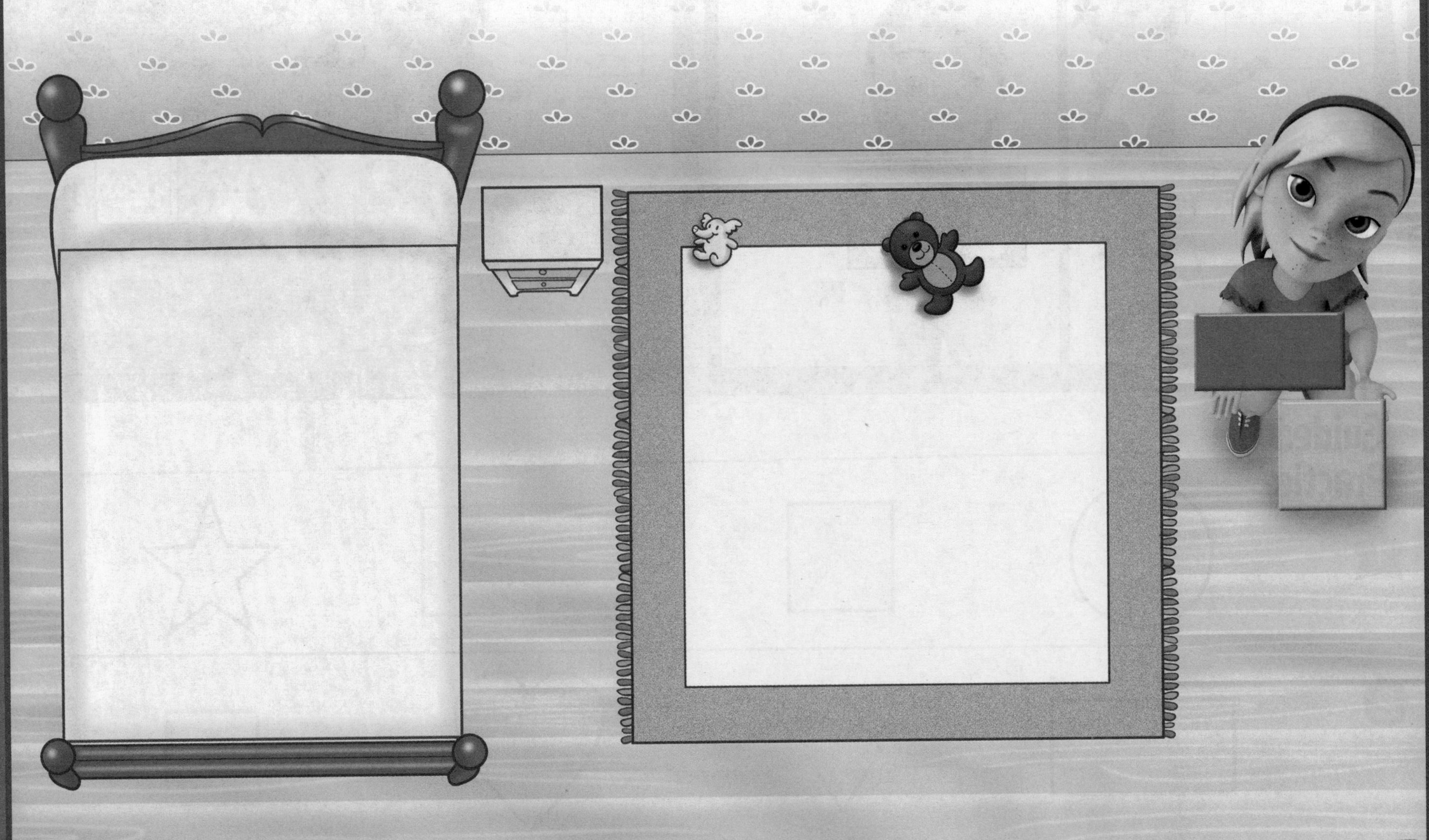

Directions Say: *Emily is holding 2 shapes. Pick either the red or the yellow shape. Draw a line from that shape to something in the room that has the same shape.*

TEKS K.6A Identify two-dimensional shapes, including circles, triangles, rectangles, and squares as special rectangles. Also, K.6, K.6D, K.6E, K.6F. **Mathematical Process Standards** K.1A, K.1F, K.1G.

Digital Resources at PearsonTexas.com

 Solve Learn A-Z Glossary Check Tools Games

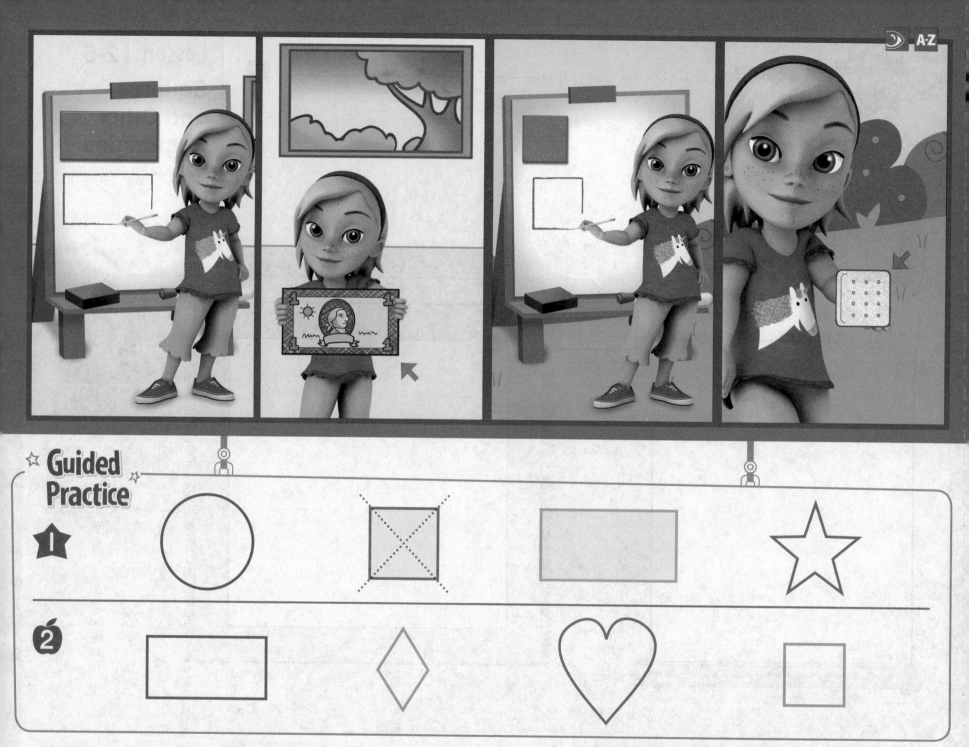

Guided Practice

1

2

Directions Remind students that squares and rectangles can be any size. Have students color the rectangles in each row, and then draw an X on each rectangle that is a square.

Name _____

Directions Have students: ③ and ④ color the rectangles in each row, and then draw an X on each rectangle that is a square; ✋ circle the objects that are shaped like a rectangle, and then draw an X on each object that is shaped like a square.

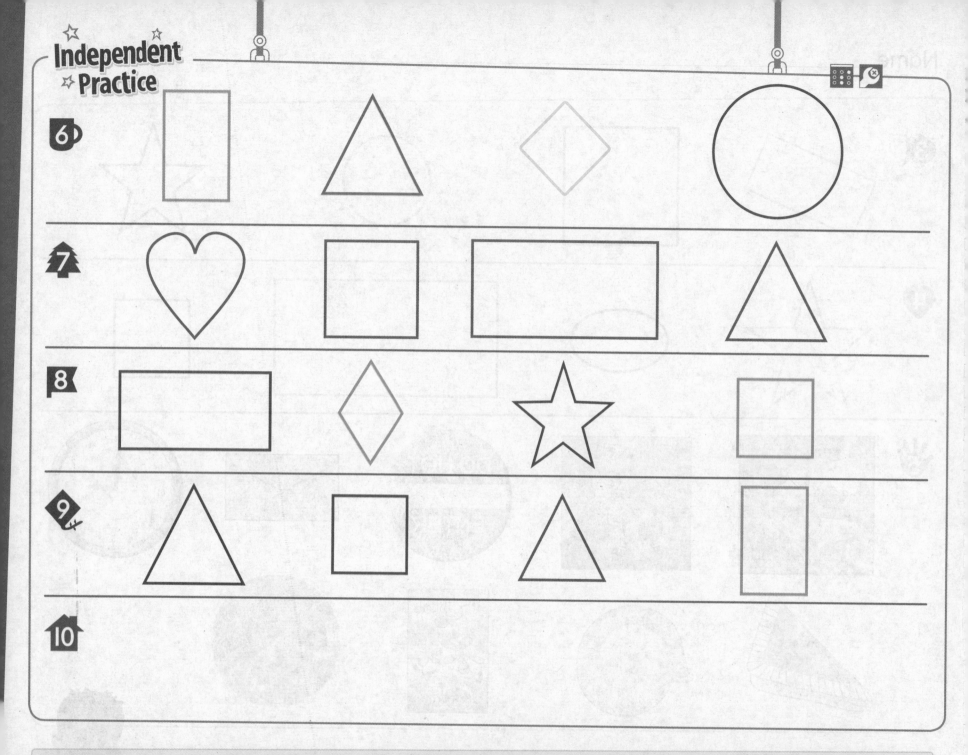

6

7

8

9

10

Directions Have students: **6**–**9** color the rectangles in each row, and then draw an X on each rectangle that is a square; **10** draw a green rectangle, and then draw a yellow square.

© Pearson Education, Inc. K

Topic 12 | Lesson 5

Name _____

Another Look

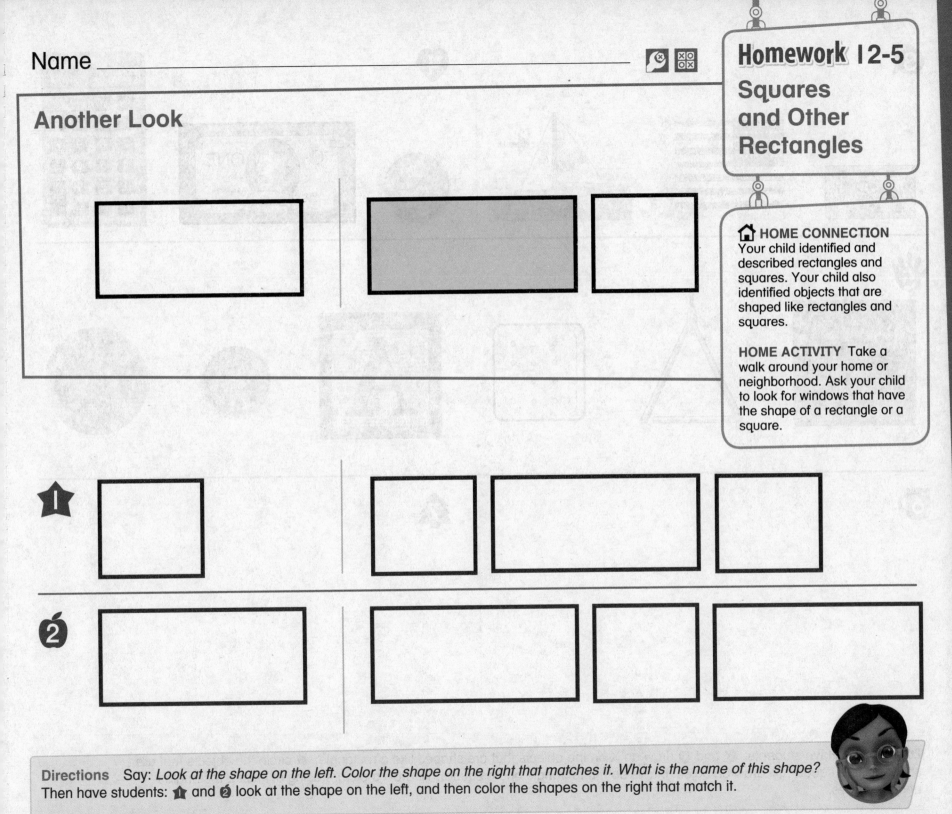

Directions Say: *Look at the shape on the left. Color the shape on the right that matches it. What is the name of this shape?* Then have students: ⭐ and 🍎 look at the shape on the left, and then color the shapes on the right that match it.

3

4

5

6

7

Directions Have students: **3** and **4** draw an X on the objects that are shaped like a rectangle; **5** circle the objects that are shaped like a square; **6** draw an object that is both a rectangle and a square; **7** draw a picture using at least 2 rectangles and 2 squares.

© Pearson Education, Inc. K

Name _____

Directions Say: *Emily wants to figure out what shape is behind the door. The shape has 4 vertices and 4 equal sides. Use the shapes above the door to help you find the mystery shape. Draw the shape on the door.*

✪ **TEKS K.6D** Identify attributes of two-dimensional shapes using informal and formal geometric language interchangeably. Also, **K.6, K.6F. Mathematical Process Standards** K.1A, K.1C, K.1D, K.1E, K.1F.

Digital Resources at PearsonTexas.com

 Solve Learn Glossary Check Tools Games

☆ **Guided Practice** ☆

1

2

Directions Have students listen to the clues, draw an X on the shapes that do **not** fit the clues, and circle the shape that the clues describe.
1 *I have 4 sides. I do* **not** *have 4 sides that are the same length. Which shape am I?* **2** *I do* **not** *have 4 sides. I do* **not** *have any vertices. Which shape am I?*

© Pearson Education, Inc. K

Name _____

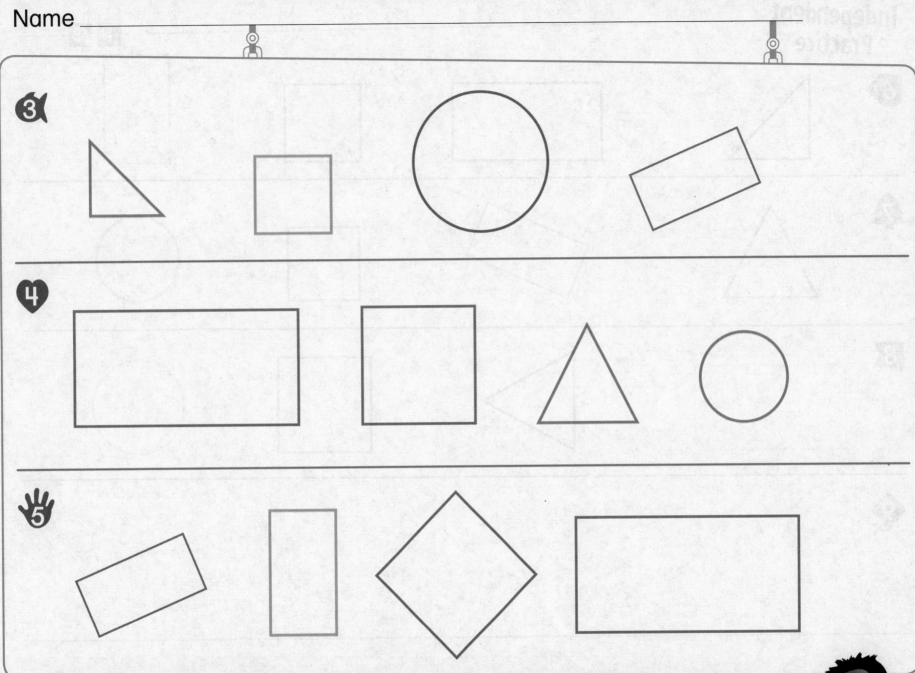

3 I am **not** round. I have 3 sides. Which shape am I?

4

5

Directions Have students listen to the clues, draw an X on the shapes that do **not** fit the clues, and circle the shape that the clues describe. **3** *I am **not** round. I have 3 sides. Which shape am I?* **4** *I am **not** a rectangle. I have 0 sides. Which shape am I?* **5** *I have 4 vertices. I am a special kind of rectangle because all my sides are the same length. Which shape am I?*

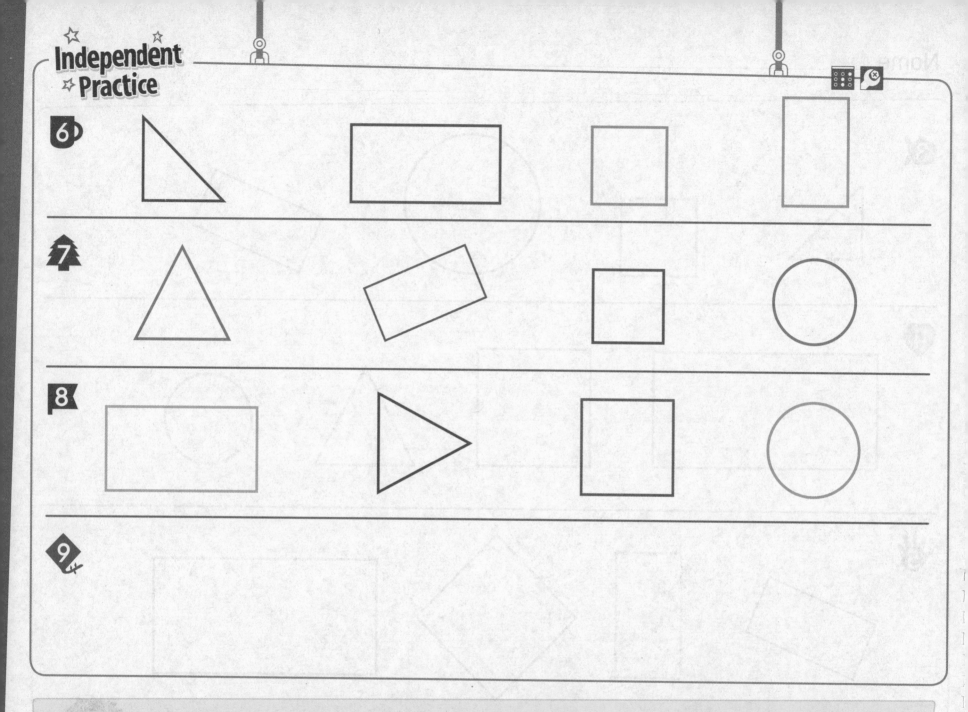

6

7

8

9

Directions Have students listen to the clues, draw an X on the shapes that do **not** fit the clues, and circle the shape that the clues describe. 6 *All of my sides are **not** the same length. I only have 3 vertices. Which shape am I?* 7 *I have 4 sides. I am the shape of a classroom door. Which shape am I?* 8 *I have less than 4 vertices. I am the shape of a wheel. Which shape am I?* Then have students listen to the clues and draw the shape the clues describe. 9 *I have more than 3 sides. I have fewer than 5 vertices. All my sides are the same length. Which shape am I?*

Topic 12 | Lesson 6

Name _____

Another Look

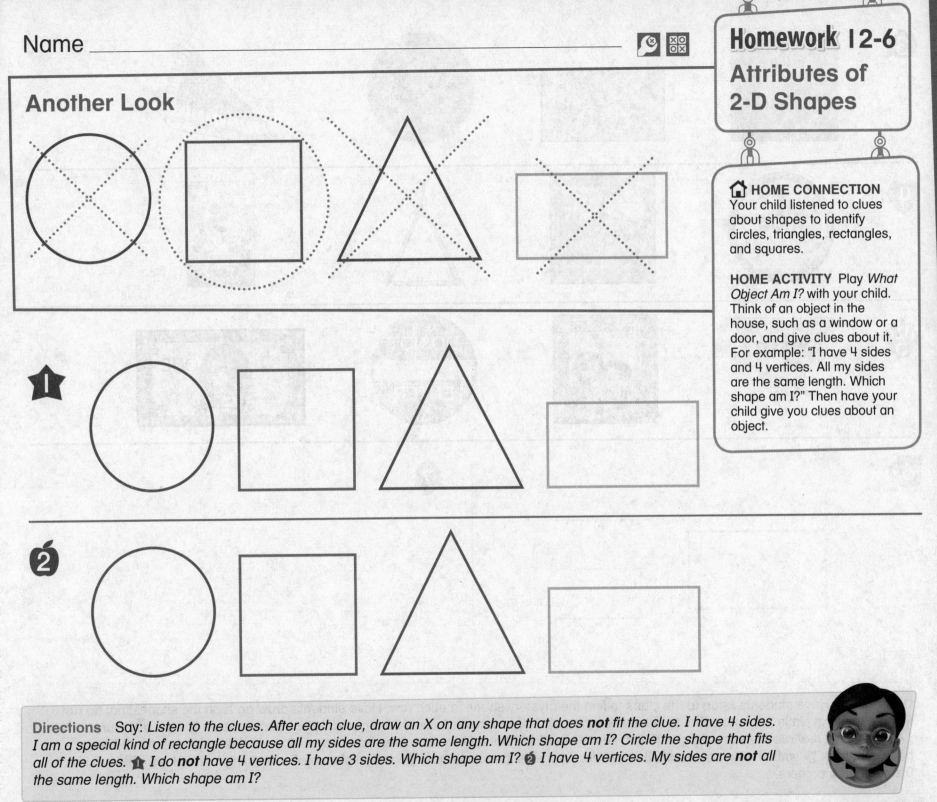

🏠 **HOME CONNECTION**
Your child listened to clues about shapes to identify circles, triangles, rectangles, and squares.

HOME ACTIVITY Play *What Object Am I?* with your child. Think of an object in the house, such as a window or a door, and give clues about it. For example: "I have 4 sides and 4 vertices. All my sides are the same length. Which shape am I?" Then have your child give you clues about an object.

⭐1

🍎2

Directions Say: *Listen to the clues. After each clue, draw an X on any shape that does **not** fit the clue. I have 4 sides. I am a special kind of rectangle because all my sides are the same length. Which shape am I? Circle the shape that fits all of the clues.* ⭐ *I do **not** have 4 vertices. I have 3 sides. Which shape am I?* 🍎 *I have 4 vertices. My sides are **not** all the same length. Which shape am I?*

3

4

5 YIELD · DO NOT ENTER · ONE

6

7

Directions Have students listen to the clues to find the mystery shape in each row. Have students draw an X on the shapes that do **not** fit the clues and circle the shape that the clues describe. **3** *I do **not** have 3 sides. I am round. Which shape am I?* **4** *I am **not** round. I have 4 sides that are the same length. Which shape am I?* **5** *I have fewer than 4 vertices. I have 3 sides. Which shape am I?* Then have students: **6** write the number that tells how many vertices the shape has; **7** draw a picture of something in the classroom that has 0 sides and 0 corners.

Name _____

Directions Say: Emily has 2 triangles. She thinks she can use them to make a shape she's learned—a circle, triangle, square, or rectangle. Try to make one of these shapes with your triangles. Tell what shape you made.

★ **TEKS K.6F** Create two-dimensional shapes using a variety of materials and drawings. **Mathematical Process Standards** K.1A, K.1C, K.1D, K.1E.

Digital Resources at PearsonTexas.com

 Solve   Learn   Glossary   Check   Tools Games

triangle

not a triangle

rectangle

not a rectangle

☆ **Guided Practice** ☆

1

2

Directions Provide students with yarn, pipe cleaners, or straws to make each shape. Students should attach any shape they make with materials to the page. Have students draw or make: **1** a square; **2** a shape that is **not** a square.

Topic 12 | Lesson 7

3

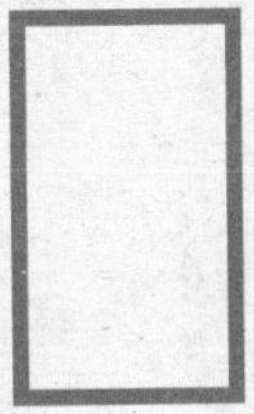

4

5

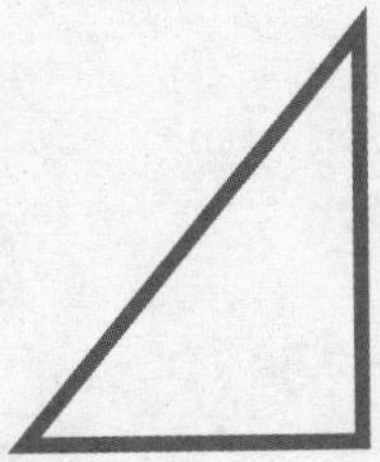

6

Directions Provide students with yarn, pipe cleaners, or straws to make each shape. Students should attach any shape they make with materials to the page. Have students draw or make: **3** a rectangle; **4** a shape that is **not** a rectangle; **5** a triangle; **6** a shape that is **not** a triangle.

7

8

9

10

Directions Have students: **7** draw a rectangle; **8** draw a triangle; **9** draw a square; **10** choose yarn, straws, or craft sticks to use to make a circle, attach it to their paper, and then explain why some materials are better for making circles.

© Pearson Education, Inc. K

Topic 12 | Lesson 7

Name _____

Another Look

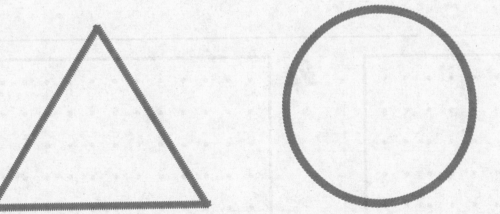

Directions Say: *This is a square. How do you know it is a square? Let's practice drawing a square.* Have students listen to the story: ⭐ *Emily made shapes out of pipe cleaners. Draw an X on the triangle.*

Directions Have students listen to each story: ② *Carlos made 6 shapes out of straws. Draw Xs on the shapes that are **not** rectangles.* ③ *Alex made 6 shapes out of pipe cleaners. Draw Xs on the shapes that are **not** triangles.* Then have students: ④ draw a circle; ⑤ draw a triangle; ⑥ draw a rectangle that is **not** a square; ⑦ draw a rectangle that is also a square.

650 six hundred fifty   © Pearson Education, Inc. K   **Topic 12** | Lesson 7

Name _____

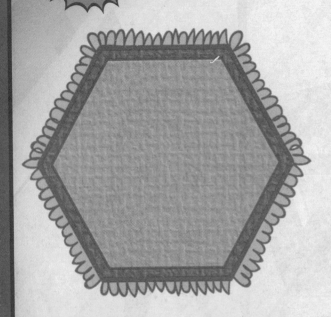

TEKS K.1C Select tools, including real objects, manipulatives, paper and pencil, and technology as appropriate, and techniques, including mental math, estimation, and number sense as appropriate, to solve problems. Also, K.6, K.6E, K.6F. **Mathematical Process Standards** K.1A, K.1B, K.1F, K.1G.

Digital Resources at PearsonTexas.com

Solve   Learn   Glossary   Check   Tools   Games

Directions Say: *Emily sees 2 rugs. She wants to find a pattern block that matches the shape of each rug. How can she solve this problem?*

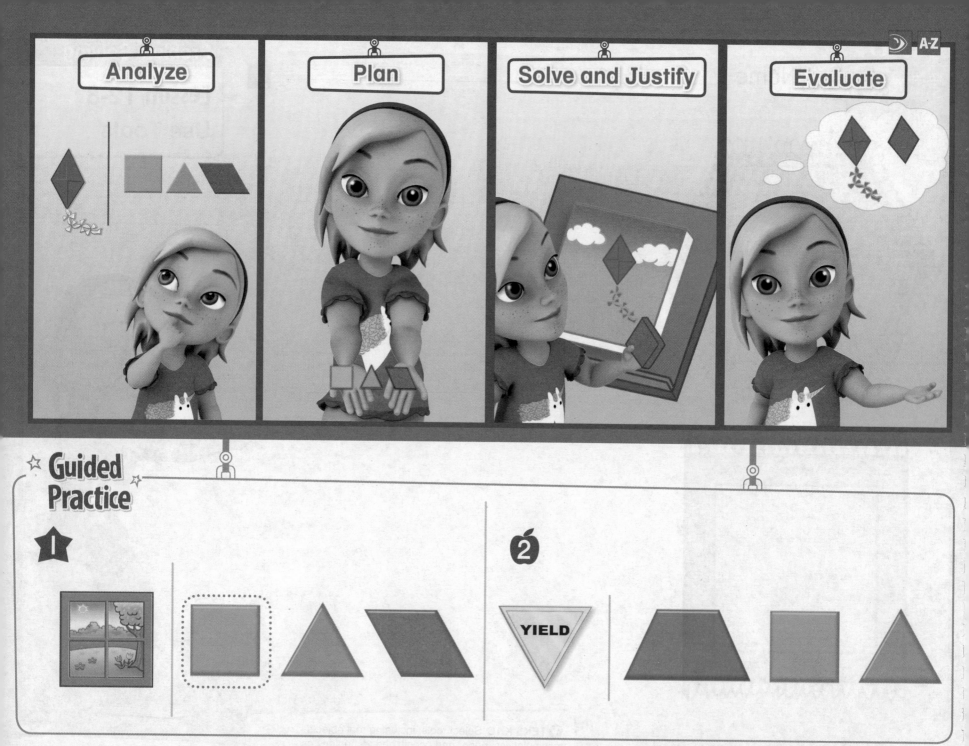

Guided Practice

1

2

YIELD

Directions Say: *How can you find the shape of an object? What can you use? How can you check?* Have students use pattern blocks to match the shape, and then circle the pattern block that matches the shape of the object.

3

4

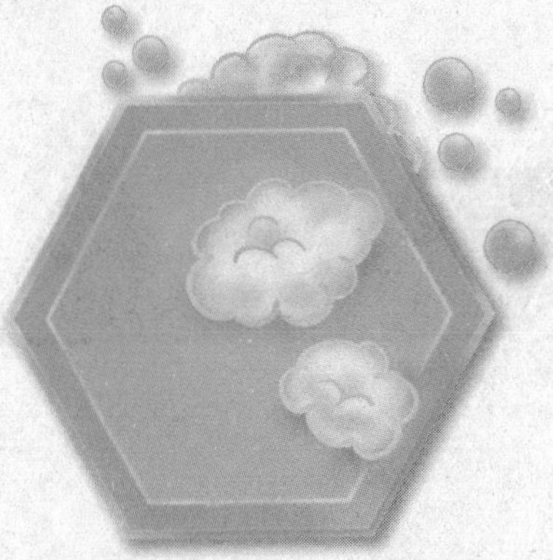

5

6

Directions Say: *How can you find the shape of an object? What can you use? How can you check?* Have students find the pattern block that matches the shape of each object, trace the pattern block, and then explain how they know that the shapes match.

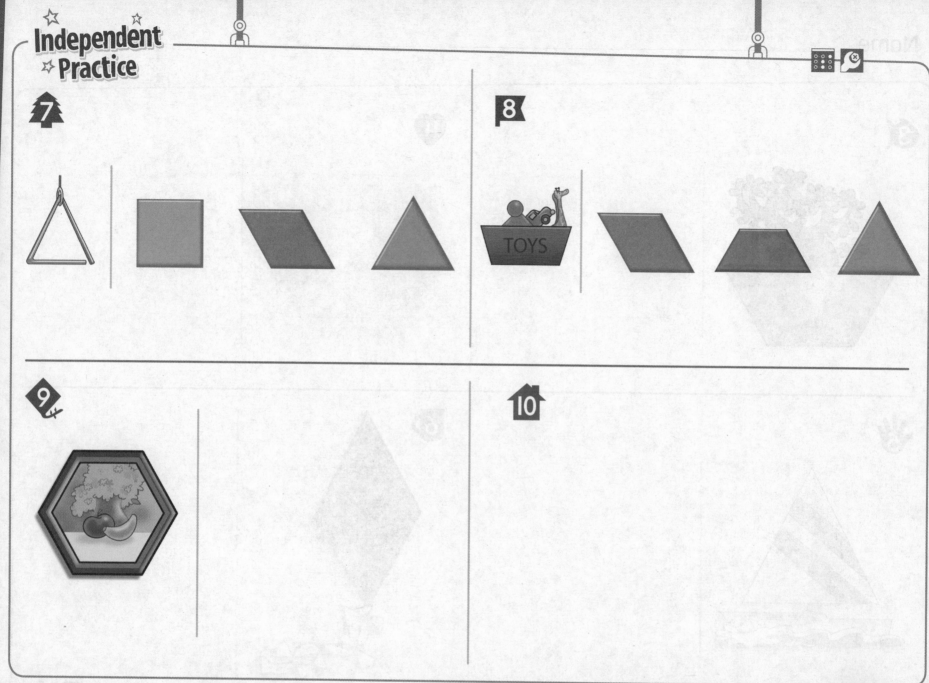

7

8

TOYS

9

10

Directions Say: *How can you find the shape of an object? What can you use? How can you check?* Have students: **7** and **8** use pattern blocks to match the shape, and then circle the pattern block that matches the shape of the object; **9** find the pattern block that matches the shape of the object, trace the pattern block, and then explain how they know that the shapes match; **10** trace any pattern block, draw an object that matches it, and then explain how they know the shapes match.

© Pearson Education, Inc. K

Topic 12 | Lesson 8

Homework 12-8
Use Tools

Another Look

  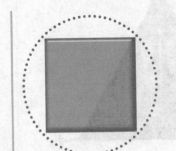 

🏠 **HOME CONNECTION**
Your child solved problems by using pattern blocks to find shapes that match pictures of real-world objects.

HOME ACTIVITY Show your child a circular plate. Look together and find objects in your home that have the same shape. Repeat the activity using triangle, square-, and rectangle-shaped objects.

 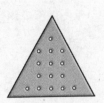  

Directions Say: *Look at the object. Use pattern blocks to match the shape. Which pattern block matches the shape of the object? Circle it.* Then have students: ⭐ and ② use pattern blocks to match the shape, and then circle the pattern block that matches the shape of the object.

656 six hundred fifty-six

Topic 12 | Lesson 8

Set A

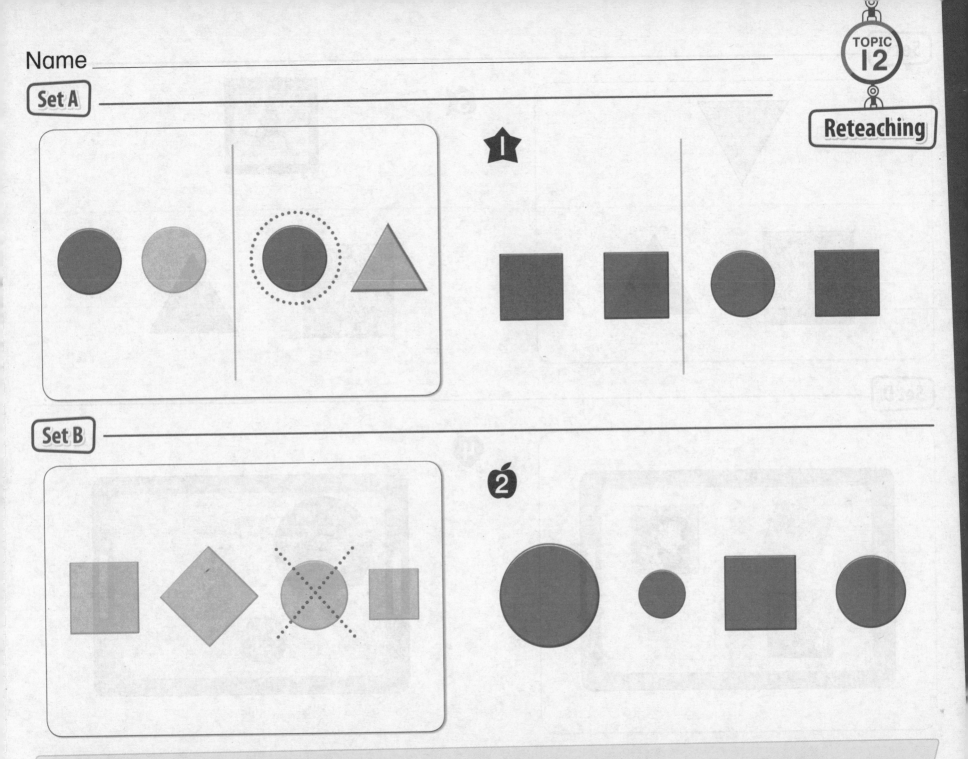

⭐ 1

Set B

🍎 2

Directions Have students: ⭐ circle the shape on the right that is the same shape as the shapes on the left; 🍎 draw an X on the shape that is different from the others.

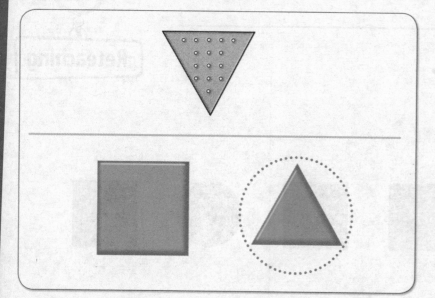

 ③

Set D

 ④

Directions Have students: ③ use pattern blocks to match the shape, and then circle the pattern block that matches the shape of the object; ④ draw an object that has the same shape as the others.

Name _____

✋ 5

triangle   not a triangle

6 ☕

no sides
no corners

Directions Have students: ✋ draw or use yarn, pipe cleaners, or straws to make a square and a shape that is **not** a square, and then attach their shapes to the page; 6 listen to the clues, draw an X on the shapes that do **not** fit the clues, and circle the shape that the clues describe. *I have 4 vertices, or corners. All of my sides have the same length. Which shape am I?*

Topic 12   six hundred fifty-nine **659**

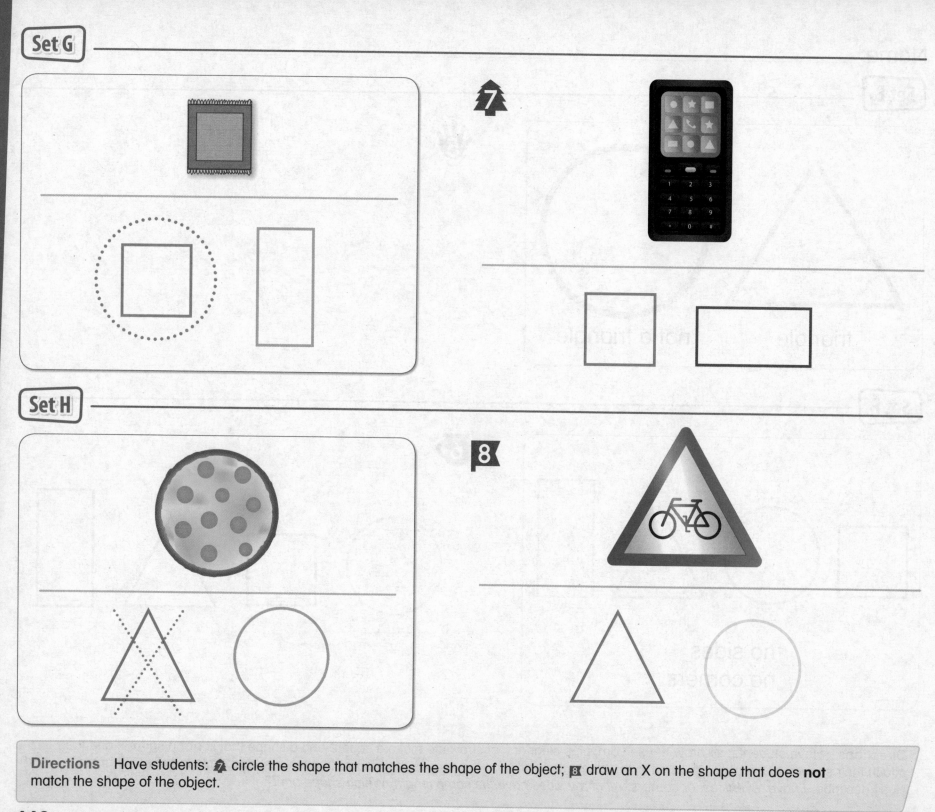

Set G

Set H

Directions   Have students: 7 circle the shape that matches the shape of the object; 8 draw an X on the shape that does **not** match the shape of the object.

© Pearson Education, Inc. K

Name _____

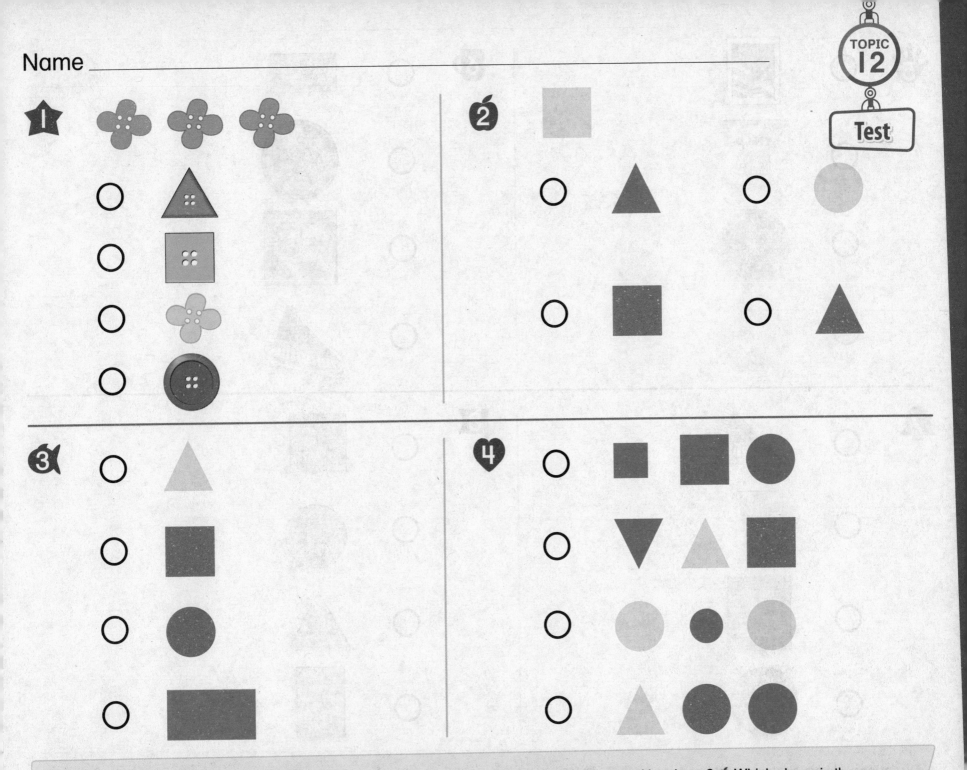

1 ○ ○ ○ ○

2 ○ ○ ○ ○

3 ○ ○ ○ ○

4 ○ ○ ○ ○

Directions Have students mark the best answer. **1** Which button belongs in the group sorted by shape? **2** Which shape is the same as the one at the top? **3** Which shape is a triangle? **4** Which group is sorted by shape?

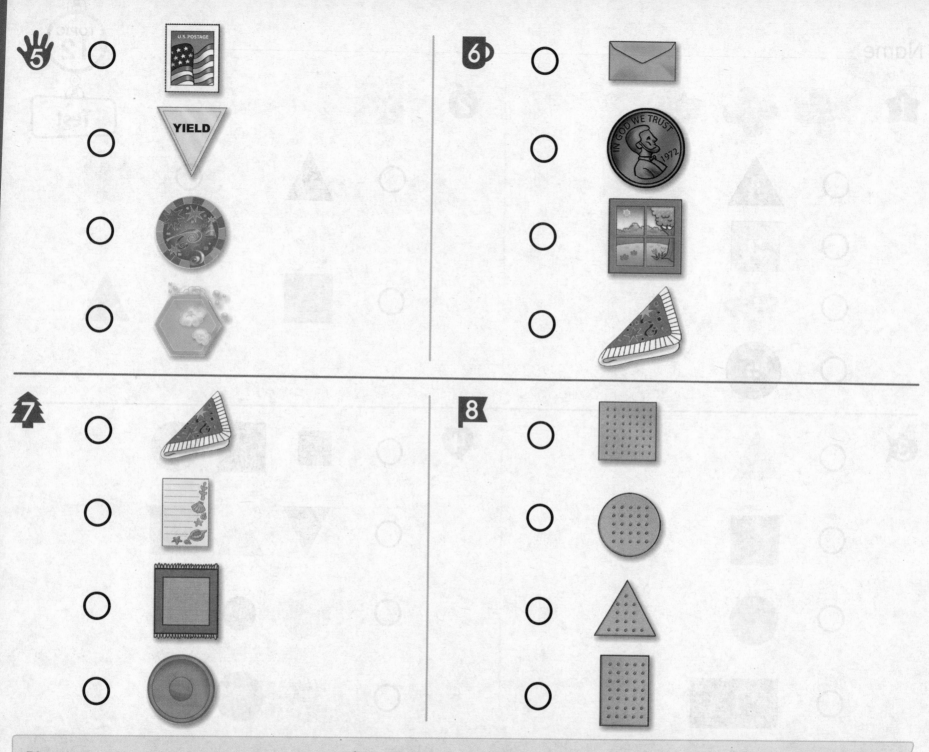

5 ○ ○ ○ ○

6 ○ ○ ○ ○

7 ○ ○ ○ ○

8 ○ ○ ○ ○

U.S. POSTAGE

YIELD

IN GOD WE TRUST 1972

Directions Have students mark the best answer. ✋ Which object is shaped like a rectangle? 6️⃣ Which object is shaped like a square? 🌲 Which object is shaped like a circle? 8️⃣ Which cracker is shaped like a triangle?

© Pearson Education, Inc. K

Name _____

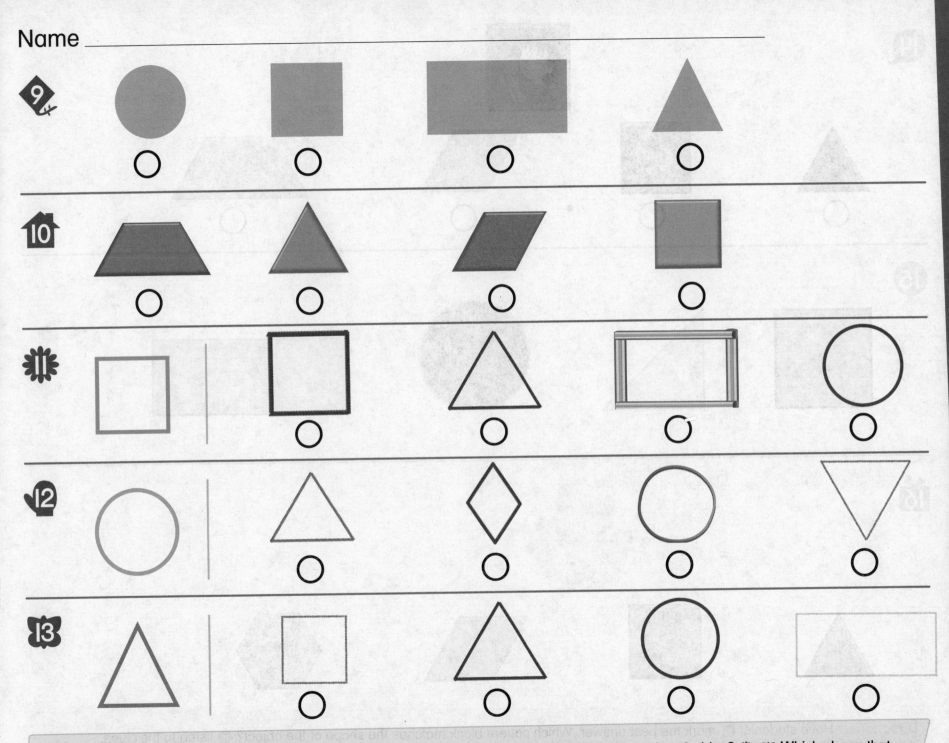

9
○　　○　　○　　○

10
○　　○　　○　　○

○　　○　　○　　○

12
○　　○　　○　　○

13
○　　○　　○　　○

Directions Have students mark the best answer. **9** Which shape is a square? **10** Which shape has 3 sides? **11–13** Which shape that was made or drawn matches the shape on the left?

Topic 12

six hundred sixty-three **663**

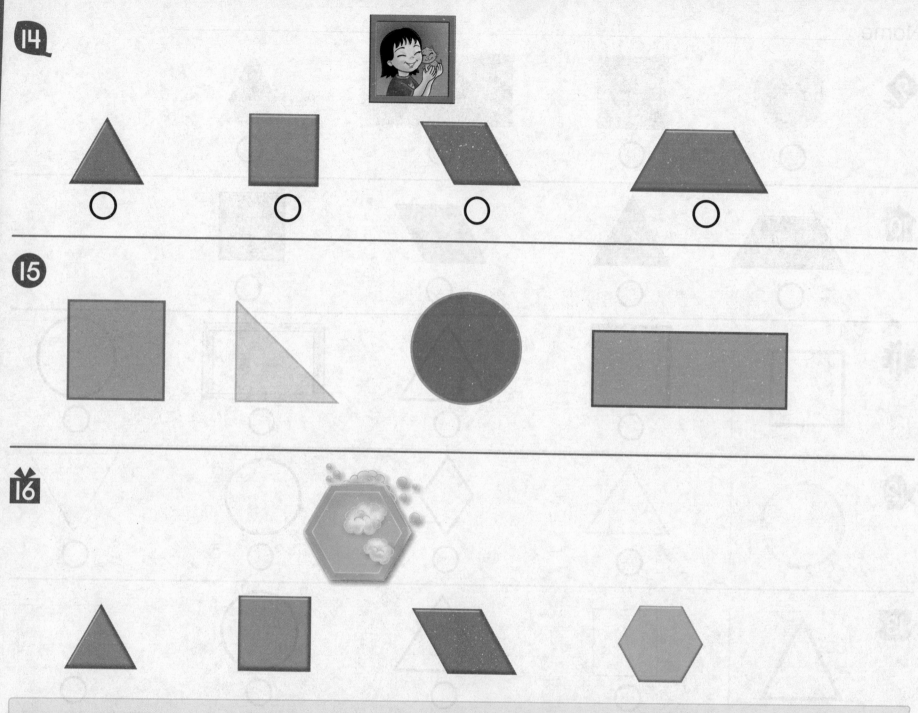

14

○　○　○　○

15

16

© Pearson Education, Inc. K

Three-Dimensional Solids

Essential Question: How can solid figures be named, described, compared, and composed?

Fun!

Balls can roll!

Math and Science Project: How Do Objects Move?

Directions Read the character speech bubbles to students. **Find Out!** Have students observe and describe how objects move using the terms *roll, stack,* and *slide.* Say: *Objects move in different ways. Talk to your friends and relatives about everyday objects that are cones, cylinders, spheres, and cubes. Ask them how they move and whether they roll, stack, or slide.* **Journal: Make a Poster** Then have students make a poster. Have them draw everyday objects that are cones, cylinders, spheres, and cubes and tell how each one moves.

Name _____

Review What You Know

1 ○ □ △

2 □ ○ △

3 □ ▭ ○

4 ▲ ■
       ▲ ♥

5 ■ ■
       ▲ ●

6 ● ●
       ■ ●

© Pearson Education, Inc. K

Topic 13

My Word Cards

Directions Have students cut out the vocabulary cards. Read the front of the card, and then ask them to explain what the word or phrase means.

A-Z

solid figure

cone

cube

cylinder

sphere

flat surface

My Word Cards

Directions Review the definitions and have students study the cards. Extend learning by having students draw pictures for each word on a separate piece of paper.

Point to the shape.
Say: *This solid figure is a* **cube**.

Point to the shape.
Say: *This solid figure is a* **cone**.

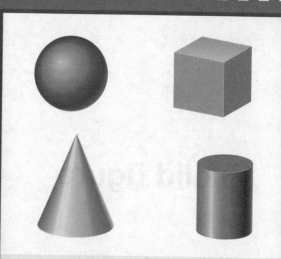

Point to the shapes.
Say: **Solid figures** *are also called three-dimensional shapes*.

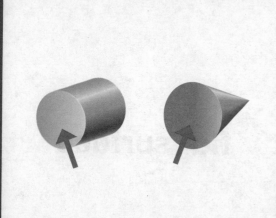

Point to the flat surface of each object.
Say: *Some solid figures have* **flat surfaces**.

Point to the shape.
Say: *This solid figure is called a* **sphere**.

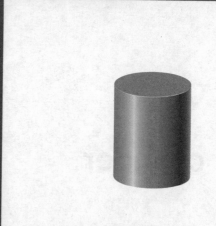

Point to the shape.
Say: *This solid figure is called a* **cylinder**.

A-Z

roll	stack	slide

My Word Cards

Directions Review the definitions and have students study the cards. Extend learning by having students draw pictures for each word on a separate piece of paper.

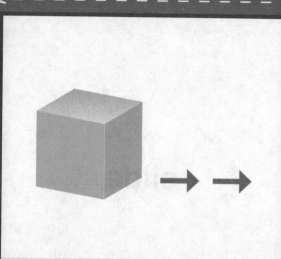

Point to the shape.
Say: *Solid figures with flat surfaces can* **slide**.

Point to the shapes.
Say: *Some solid figures can* **stack** *on each other.*

Point to the shape.
Say: *Some solid figures can* **roll**.

Solve & Share Name ______________________________

Lesson 13-1
Sorting 3-D Figures

One Way

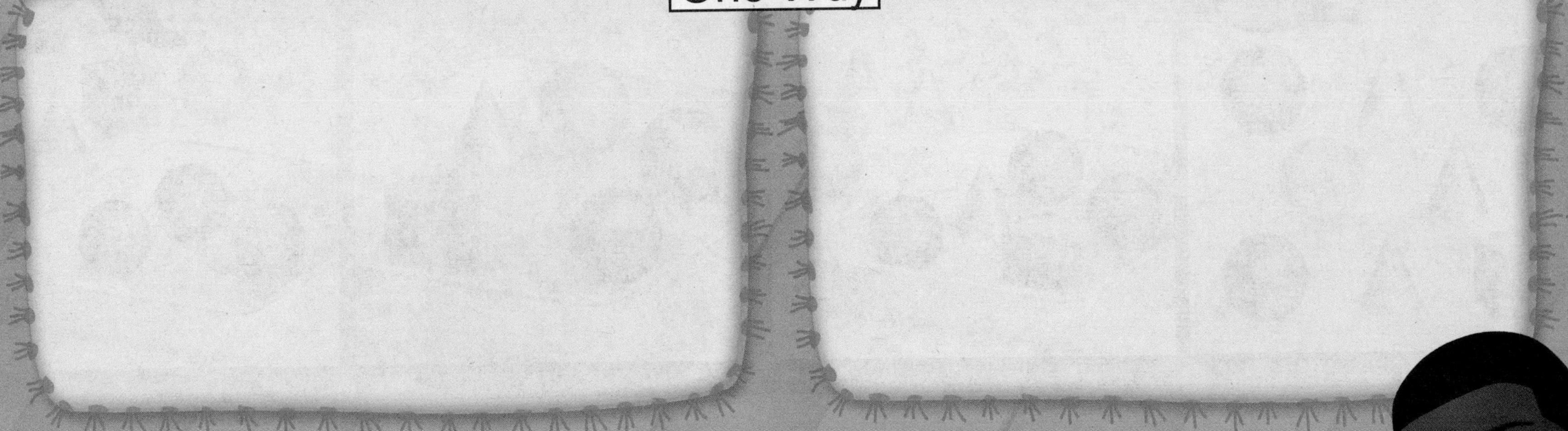

Another Way

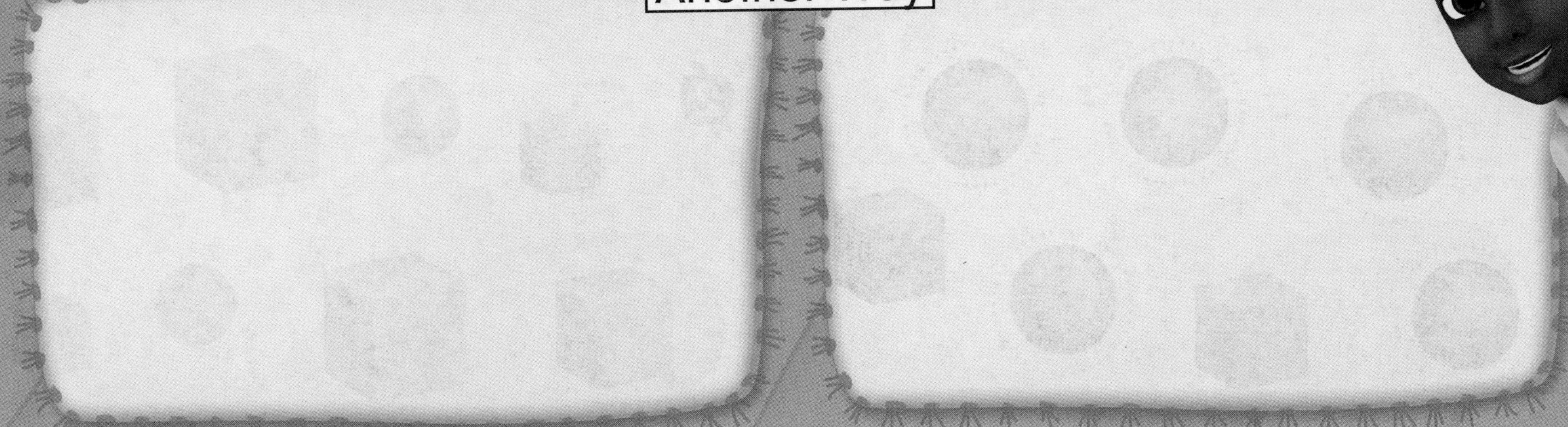

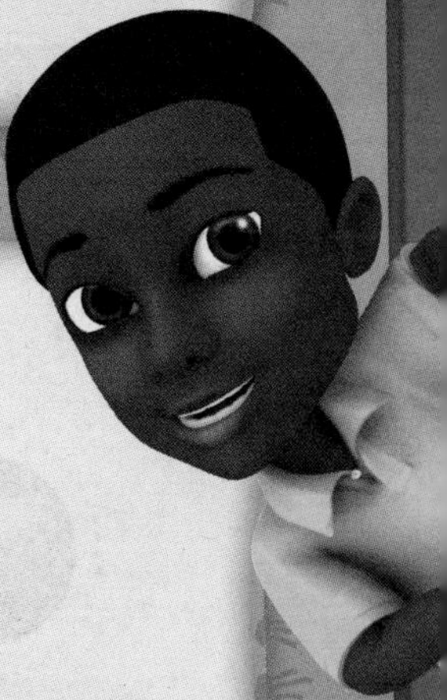

Directions Say: *Jackson puts 2 green blocks and 2 blue blocks on a rug. He wants to make 2 groups of blocks in 2 different ways. How can he sort the blocks? Glue blocks onto your mat to show the different ways.*

TEKS K.6E Classify and sort a variety of regular and irregular two- and three-dimensional figures regardless of orientation or size. Also, K.6. **Mathematical Process Standards** K.1A, K.1C, K.1D.

Digital Resources at PearsonTexas.com

Solve Learn Glossary Check Tools Games

Guided Practice

1

2

Directions Have students: 1 circle the shapes that are round; 2 circle the shapes that are **not** round.

© Pearson Education, Inc. K

Topic 13 | **Lesson 1**

Name _____

3

4

5

6

7

8

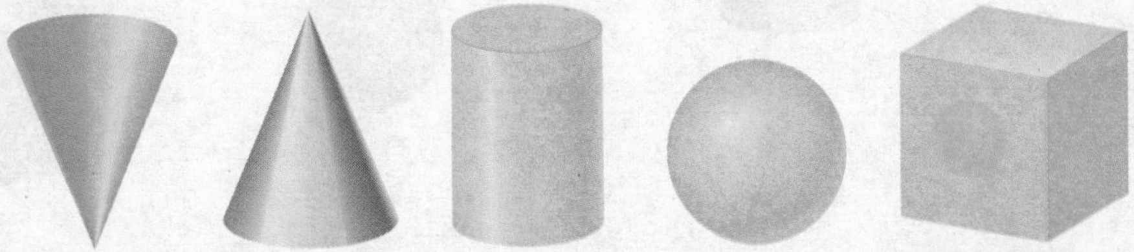

Independent Practice

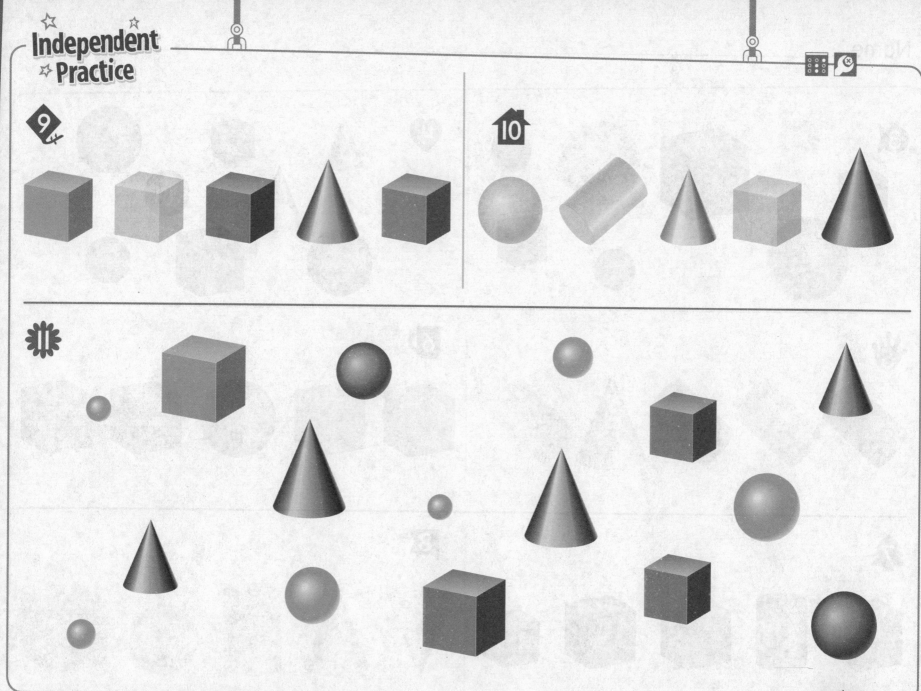

Directions Have students: 9 and 10 draw an X on the shape that does **not** belong in the group; 11 find 2 different ways to sort the shapes, circle shapes to show one way to sort, draw Xs on shapes to show another way to sort, and then explain their reasoning.

674 six hundred seventy-four

© Pearson Education, Inc. K

Topic 13 | Lesson 1

Name _____

Another Look

🏠 **HOME CONNECTION**
Your child learned to sort objects by different attributes, such as shape and color.

HOME ACTIVITY Set out a variety of simple objects, such as marbles in different colors and sizes, and ask your child to sort the objects into groups in at least 2 different ways. Ask your child to tell what is alike about all of the objects in each group. For example, your child may sort all of the large marbles into a group and then sort all of the blue marbles into a group.

⭐ 1

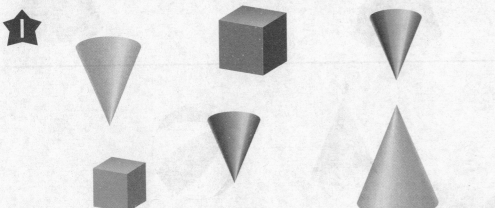

🍎 2

Directions Say: *You can sort shapes and objects in different ways. Circle all of the red boxes to sort by shape and color.* Then have students: ⭐ circle all of the boxes to sort by shape; 🍎 circle all of the yellow shapes to sort by color.

Directions Have students: **3** circle the small shapes to sort by size; **4** find 2 different ways to sort the shapes, circle shapes to show one way to sort, draw Xs on shapes to show another way to sort, and then explain their reasoning; **5** find 2 different ways to sort the objects, circle objects to show one way to sort, draw Xs on objects to show another way to sort, and then explain their reasoning.

Topic 13 | Lesson 1

Directions Say: *Jackson wants to find objects that have the same shape as these solid figures. How can he find objects that have the same shape? Draw objects below the solid figure with the same shape.*

⊕ **TEKS K.6B** Identify three-dimensional solids, including cylinders, cones, spheres, and cubes, in the real world. Also, K.6. **Mathematical Process Standards** K.1C, K.1D, K.1F, K.1G.

Digital Resources at PearsonTexas.com

Solve   Learn   Glossary   Check   Tools   Games

Topic 13 | Lesson 2

six hundred seventy-seven   **677**

Guided Practice

1

2

Directions Have students: ⭐ and 🍎 name the solid figure on the left, and then circle the solid figure on the right that has the same shape.

Topic 13 | Lesson 2

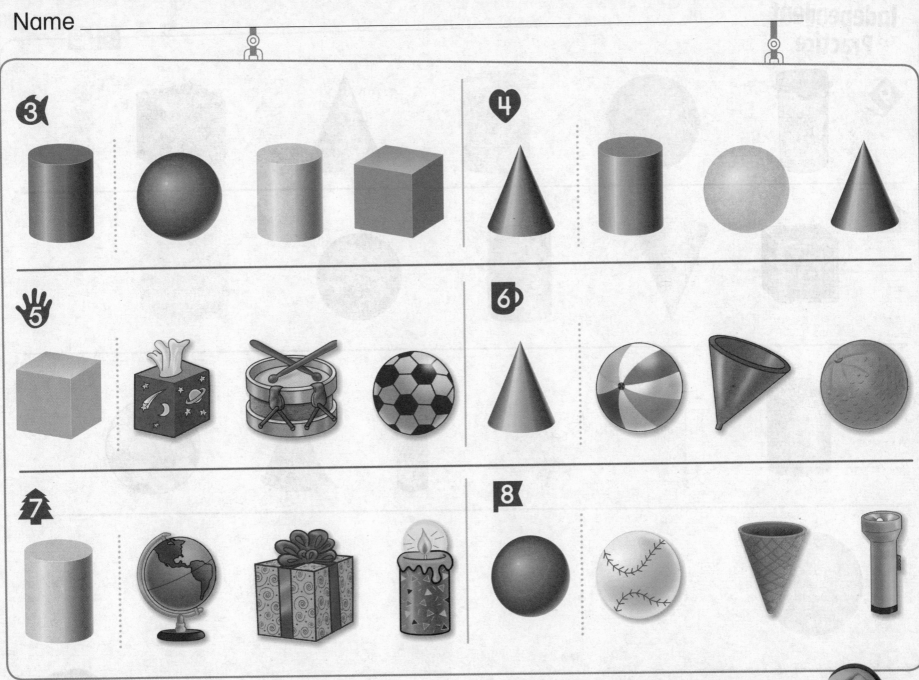

3

4

5

6

7

8

Directions Have students: **3–8** name the solid figure on the left, and then circle the object or solid figure on the right that has the same shape.

Independent Practice

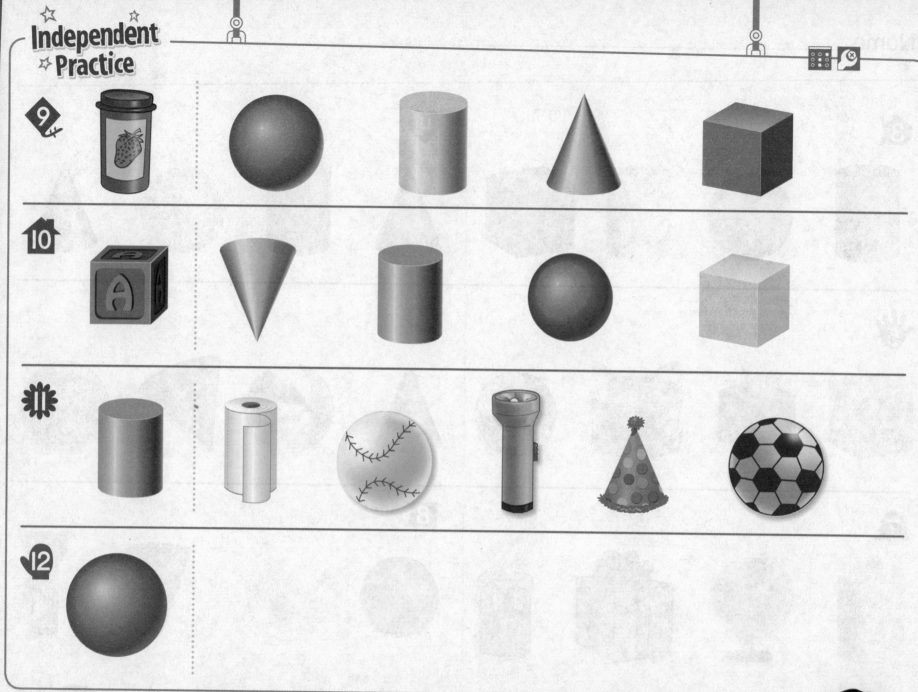

9

10

11

12

Directions Have students: **9** and **10** look at the object on the left, and then circle the solid figure on the right that has the same shape; **11** name the solid figure on the left, and then circle the 2 objects on the right that have the same shape; **12** name the solid figure on the left, and then draw 2 more objects that have the same shape.

680 six hundred eighty

© Pearson Education, Inc. K

Topic 13 | Lesson 2

Name _____

Another Look

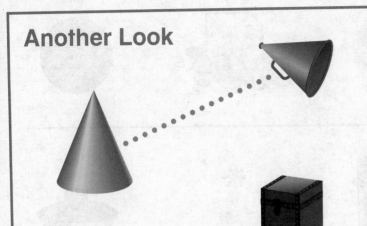

🏠 **HOME CONNECTION**
Your child learned to identify four solid figures: cube, cylinder, sphere, and cone.

HOME ACTIVITY Show your child several objects shaped like cubes, cylinders, spheres, or cones. Ask your child to name the solid figure that has the same shape. For example, show your child a ball and ask your child to name the shape (sphere).

⭐ 1

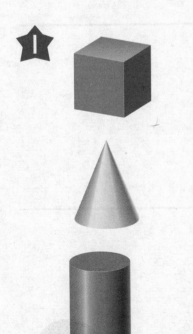

2️⃣

Directions Say: *This solid figure is a cone. Draw a line from the cone to the object that has the same shape. Draw a line from the cylinder to the object that has the same shape.* Then have students: ⭐ and 2️⃣ draw a line from each solid figure to the object that has the same shape.

3

4

5

6

© Pearson Education, Inc. K

Directions Have students: **3** and **4** circle the 4 objects that have the same shape, and then name the shape; **5** and **6** look at the solid figure on the left, and then draw 2 more objects that have the same shape.

Solve & Share Name _____

Directions Provide groups of students with cube, cone, and cylinder geometric solids. Say: *Jackson needs to draw this shape for a project. This is a circle. Which solid figures create this shape when traced? Trace those solid figures to show you are correct.*

⬥ **TEKS K.6C** Identify two-dimensional components of three-dimensional objects. Also, K.6, K.6A, K.6B. **Mathematical Process Standards** K.1C, K.1E, K.1F.

Digital Resources at PearsonTexas.com

Solve Learn Glossary Check Tools Games

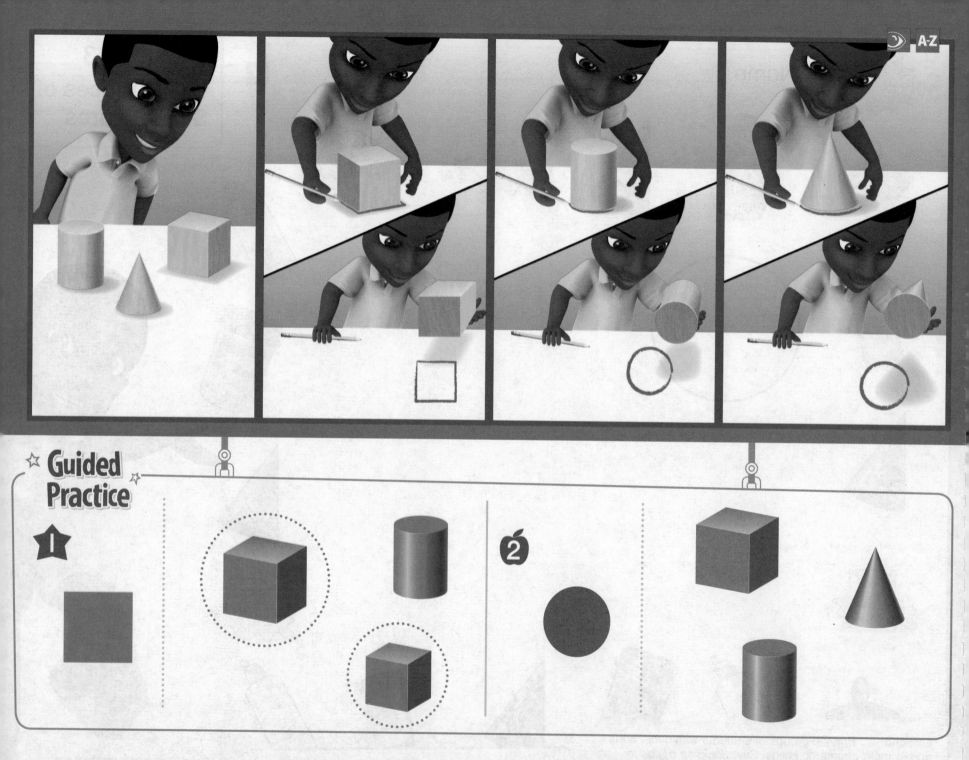

Guided Practice

1

2

Directions Have students: **1** and **2** look at the shape on the left, and then circle the solid figures that have a flat surface with that shape.

© Pearson Education, Inc. K

Topic 13 | Lesson 3

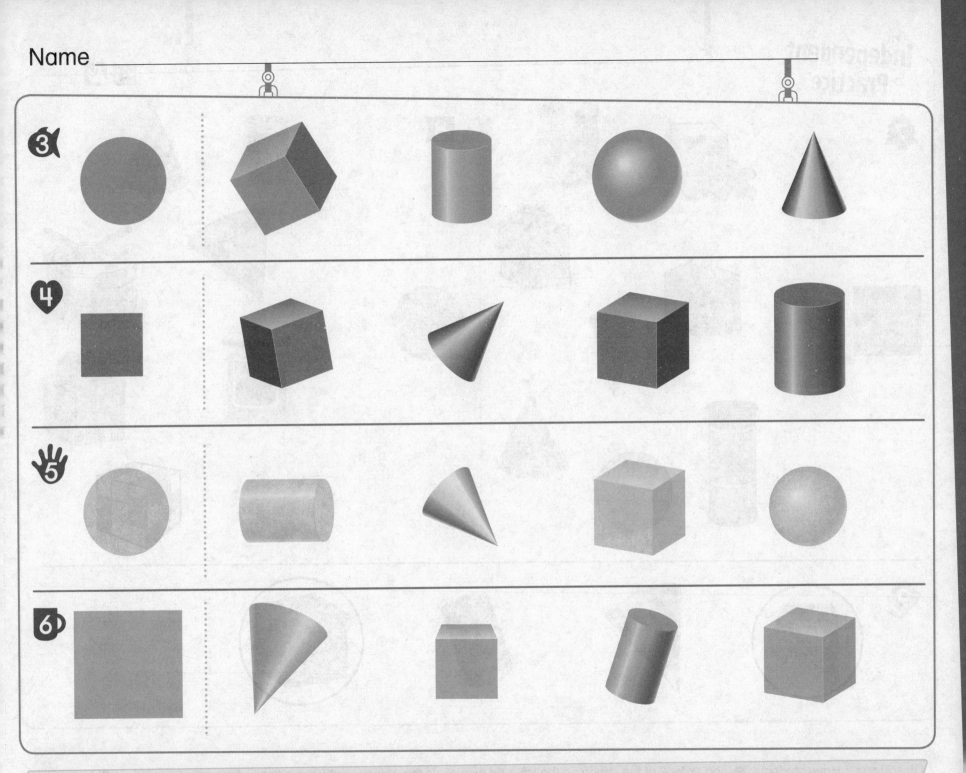

3

4

5

6

Directions Have students: **3–6** look at the shape on the left, and then circle the solid figures that have a flat surface with that shape.

Topic 13 | Lesson 3

six hundred eighty-five **685**

Independent Practice

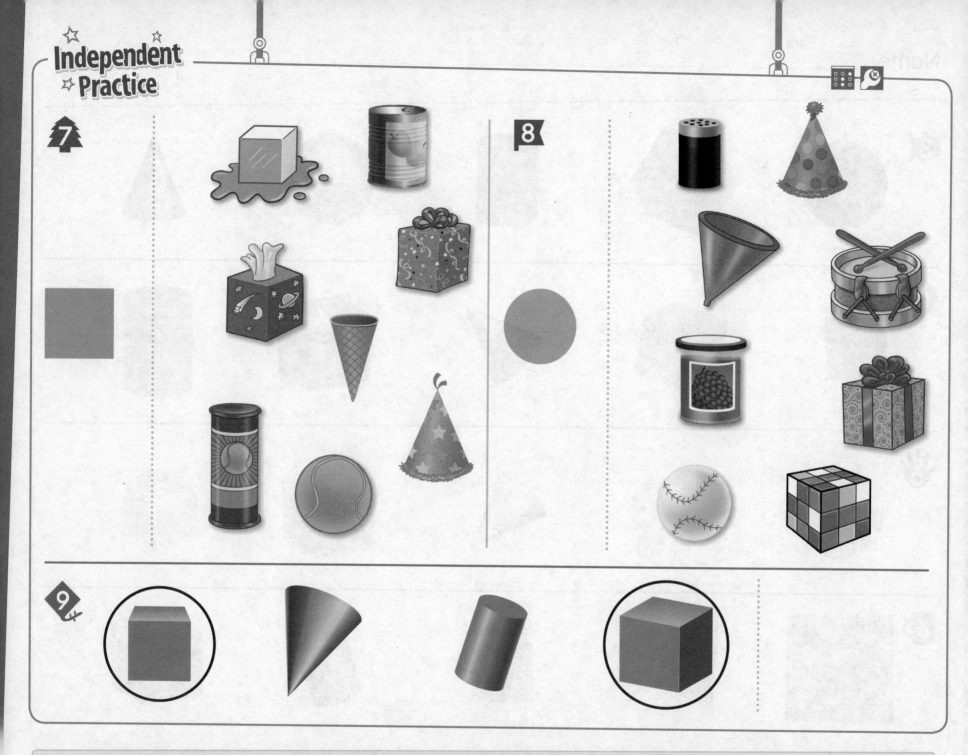

7

8

9

Directions Have students: **7** and **8** look at the shape on the left, and then circle the objects that have a flat surface with that shape; **9** look at the solid figures that are circled on the left, and then draw the shape of the flat surfaces for these solid figures on the right.

686 six hundred eighty-six

© Pearson Education, Inc. K

Topic 13 | Lesson 3

Name _____

Another Look

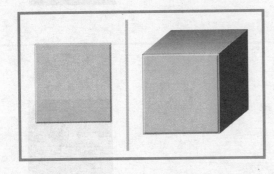

🏠 **HOME CONNECTION**
Your child identified the flat surfaces of solid figures.

HOME ACTIVITY Show your child a can and ask him or her to identify the flat surfaces (circles). Show your child a box shaped like a cube and ask him or her to identify the flat surfaces (squares). Take turns identifying other objects that have flat surfaces that are circles or squares.

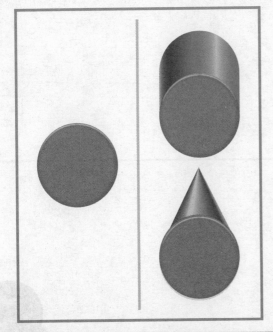

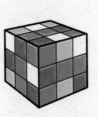

Directions Say: *A cube has square flat surfaces. Circle the objects that have a square flat surface.* Then have students: 🌟 look at the cylinder and cone in the blue box, identify the shape of their flat surfaces, and then draw Xs on the objects that have a flat surface that is a circle.

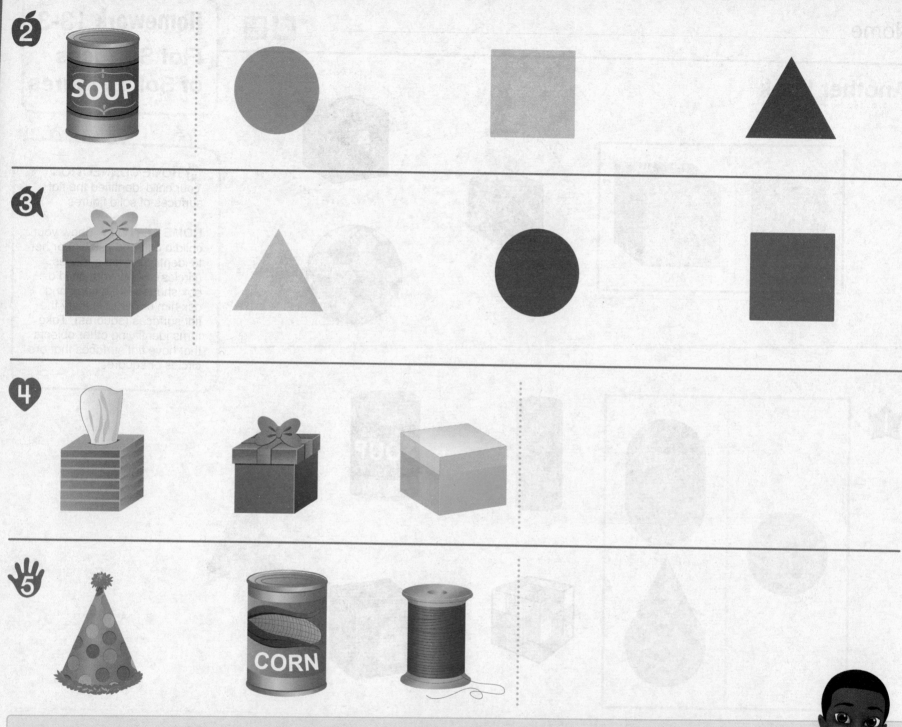

2

3

4

5

Directions Have students: **2** and **3** look at the object on the left, and then circle the shape of its flat surfaces; **4** and **5** look at the objects on the left, and then draw the shape of their flat surfaces.

688 six hundred eighty-eight

© Pearson Education, Inc. K

Topic 13 | Lesson 3

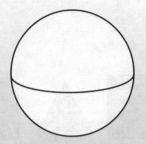

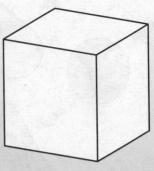

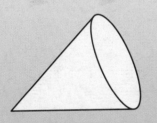

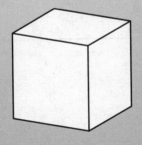
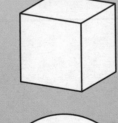

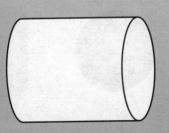
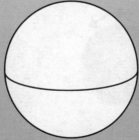
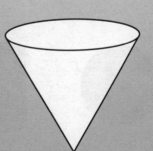

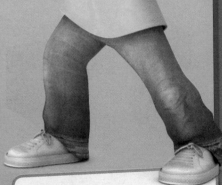

Directions Say: *Jackson wants to build a tower with solid figures. Color the solid figures he can use to build his tower.*

★ **TEKS K.6E** Classify and sort a variety of regular and irregular two- and three-dimensional figures regardless of orientation or size. Also, K.6. **Mathematical Process Standards** K.1A, K.1D, K.1F, K.1G.

Digital Resources at PearsonTexas.com

Solve   Learn   Glossary   Check   Tools   Games

Guided Practice

1

2

Directions Have students: **1** look at the stacked solid figures on the left, and then circle the other solid figures that stack; **2** look at the rolling solid figure on the left, and then circle the other solid figures that roll.

© Pearson Education, Inc. K

Name _____

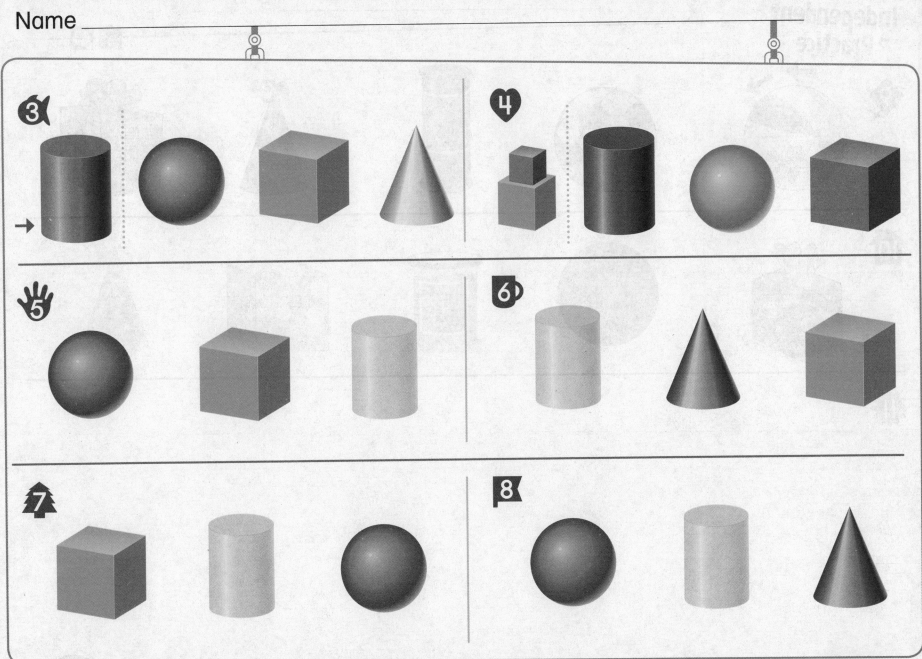

3

4

5

6

7

8

Topic 13 | Lesson 4

9

10

✻

© Pearson Education, Inc. K

Directions Have students: 9 look at the rolling object on the left, and then circle the other objects that roll; 10 look at the sliding object on the left, and then circle the other objects that slide; ✻ draw 2 solid figures that can stack on each other.

Name _____

Another Look

🏠 **HOME CONNECTION**
Your child compared solid
figures. Your child learned
that some solid figures can
stack, some can roll, and
some can slide.

HOME ACTIVITY Show your
child a ball, a can, and a cube-
shaped block. Ask him or her
to compare the features of
each object, such as which
objects can stack, which can
roll, and which can slide. Have
your child point to the flat
surfaces on the objects.

⭐ ➡️ ➡️

②

Directions Say: *A cube can stack on top of another cube. Circle the other solid figures that can also be stacked on top of a cube.* Then have students: ⭐ look at the rolling solid figure on the left, and then circle the other solid figures that can roll; ② look at the sliding solid figure on the left, and then circle the other solid figures that can slide.

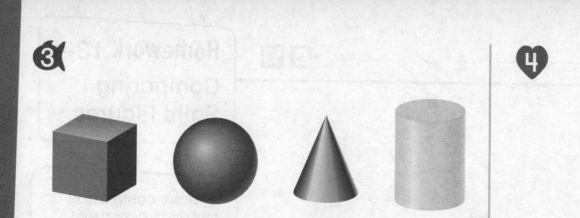

✋

Directions Have students: ③ draw Xs on the solid figures that can both roll **and** slide; ❤ draw 2 solid figures that can roll; ✋ draw a castle made of blocks that uses **all** of the 3 solid figures that can stack, and then explain why cones can only stack on top of other shapes.

© Pearson Education, Inc. K

Topic 13 | Lesson 4

 **Name** _____

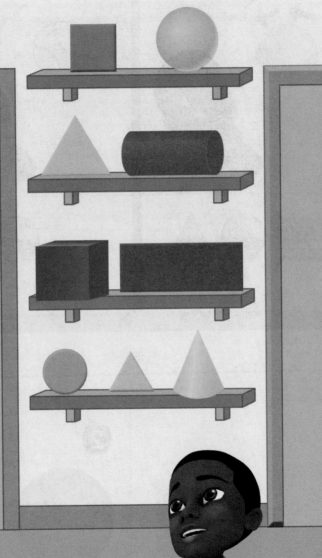

Directions Say: *Jackson wants to put flat shapes behind Door 1 and solid figures behind Door 2. Draw a line from each shape to the correct door to show how he should sort his shapes.*

⭐ **TEKS K.1B** Use a problem-solving model that incorporates analyzing given information, ... **TEKS K.1D** Communicate mathematical ideas, reasoning, and their implications using . . . language as appropriate. Also, **K.6, K.6D, K.6E. Mathematical Process Standards K.1A, K.1F, K.1G.**

Digital Resources at PearsonTexas.com

 Solve   Learn   **A-Z** Glossary   Check   Tools   Games

Analyze

Plan

Solve and Justify

Evaluate

Guided Practice

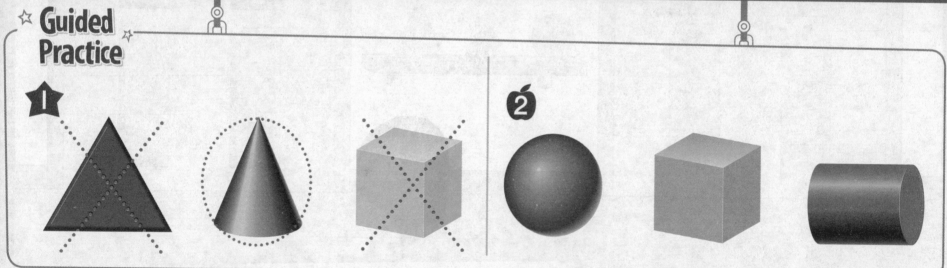

1

2

Directions Read the clues to students. Have them draw Xs on the shapes that do **not** fit the clues and circle the shape that the clues describe. **1** *I am a solid figure. I can roll. I have only 1 flat surface. Which shape am I?* **2** *I am a solid figure. I can roll. I can also stack. Which shape am I?*

696 six hundred ninety-six

© Pearson Education, Inc. K

Topic 13 | Lesson 5

Name _____

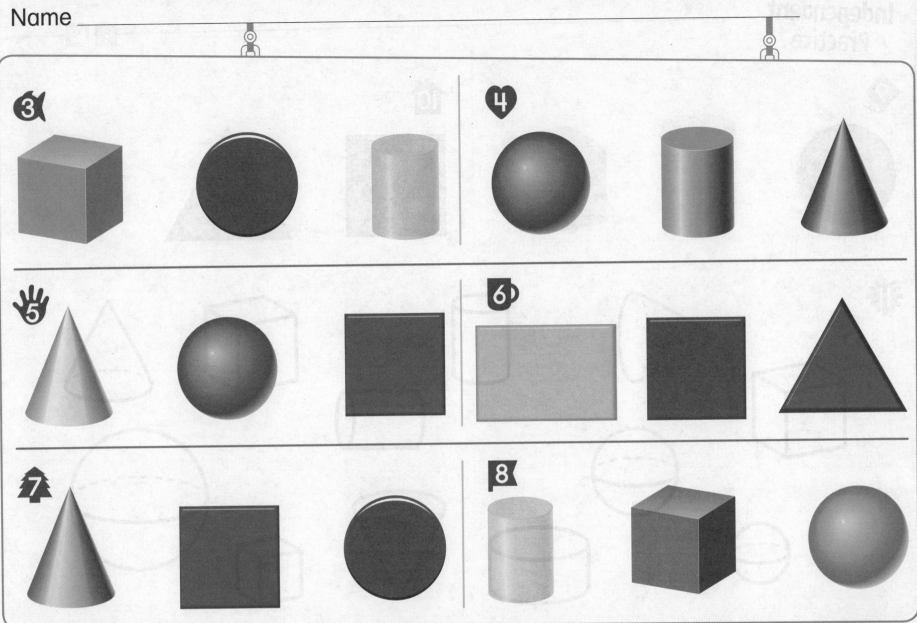

3

4

5

6

7

8

Directions Read the clues to students. Have them draw Xs on the shapes that do **not** fit the clues and circle the shape that the clues describe. Have students name the shape. **3** *I am a solid figure. I can stack and slide. I have 6 flat surfaces. Which shape am I?* **4** *I am a solid figure. I can slide. I have only 1 flat surface. Which shape am I?* **5** *I am a solid figure. I can roll. I do **not** have any flat surfaces. Which shape am I?* **6** *I am a flat shape. I have 4 sides. All of my sides are the same length. Which shape am I?* **7** *I am a flat shape. I do **not** have any straight sides. Which shape am I?* **8** *I am a solid figure. I can roll. I have 2 flat surfaces. Which shape am I?*

Topic 13 | Lesson 5

six hundred ninety-seven **697**

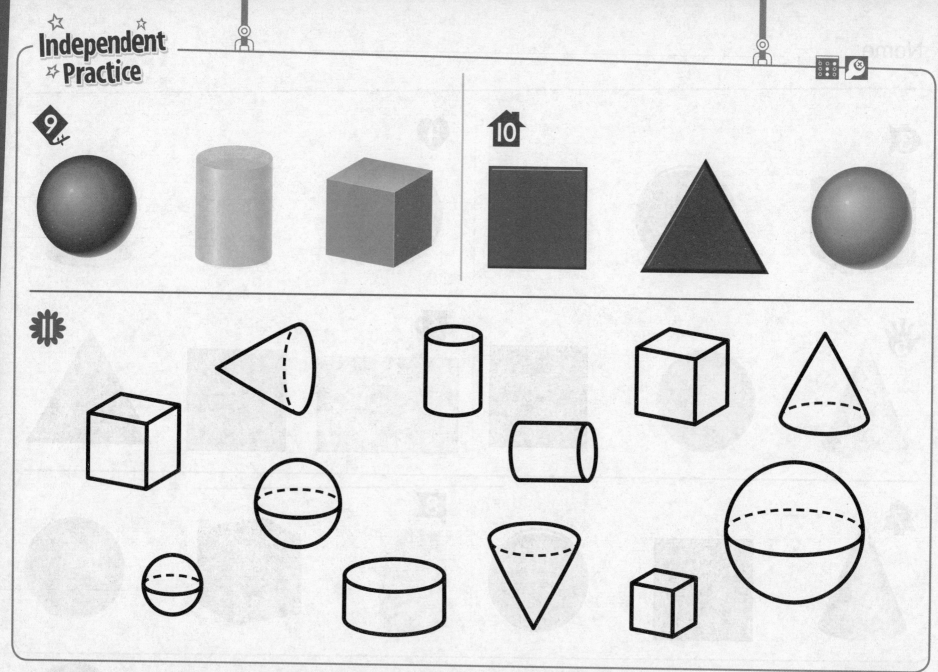

9

10

Directions Read the clues to students. Have them draw Xs on the shapes that do **not** fit the clues and circle the shape that the clues describe. Have students name the shape. **9** *I am a solid figure. I can slide. All of my flat surfaces are squares. Which shape am I?* **10** *I am a flat shape. I have 3 vertices. Which shape am I?* Then have students: **☀** color all the solid figures that can stack on a cube, circle all the solid figures that can roll, and draw Xs on all the solid figures that have 2 flat surfaces that are circles.

Topic 13 | Lesson 5

Another Look

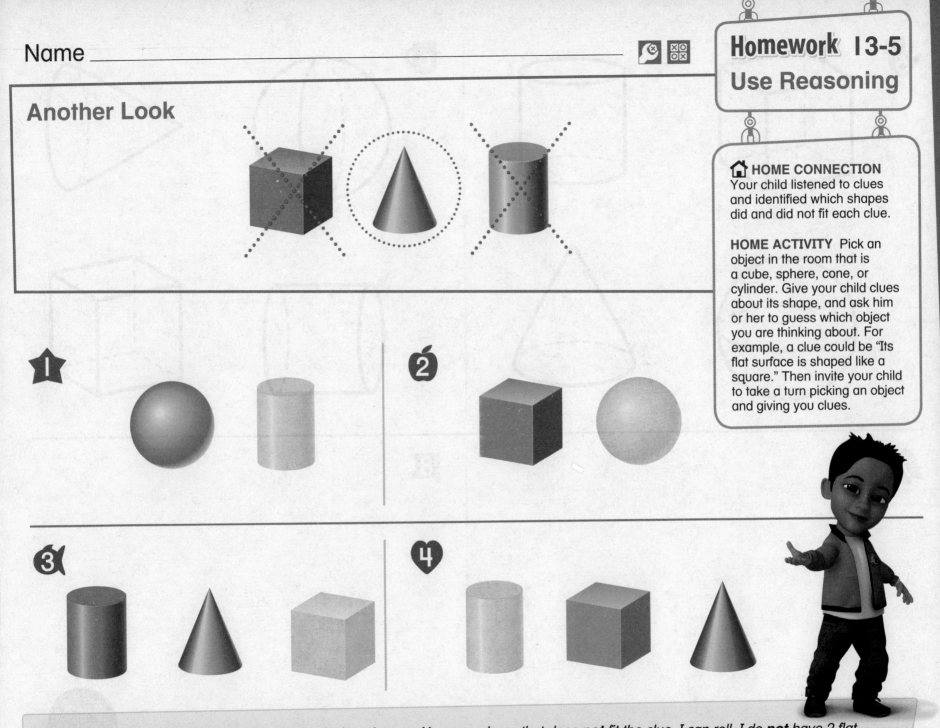

🏠 **HOME CONNECTION**
Your child listened to clues and identified which shapes did and did not fit each clue.

HOME ACTIVITY Pick an object in the room that is a cube, sphere, cone, or cylinder. Give your child clues about its shape, and ask him or her to guess which object you are thinking about. For example, a clue could be "Its flat surface is shaped like a square." Then invite your child to take a turn picking an object and giving you clues.

⭐ 1

🍎 2

🌀 3

❤️ 4

Directions Say: *Listen to the clues. After each clue, draw an X on any shape that does **not** fit the clue. I can roll. I do **not** have 2 flat surfaces. Which shape am I? Circle the shape that fits all of the clues.* Then read the clues to students. Have them draw Xs on the shapes that do **not** fit the clues and circle the shape that the clues describe. ⭐ *I can roll. I **cannot** stack. Which shape am I?* 🍎 *I can stack. I can slide. Which shape am I?* 🌀 *I can roll. I have only 1 flat surface. Which shape am I?* ❤️ *I can stack. I **cannot** roll. Which shape am I?*

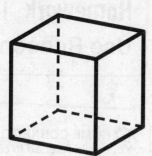

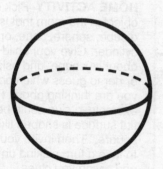
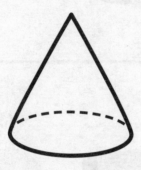

6

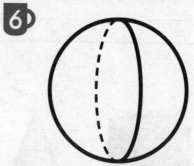

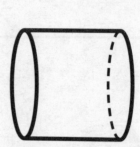
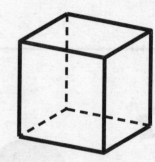

7

8

Directions Read the clues. Have students color the shape the clues describe, and then name the shape. ✋ *I have more than 2 flat surfaces. I can stack but I **cannot** roll. Which shape am I?* ☕ *I can roll and I can stack. I do **not** have more than 1 flat surface. Which shape am I?* Then have students listen to the clues, and then draw the shape that the clues describe. 🌲 *I can roll and I can slide. I do **not** have 2 flat surfaces. Which shape am I?* 🚩 *I can roll. I have no flat surfaces. Which shape am I?*

Topic 13 | Lesson 5

Name _____

Set A

⭐ 1

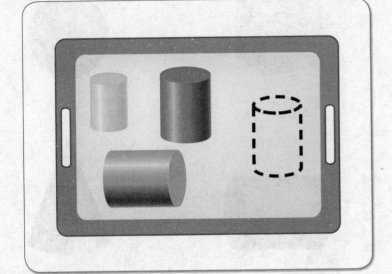

Set B

🍎 2

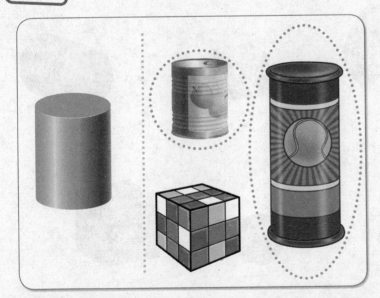

Directions Have students: ⭐ tell how the shapes are sorted, and then draw another shape that belongs in the group; 🍎 look at the solid figure on the left, and then circle the objects on the right that have the same shape.

Directions Have students: ❸ look at the shape on the left, and then circle the solid figures that have that a flat surface with that shape; ❹ circle the solid figures that can stack on top of another solid figure to build something.

© Pearson Education, Inc. K

Name _____

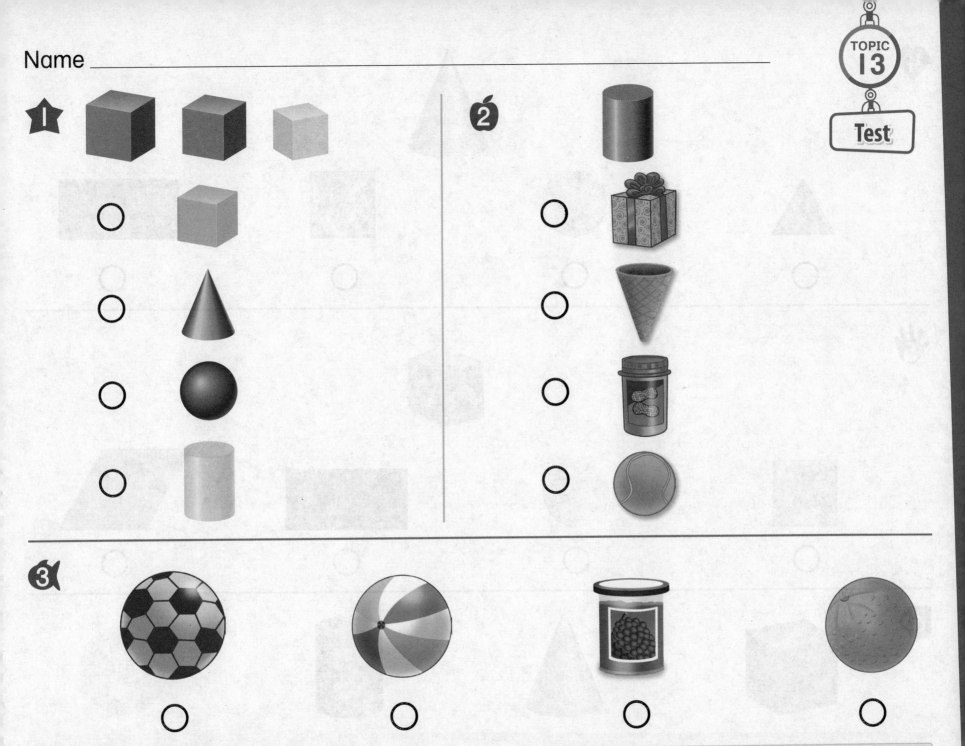

Directions Have students mark the best answer. ⭐ Which shape belongs in this group? 🍎 Which object has the same shape?
◆ Which object can stack?

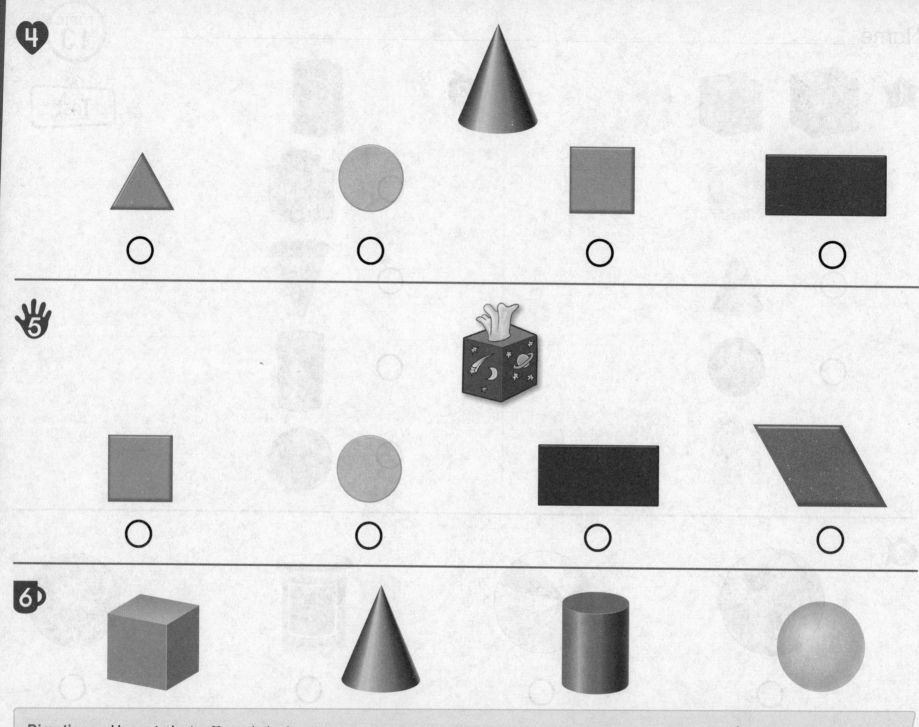

Directions Have students: ❹ mark the best answer. Which shape matches the flat surface of the solid figure? ✋ mark the best answer. Which shape matches the flat surface of the object? ❻ listen to the clues, and then circle the solid figure that the clues describe. Say: *I can roll. I **cannot** stack. Which shape am I?*

© Pearson Education, Inc. K

Topic 13

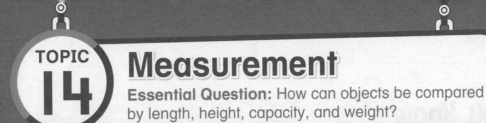

Measurement

Essential Question: How can objects be compared by length, height, capacity, and weight?

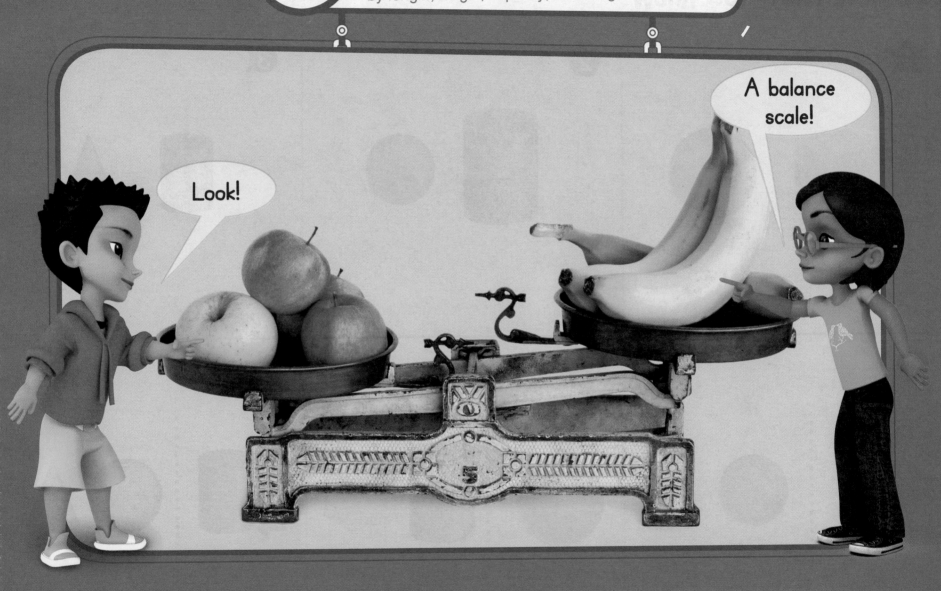

Math and Science Project: Tools for Measuring

Directions Read the character speech bubbles to students. **Find Out!** Have students find out about different tools for measuring. Say: *Talk to friends and relatives about measuring tools. Ask how they measure the length, height, or weight of objects.* **Journal: Make a Poster** Then have students make a poster. Have them draw a picture of an object and a tool they could use to measure it.

Name _____

Review What You Know

1

2

3

4

5

6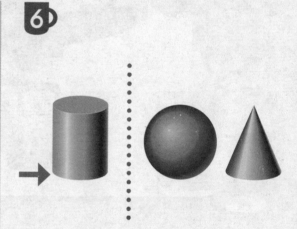

© Pearson Education, Inc. K

Directions Say: *These are 2 tools for measuring. What can you measure with the cup? What can you measure with the cube train? Draw an object you can measure with each tool.*

⭐ **TEKS K.7A** Give an example of a measurable attribute of a given object, including length, capacity, and weight. Also, K.7. **Mathematical Process Standards K.1A, K.1B, K.1C, K.1F.**

Digital Resources at PearsonTexas.com

 Solve Learn **A-Z** Glossary Check Tools Games

☆ **Guided Practice** ☆

1

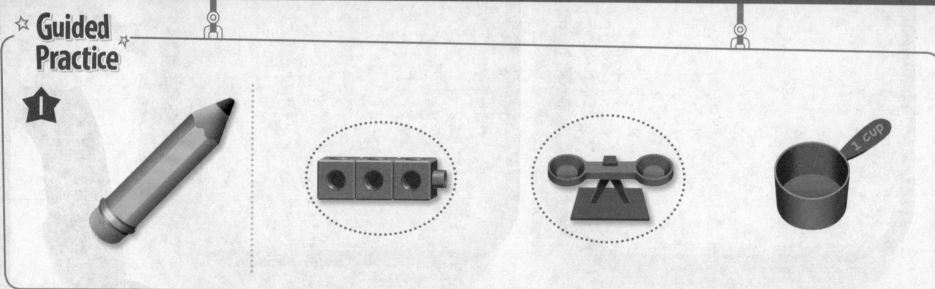

Directions Have students look at the object on the left, identify the attributes that can be measured, and then circle the tools that could be used to tell about those attributes.

712 seven hundred twelve   © Pearson Education, Inc. K   **Topic 14 | Lesson 1**

Name _____

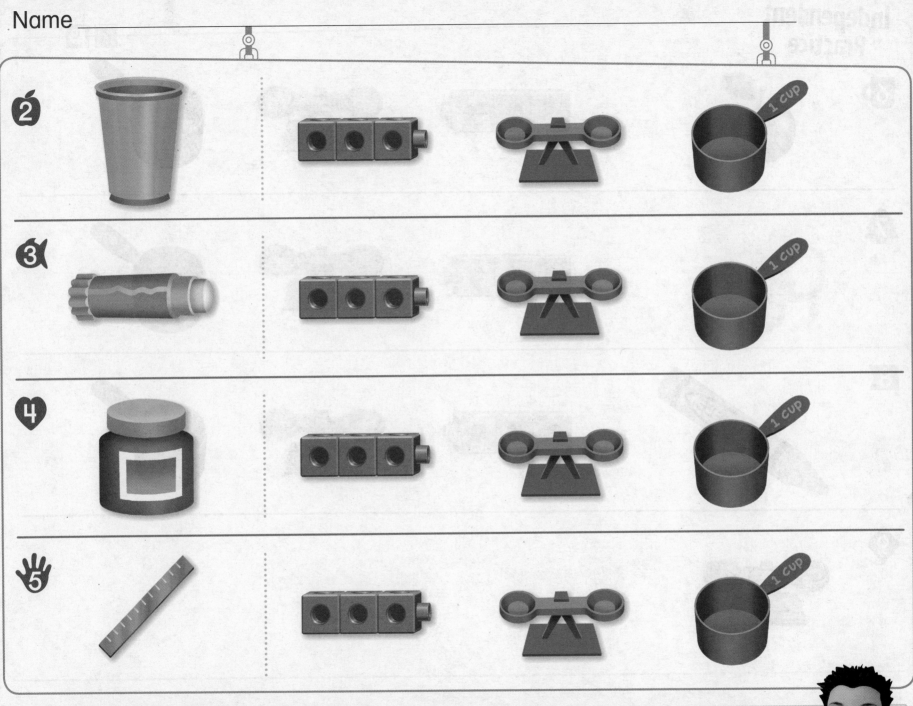

2

3

4

5

Directions Have students look at the object on the left, identify the attributes that can be measured, and then circle the tools that could be used to tell about those attributes.

Independent Practice

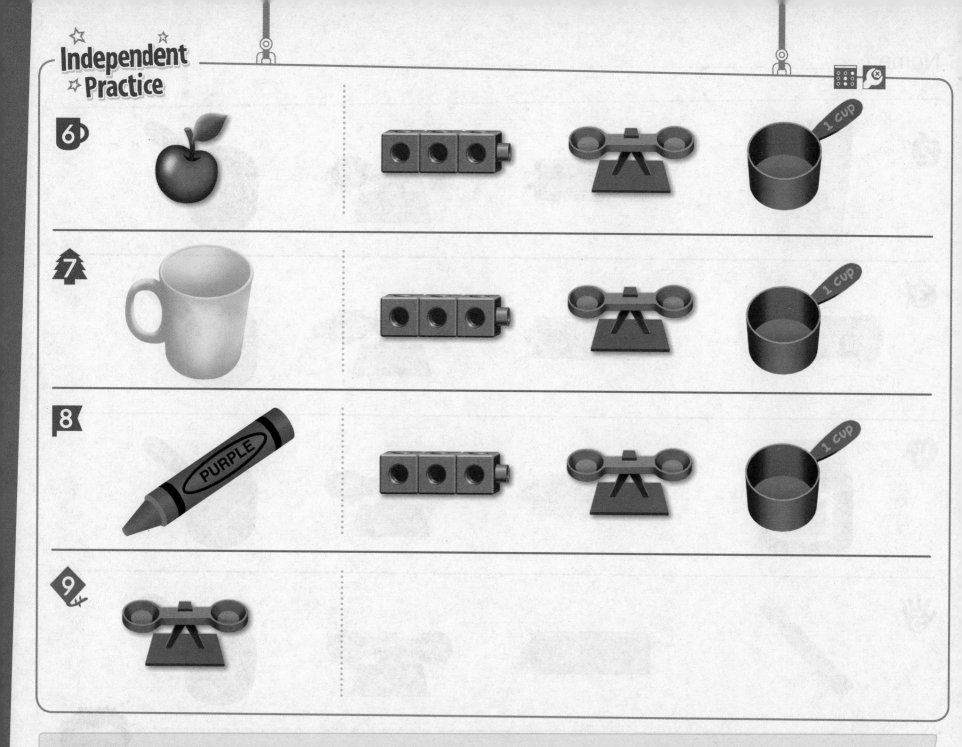

6 🍎

7 🌲 ☕

8 🚩 PURPLE

9 🔶

Topic 14 | Lesson 1

Name _____

Another Look

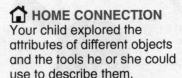 **HOME CONNECTION**
Your child explored the attributes of different objects and the tools he or she could use to describe them.

HOME ACTIVITY Choose a few small objects, such as a cup, a book, and a spoon. Ask your child to describe each object, and then name tools that could be used to tell about different attributes of the object (e.g., balance scale, cube trains, measuring cup).

Directions Say: *Attributes like how long something is, how heavy something is, or how much something holds can be measured using tools. What attributes does a carton of milk have? Circle the tools that could be used to tell about these attributes.* Then have students: ⭐ and ② look at the object on the left, identify the attributes that can be measured, and then circle the tools that could be used to tell about those attributes.

3

4

5

6

Directions Have students: ❸ and ❹ identify what attribute the tool on the left can measure, and then circle the objects that could be measured with that tool; ✋ identify the attribute that can be measured using the tool on the left, and then draw 2 objects that could be measured using that tool; ❻ draw an object that could be measured by the attributes of length, weight, and capacity.

716 seven hundred sixteen   © Pearson Education, Inc. K   **Topic 14** | Lesson 1

Data

Essential Question: How can graphs be used to show data and answer questions?

Look!

We can make surveys about animals!

Math and Science Project: Organizing Data

Directions Read the character speech bubbles to students. **Find Out!** Have students find out how scientists collect and organize data.
Say: *You can organize data using pictures, numbers, and words. Talk to friends and relatives about situations where you would need to organize data.*
Journal: Make a Poster Then have students make a poster. Ask them to draw 2 different animals and then ask 5 classmates which of the 2 animals they like better. Have them organize their classmates' responses in a picture graph.

Name _____

Review What You Know

1

2

3

4

5

6

Directions Have students: **1** circle the tool used to measure weight; **2** circle the tool that measures height or length; **3** circle the tool that measures how much a container can hold; **4** circle the cube train that is longer; **5** circle the flower that is shorter; **6** circle the elephant that is heavier.

© Pearson Education, Inc. K

Name _____

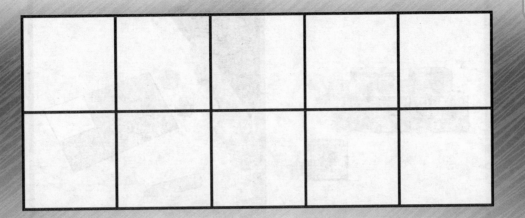

Directions Say: Daniel has a group of red cubes and a group of blue cubes. How can you find out which group has more cubes?

⭐ **TEKS K.8A** Collect, sort, and organize data into two or three categories. Also, **K.8. Mathematical Process Standards** K.1D, K.1E, K.1F.

Digital Resources at PearsonTexas.com

↗ Solve | 👁 Learn | A-Z Glossary | ⠿ Check | ⚙ Tools | ⊠⊠ Games

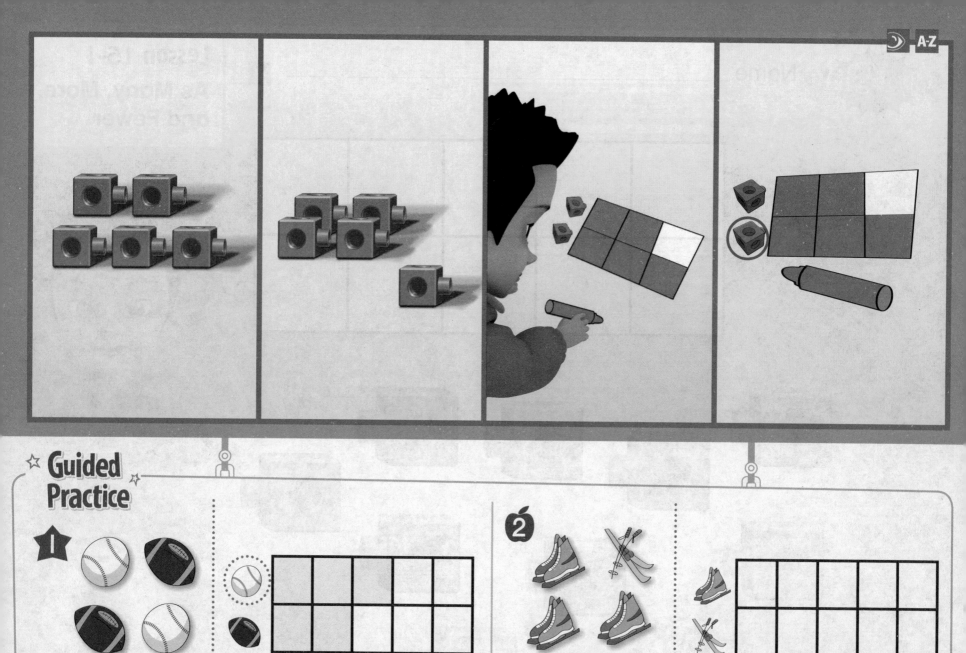

✩ Guided Practice ✩

1

2

Directions Have students color a box on the graph for each object, and then circle the object next to the row with more objects or circle the exercise number if the number of objects is the same.

© Pearson Education, Inc. K

Topic 15 | Lesson 1

Name _____

3

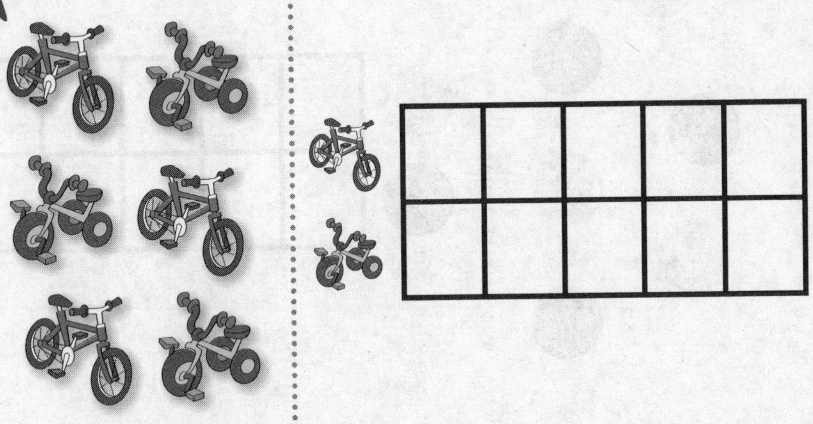

4

5

6

Directions Have students color a box on the graph for each object, and then circle the object next to the row with fewer objects or circle the exercise number if the number of objects is the same.

Topic 15 | Lesson 1

seven hundred sixty-one **761**

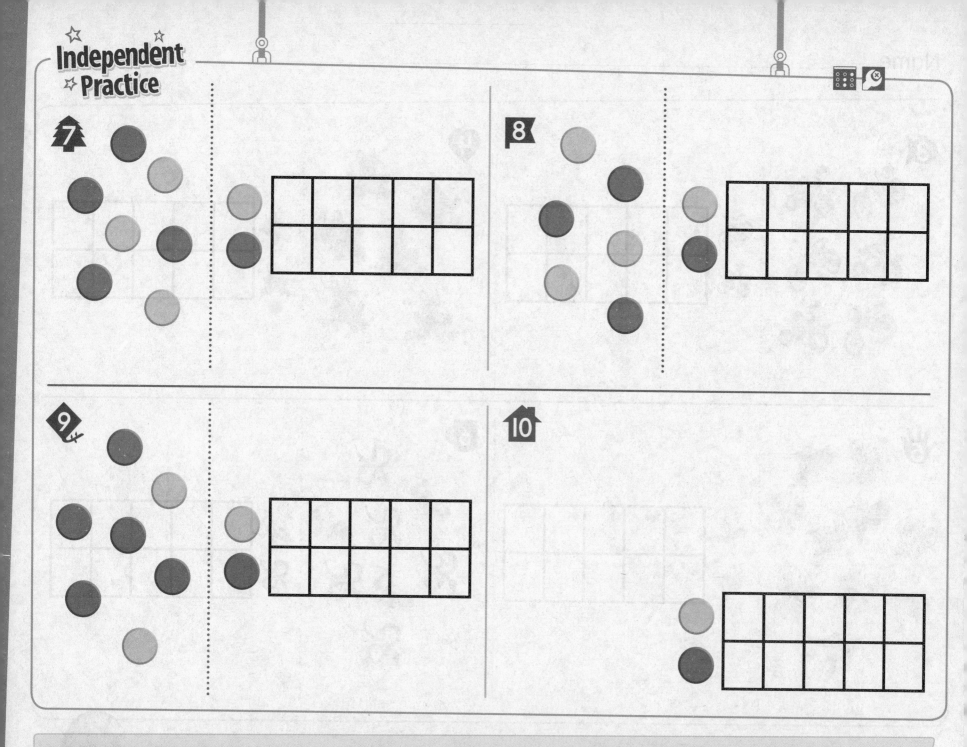

Directions Have students: **7**–**9** color a box on the graph for each object, and then circle the object next to the row with more objects or circle the exercise number if the number of objects is the same; **10** draw a set of yellow counters that has 2 fewer than a set of red counters, color a box on the graph for each counter, and then circle the object next to the row with more counters.

© Pearson Education, Inc. K

Topic 15 | Lesson 1

Name _____

Another Look

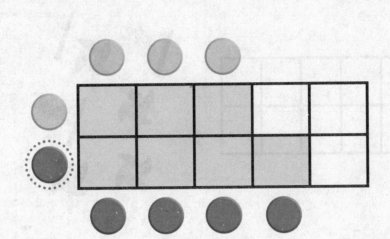

🏠 **HOME CONNECTION**
Your child learned to organize data for 2 groups of objects in order to compare the number of objects and determine which group has more, fewer, or if the groups have the same number of objects.

HOME ACTIVITY Set out a group of 1–5 forks and a group of 1–5 spoons. Have your child decide which group has more by matching each fork to a spoon. Repeat with different quantities of forks and spoons.

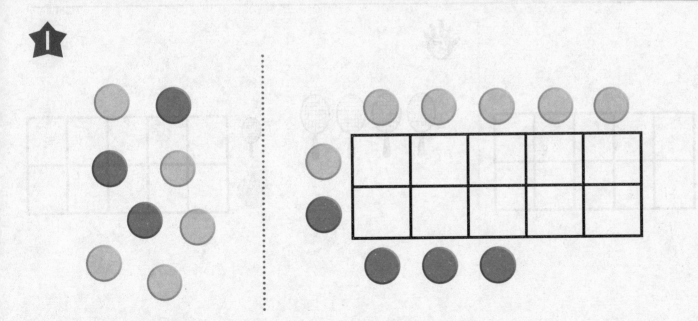

Directions Say: *Color a box on the graph for each object, and then circle the object next to the row with more objects.*
Then have students: ⭐ color a box on the graph for each object, and then circle the object next to the row with more objects.

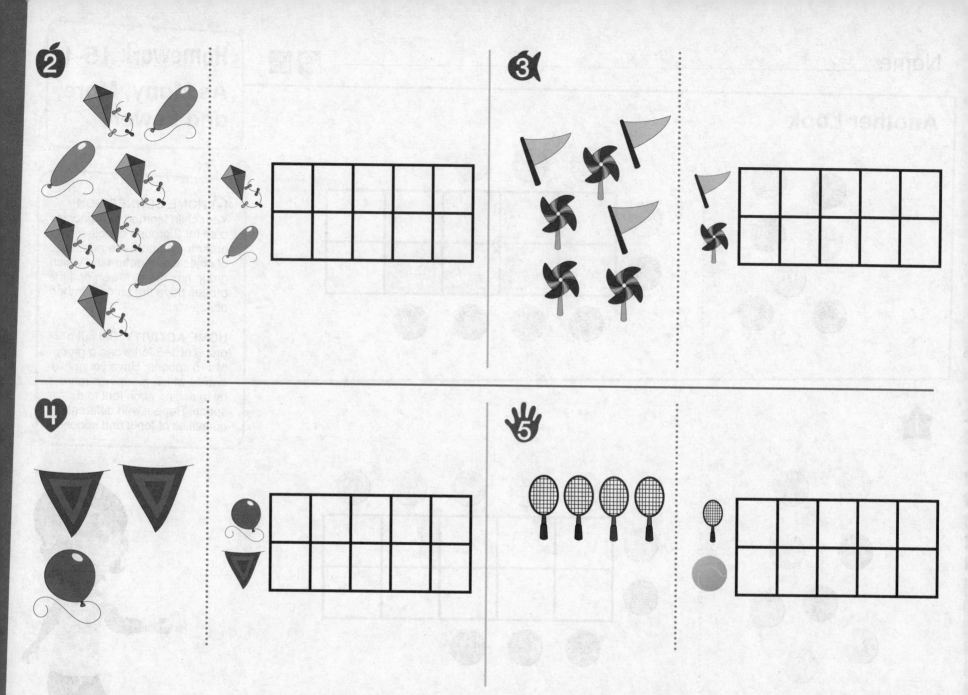

Directions Have students: ❷ and ❸ color a box on the graph for each object, and then circle the object next to the row with fewer objects or circle the exercise number if the number of objects is the same; ❹ draw more balloons to make the same number of each decoration, and then color a box on the graph for each object; ✋❺ draw more tennis balls than there are rackets, color a box on the graph for each object, circle the object next to the row with more objects, and then explain how they know that there are more balls than rackets.

© Pearson Education, Inc. K

Topic 15 | Lesson 1

Solve & Share   Name _____

Directions Say: *Ask your classmates which instrument they like better, a drum or a horn. Find a way to show their answers on your workmat.*

⭐**TEKS K.8A** Collect, sort, and organize data into two or three categories. Also, K.8. **Mathematical Process Standards** K.1A, K.1D, K.1E, K.1F.

Digital Resources at PearsonTexas.com

Solve   Learn   Glossary   Check   Tools   Games

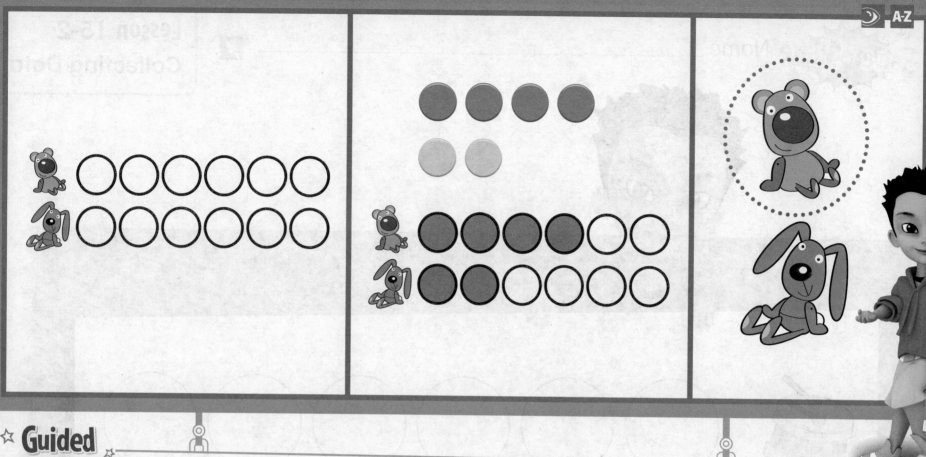

Guided Practice

1

2

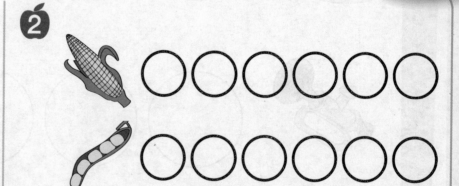

Directions Have students survey 6 classmates to find out which foods they like better, color circles to show each response, and then answer the survey questions by circling the foods more students like. If the same number of classmates like both foods, have students circle the exercise number.

766 seven hundred sixty-six

Topic 15 | Lesson 2

Name _____

3 🐟

⚪⚪⚪⚪⚪⚪

⚪⚪⚪⚪⚪⚪

4 ❤️

⚪⚪⚪⚪⚪⚪

⚪⚪⚪⚪⚪⚪

5 ✋

⚪⚪⚪⚪⚪⚪

⚪⚪⚪⚪⚪⚪

6 ☕

⚪⚪⚪⚪⚪⚪

⚪⚪⚪⚪⚪⚪

Directions Have students survey 6 classmates to find out which foods or drinks they like better, color circles to show each response, and then answer the survey questions by circling the foods or drinks more students like. If the same number of classmates like both foods or drinks, have students circle the exercise number.

Independent Practice

7
○○○○○○
○○○○○○

8
○○○○○○
○○○○○○

9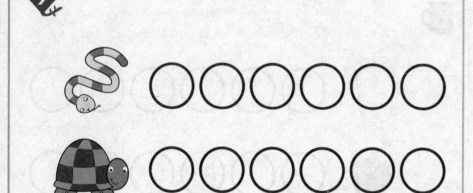
○○○○○○
○○○○○○

10
○○○○○○
○○○○○○
○○○○○○

Directions Have students: **7**—**9** survey 6 classmates to find out which toy they like better, color circles to show each response, and then answer the survey questions by circling the toy more students like or circling the exercise number if the same number of classmates like both toys; **10** survey 6 classmates to see which toy they would like to own, color circles to show each response, and then answer the survey question by circling the toy most students would like to own.

© Pearson Education, Inc. K

Topic 15 | Lesson 2

Name _____

Another Look

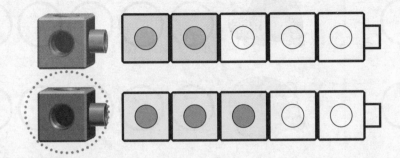

🏠 **HOME CONNECTION**
Your child learned to organize data from surveys.

HOME ACTIVITY Help your child conduct a survey in your family or neighborhood to find out which food people like best for dinner. Choose 2 dinners. Draw pictures of each dinner beside an empty box graph. Then have him or her fill in boxes for each response and circle the dinner that had the most responses to answer the survey.

 ⭐

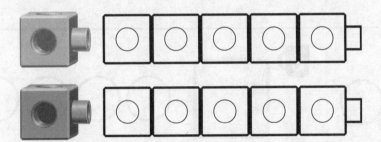

❷

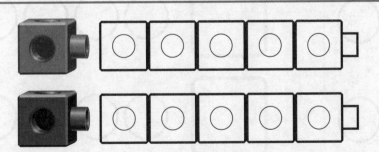

Directions Say: *5 people were asked if they liked the color orange or blue better. 2 people said they liked orange more and 3 people said they liked blue more. Color 2 of the cubes next to the orange cube to show that 2 people like orange more. Color 3 of the cubes next to the blue cube to show that 3 people like blue more. Circle the blue cube because more people liked the color blue.* Then have students: ⭐ and ❷ ask 5 friends or family members which color they like better, color a cube for each response, and then circle the colored cube that more people like.

3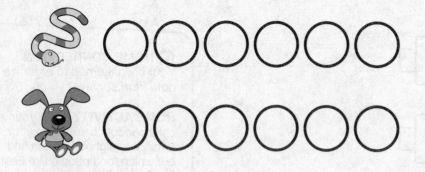

○ ○ ○ ○ ○ ○

○ ○ ○ ○ ○ ○

4

○ ○ ○ ○ ○ ○

○ ○ ○ ○ ○ ○

5

○ ○ ○ ○ ○ ○

○ ○ ○ ○ ○ ○

○ ○ ○ ○ ○ ○

6

○ ○ ○ ○ ○ ○

○ ○ ○ ○ ○ ○

○ ○ ○ ○ ○ ○

Directions Have students: **3** and **4** survey 6 friends or family members to find out which toy they like better, color circles to show each response, and then answer the survey questions by circling the toy more people like or circling the exercise number if the same number of people like both toys; **5** ask 6 friends or family members which color they like best, record each response by coloring a circle, and then answer the survey question by circling the color most people like; **6** design a survey by drawing different foods, animals, or colors in the boxes, ask 6 friends or family members which they like best, record each response by coloring a circle, and then answer the survey question by circling the item most people like.

© Pearson Education, Inc. K

Solve & Share Name _____

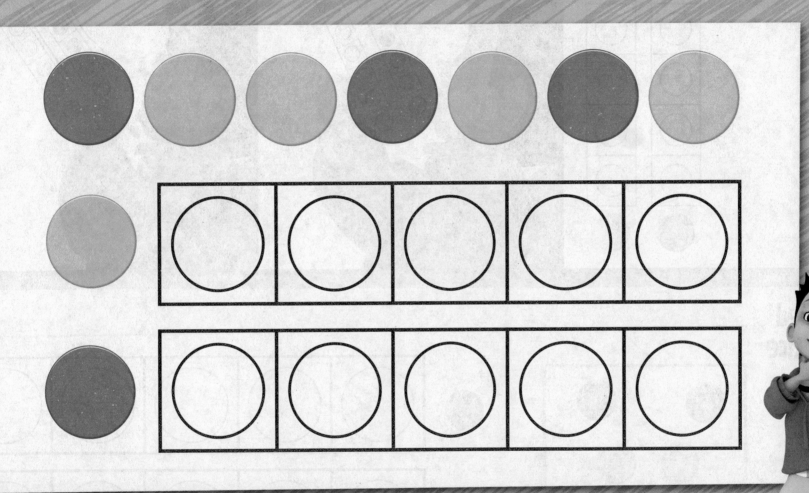

⭐ **TEKS K.8B** Use data to create real-object and picture graphs.
TEKS K.8C Draw conclusions from real-object and picture graphs. Also, **K.8, K.8A. Mathematical Process Standards** K.1C, K.1E, K.1F.

Directions Say: *Daniel's teacher gave him 2 groups of counters. How can you find out which group of counters has more, red or yellow?*

Digital Resources at PearsonTexas.com

 Solve   Learn   Glossary   Check   Tools   Games

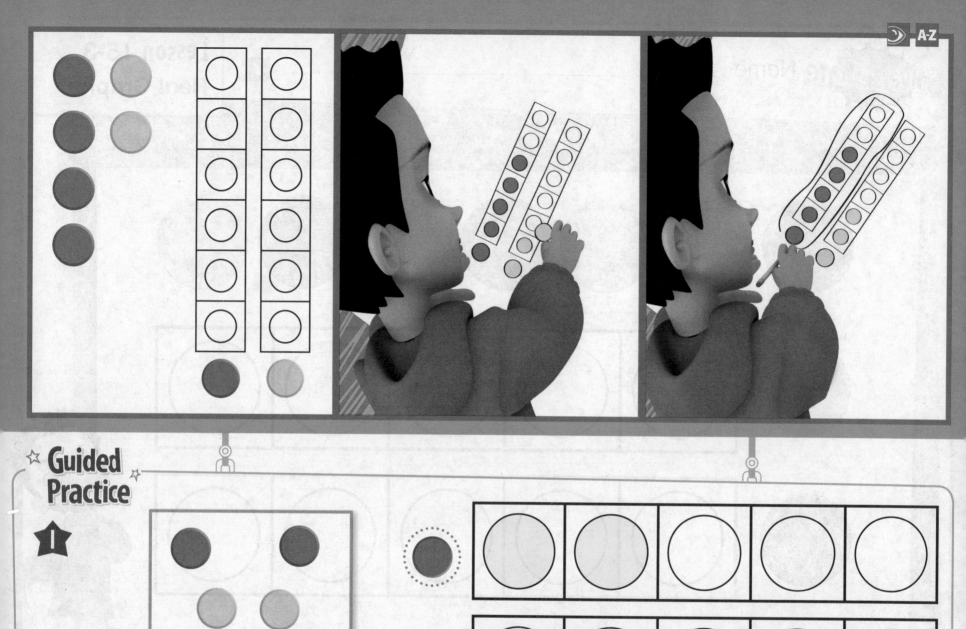

Guided Practice

1

Directions Have students get the same numbers of red and yellow counters as shown on the mat, move the counters to the graph, color the graph to show the counters, and then circle the counter that shows which group has fewer.

© Pearson Education, Inc. K

Name _____

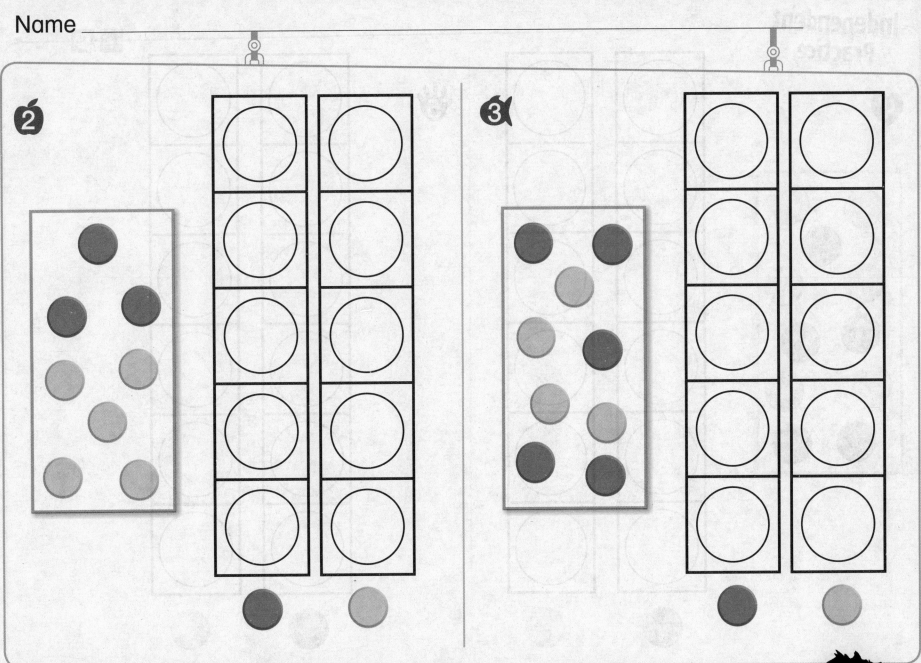

2

3

Directions Have students get the same numbers of red and yellow counters as shown on the mat, move the counters to the graph, color the graph to show the counters, and then circle the counter that shows which group has fewer.

4

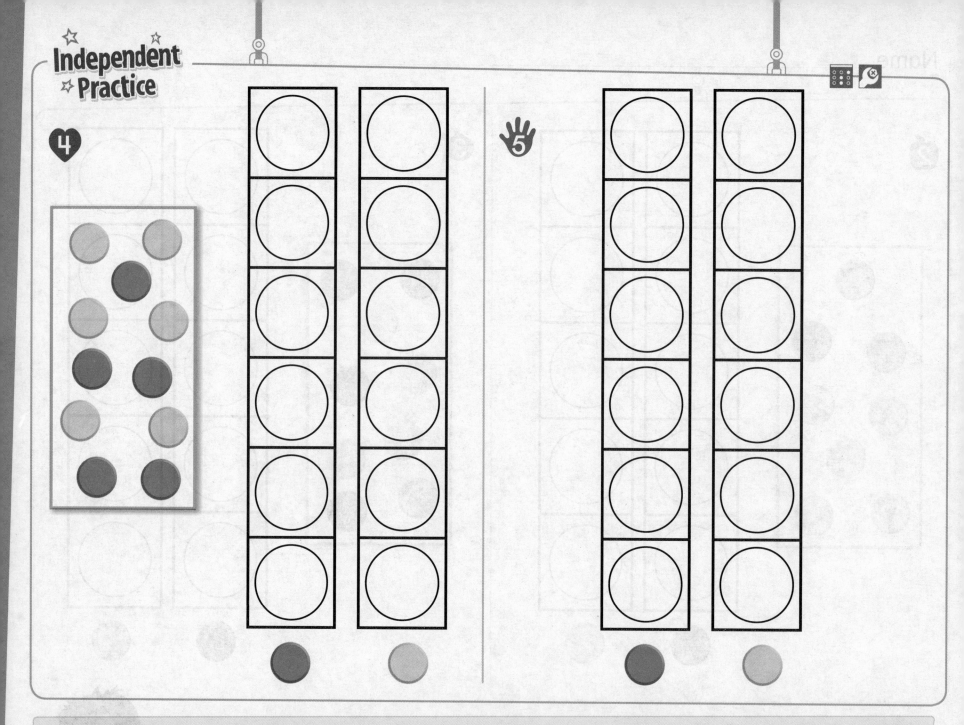

5

Directions Have students: **4** get the same numbers of red and yellow counters as shown on the mat, move the counters to the graph, color the graph to show the counters, and then circle the counter below the column that shows which group has more; **5** toss a two-color counter and color one counter red or yellow on the graph to show how it landed, repeat tossing the counter and coloring the graph until one column is full, tell the results as more red or more yellow counters, and then circle the counter below the column that shows which group has more.

774 seven hundred seventy-four   © Pearson Education, Inc. K   **Topic 15 | Lesson 3**

Name _____

Another Look

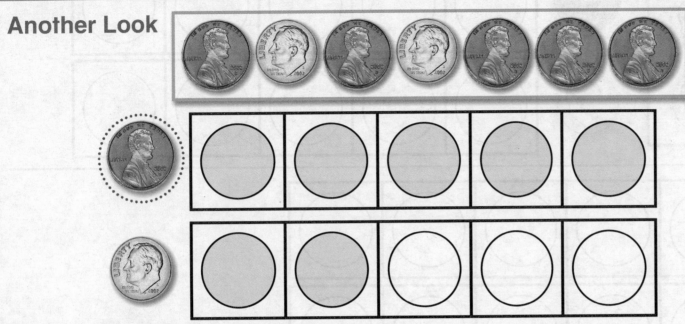

🏠 **HOME CONNECTION**
Your child learned how to create real-object graphs to compare the number of objects in 2 different groups.

HOME ACTIVITY Have your child flip 10 pennies and create a real graph to compare the number of heads and tails. Line up all of the pennies showing heads to form one column and all of the pennies showing tails to form another column. Ask your child to tell which column has more.

 1

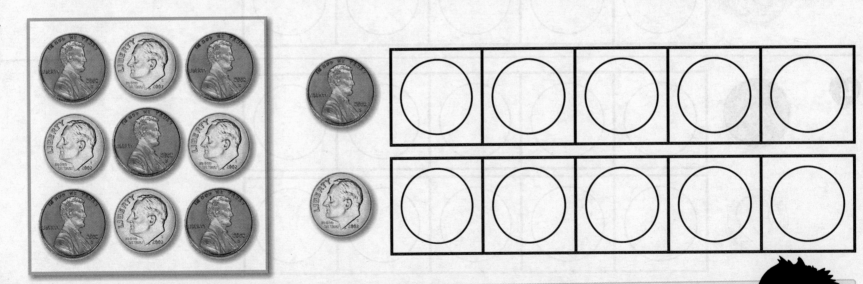

Directions Say: *Get the same numbers of pennies and dimes as shown on the mat, move the coins to the graph, color the graph to show the coins, and then circle the coin that shows which group has more.* Then have students: 🔺 *get the same numbers of pennies and dimes as shown on the mat, move the coins to the graph, color the graph to show the coins, and then circle the coin that shows which group has more.*

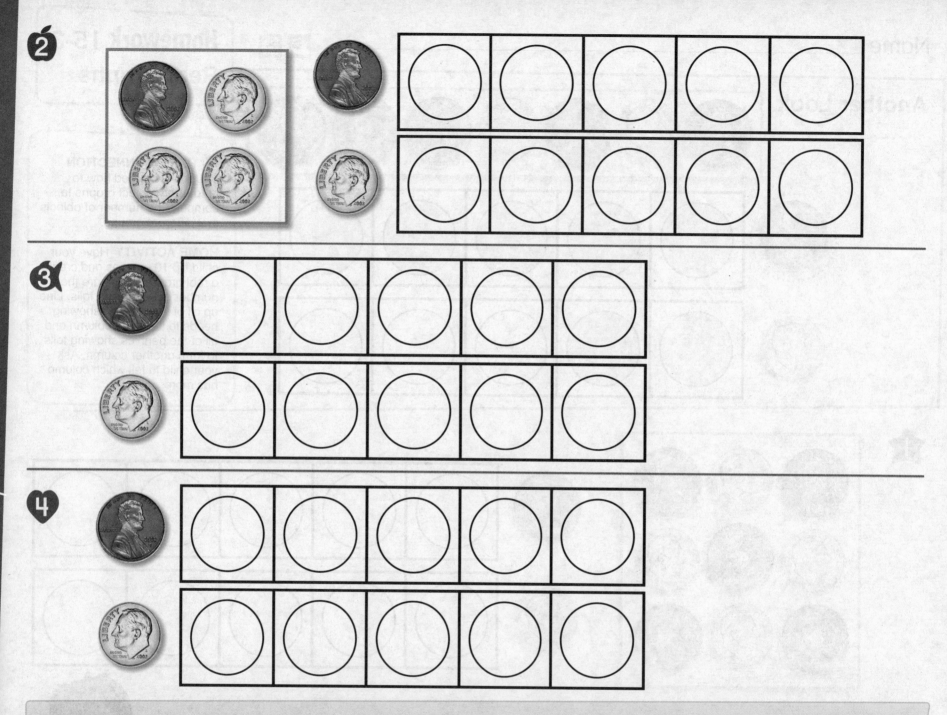

2

3

4

Directions Have students: **2** get the same numbers of pennies and dimes as shown on the mat, move the coins to the graph, color the graph to show the coins, and then circle the coin that shows which group has more; **3** get 5 dimes and 1 fewer penny, move the coins to the graph, color the graph to show the coins, and then circle the coin that shows which group has more; **4** get 5 dimes and 2 fewer pennies, move the coins to the graph, color the graph to show the coins, and then circle the coin that shows which group has fewer.

Solve & Share   Name _____

Directions Say: *Daniel's teacher gave him a handful of shapes. How can you make a graph with the information you have? Are there more orange or green shapes?*

⟳**TEKS K.8B** Use data to create real-object and picture graphs.
TEKS K.8C Draw conclusions from real-object and picture graphs. Also, K.8, K.8A. **Mathematical Process Standards** K.1D, K.1E, K.1F, K.1G.

Digital Resources at PearsonTexas.com

Guided Practice

1

2

Directions Have students look at the objects in the group on the left, color a picture on the graph for each object, and then circle the object next to the row that shows which group has more.

© Pearson Education, Inc. K

3

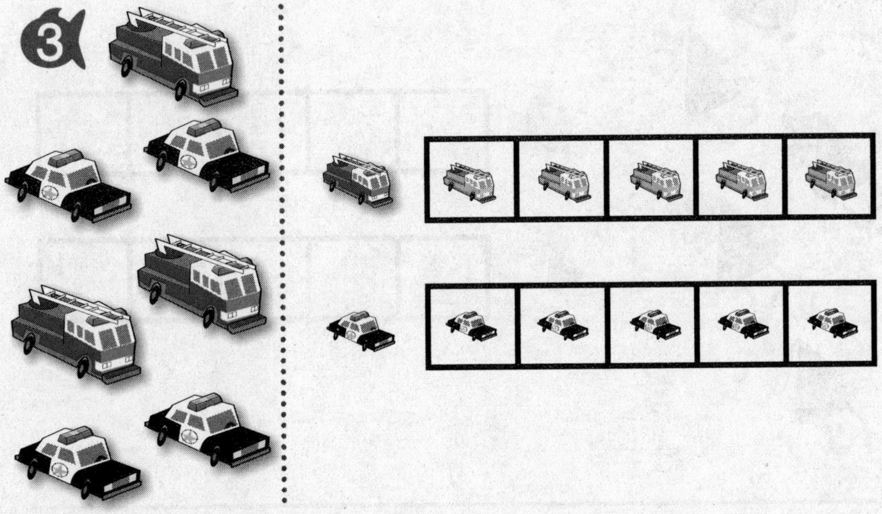

4

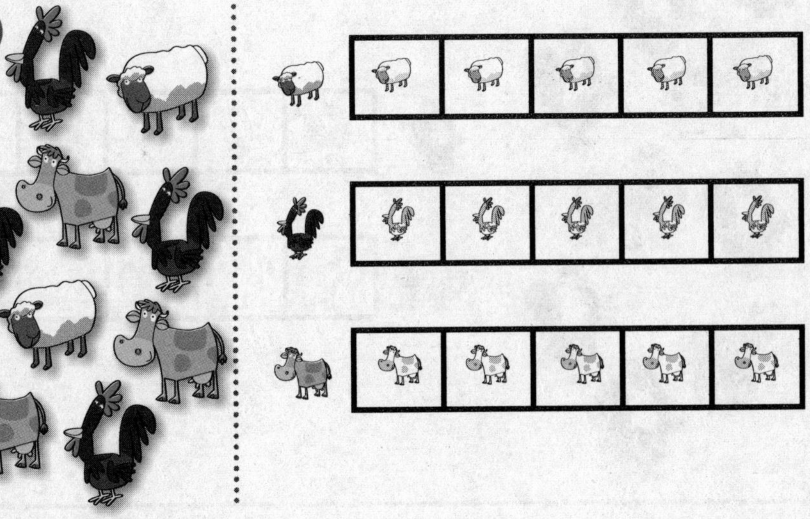

5

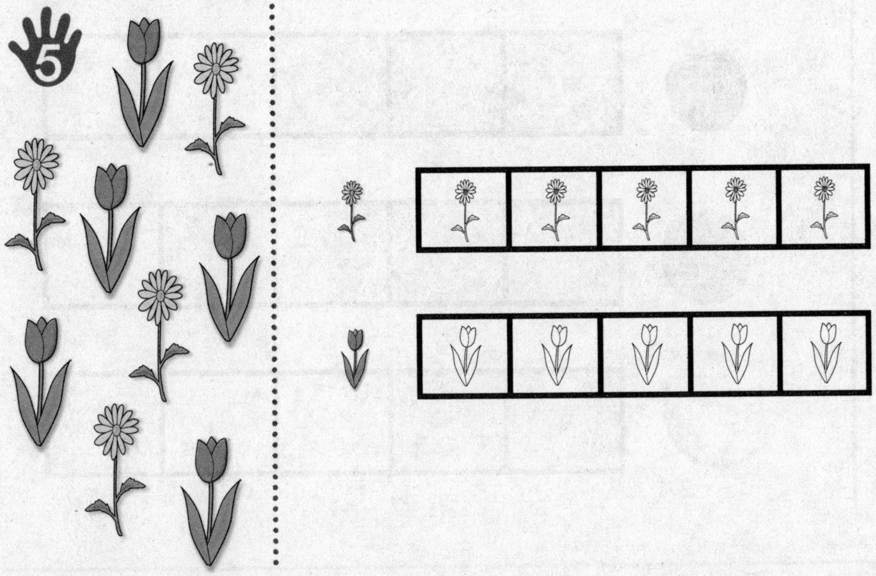

6

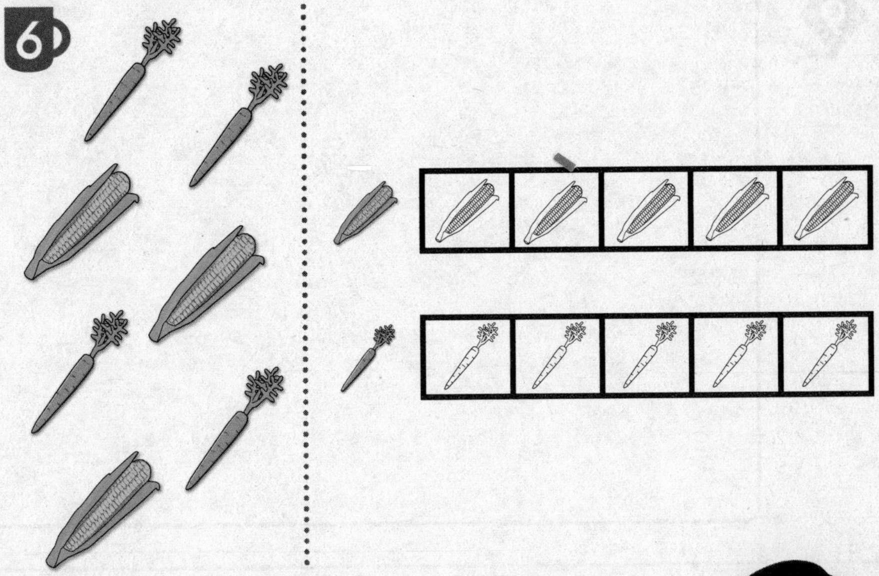

Directions Have students look at the objects in the group on the left, color a picture on the graph for each object, and then circle the object next to the row that shows which group has fewer or the fewest.

Topic 15 | Lesson 4

seven hundred seventy-nine **779**

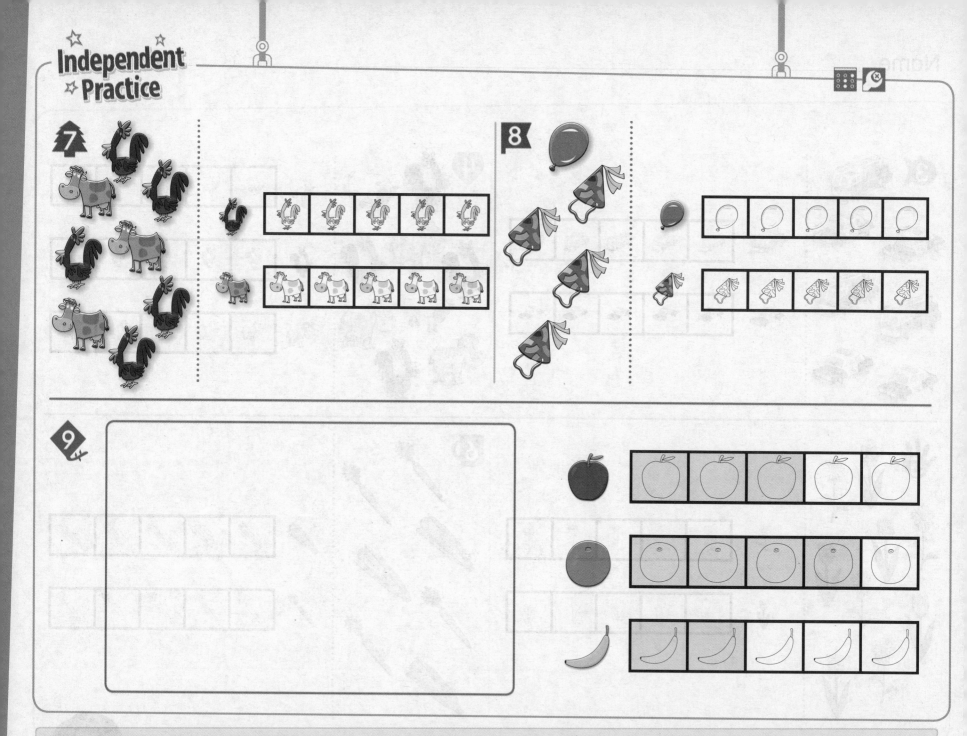

Directions Have students: **7** and **8** look at the objects in the group on the left, color a picture on the graph for each object, and then circle the object next to the row that shows which group has more; **9** draw a picture using the same numbers of apples, oranges, and bananas as shown on the graph, circle the fruit next to the row that shows which group has the most, and then draw an X on the fruit that shows which group has the fewest.

Topic 15 | Lesson 4

Another Look

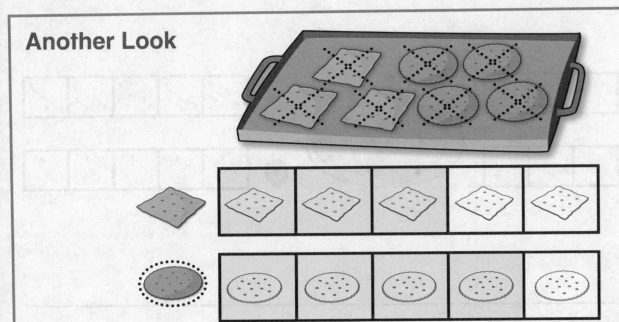

🏠 **HOME CONNECTION**
Your child learned to use picture graphs to organize data and compare the number of objects in groups.

HOME ACTIVITY Create a picture graph with your child. Set out several plates and cups. Have your child line up the plates in one row and the cups in another row. Help your child create a picture graph by drawing one picture for each object. Ask your child to explain what the graph shows.

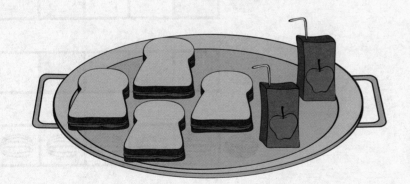

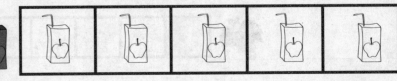

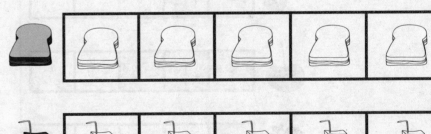

Directions Say: *Look at the crackers on the tray. Draw an X on each item on the tray as you color a picture on the graph to match. Circle the cracker next to the row that shows which group has more.* Then have students: 🌟 look at the objects on the tray, draw an X on each item as they color a picture on the graph to match, and then circle the object next to the row that shows which group has more.

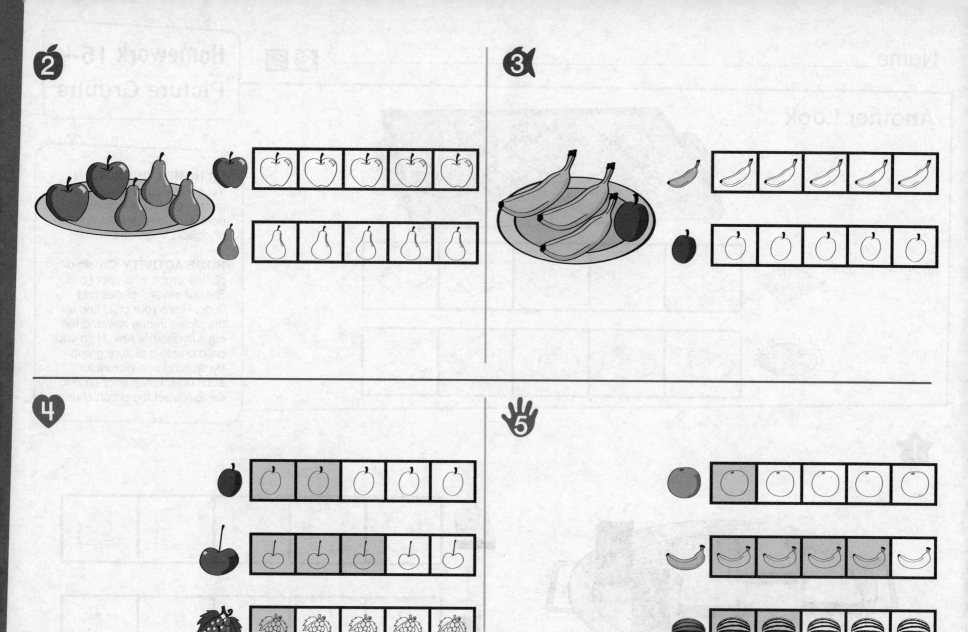

Directions Have students: ② and ③ look at the pieces of fruit on each plate, color a picture on the graph for each piece of fruit, and then circle the fruit next to the row that shows which group has more; ④ draw a picture with the same number of pieces of fruit as shown on the graph, and then circle the fruit next to the row that shows which group has the most; ⑤ draw a picture with the same number of pieces of fruit as shown on the graph, and then circle the fruit next to the row that shows which group has the fewest.

© Pearson Education, Inc. K

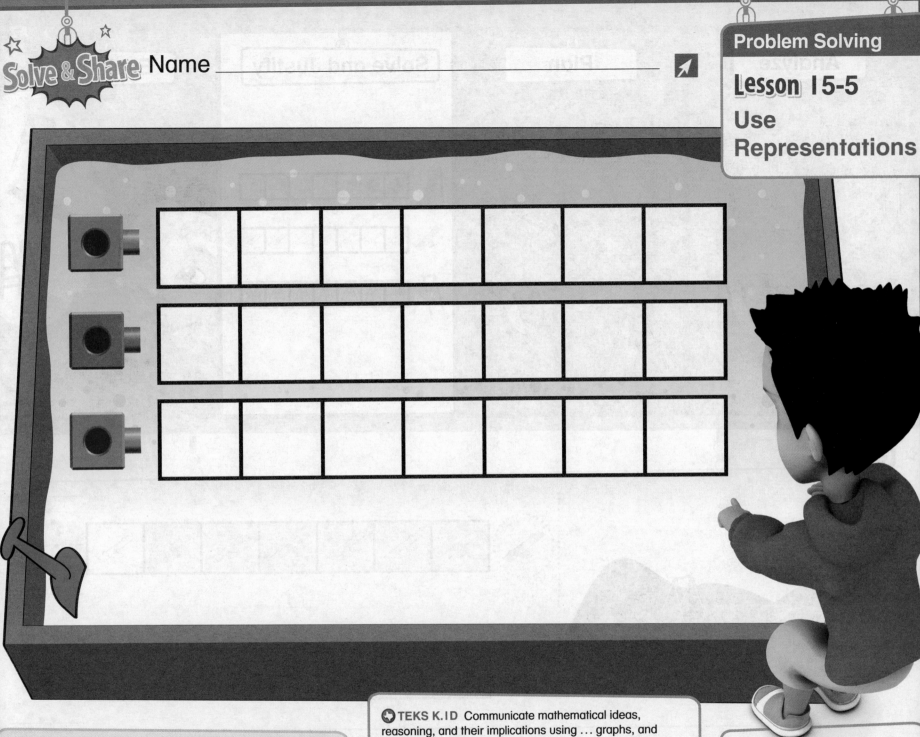

☆ ☆ **Solve & Share** Name _____

Directions Say: *Ask 7 friends what their favorite color is of these 3 cube colors: red, blue, or green. Organize the data you collected on the graph, and then circle the picture of the cube that has the most.*

⭐ **TEKS K.1D** Communicate mathematical ideas, reasoning, and their implications using ... graphs, and language as appropriate.
TEKS K.8A Collect, sort, and organize data into two or three categories. Also, K.8, K.8B, K.8C. **Mathematical Process Standards** K.1, K.1B, K.1E, K.1G.

Digital Resources at PearsonTexas.com

Solve   Learn   Glossary   Check   Tools   Games

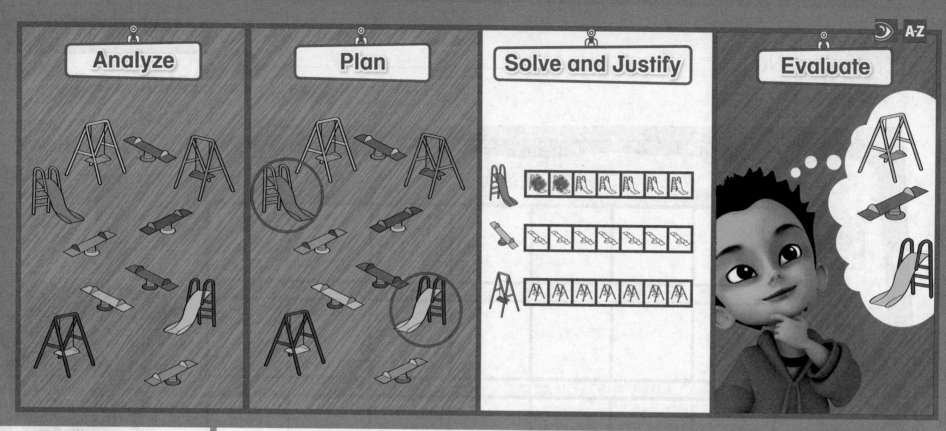

Analyze

Plan

Solve and Justify

Evaluate

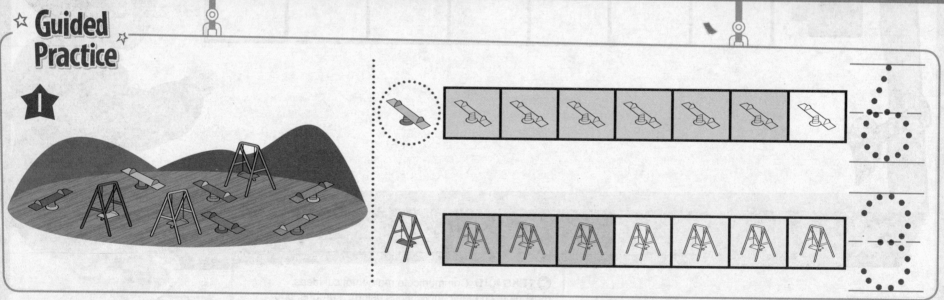

☆ **Guided Practice** ☆

1

Directions Have students look at the picture on the left, color the graph for each object, write the number of each object, and then circle the object that answers the question. Ask: *Which kind of playground object does the park have more of?*

© Pearson Education, Inc. K

Topic 15 | Lesson 5

Name _____

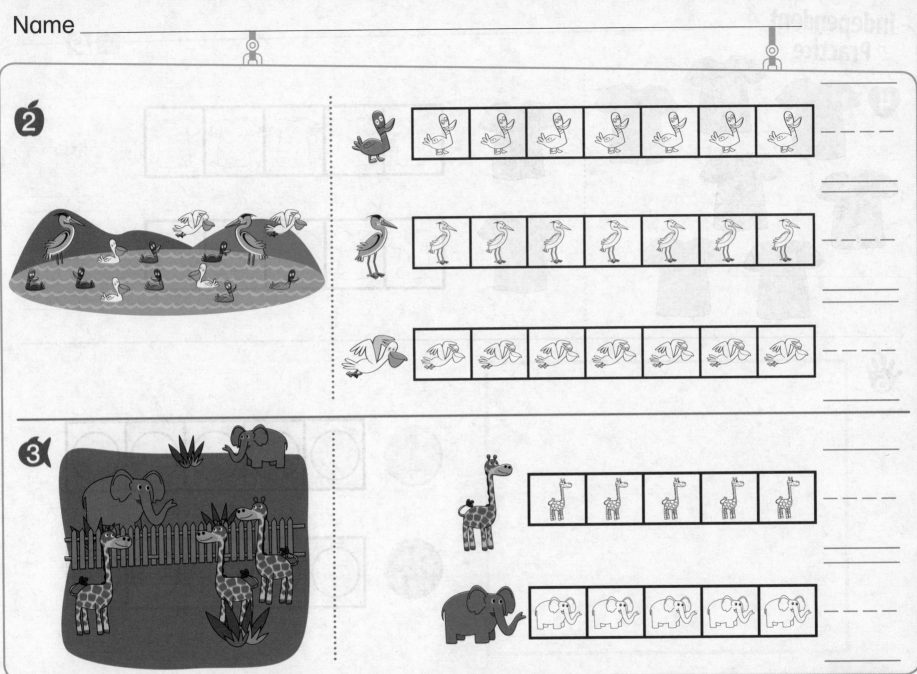

Directions Have students look at the picture on the left, color the graph for each animal, write the number of each animal, and then circle the animal that answers the question. ❷ *Which kind of bird are there the fewest of at the lake?* ❸ *Which kind of animal are there more of at the zoo?*

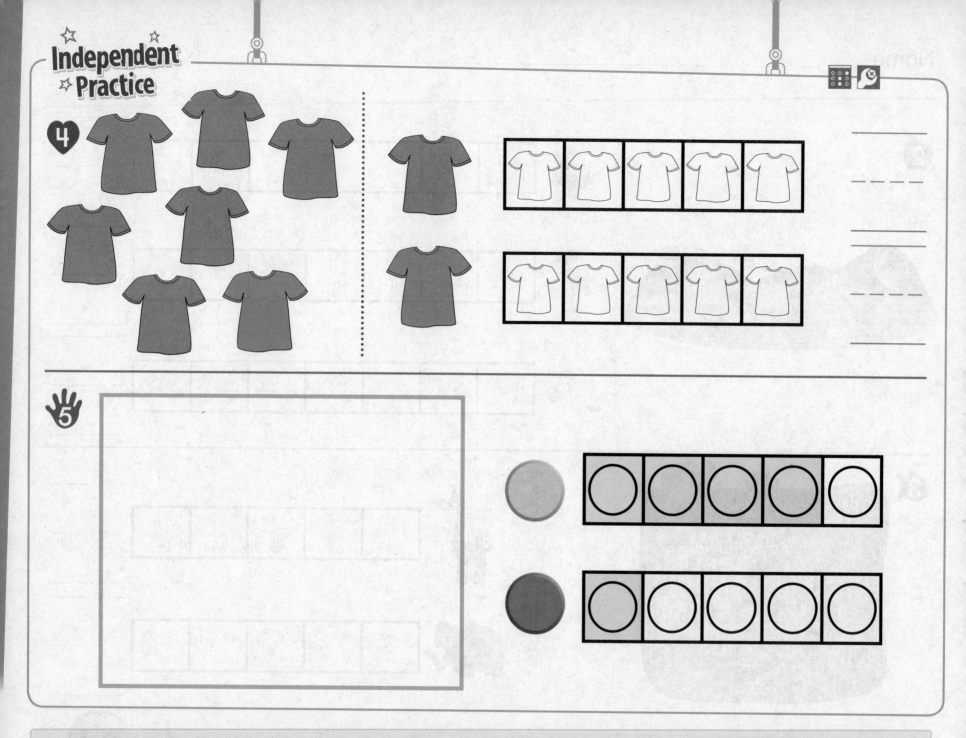

4

5

Another Look

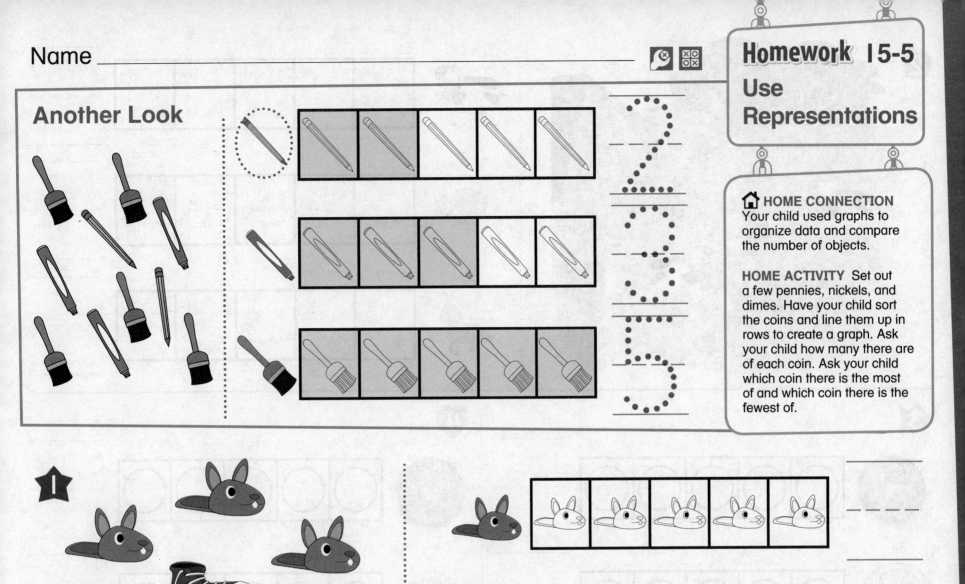

HOME CONNECTION
Your child used graphs to organize data and compare the number of objects.

HOME ACTIVITY Set out a few pennies, nickels, and dimes. Have your child sort the coins and line them up in rows to create a graph. Ask your child how many there are of each coin. Ask your child which coin there is the most of and which coin there is the fewest of.

Directions Say: *Look at the picture of different school supplies. To find out which school supply there are the fewest of, color the graph for each pencil, marker, and paintbrush. Then write the number of each school supply and circle the picture next to the row that shows which group has the fewest.* Then have students: ⭐ *look at the picture on the left, color the graph for each shoe, write the number of each shoe, and then circle the shoe that answers the question. Ask: Which kind of shoe are there fewer of?*

2

3

4

Directions Have students: **2** look at the picture on the left, color the graph for each animal, write the number of each animal, and then circle the animal that answers the question. Ask: *Which kind of animal is there the most of at the farm?* **3** pick coins from 5 pennies and 5 nickels to make their own graph, color the graph for each coin and write the number of each coin, and then circle the coin next to the row that shows which group has fewer; **4** pick coins from 5 pennies and 5 dimes to make their own graph, color the graph for each coin and write the number of each coin, and then circle the coin next to the row that shows which group has more.

© Pearson Education, Inc. K

Set A

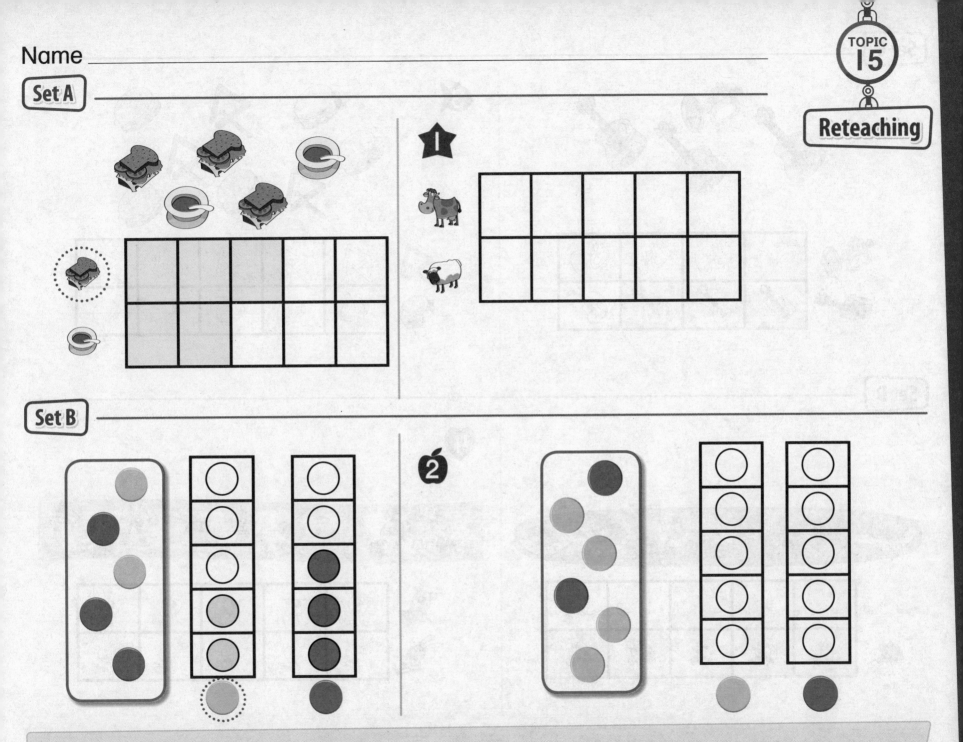

Set B

Directions Have students: ⭐ ask 5 people whether they like cows or sheep more, color in the graph to share their results, and then circle the animal people like more; ❷ use counters at their desk to make the real graph, color the graph to show the counters, and then circle the counter that shows which group has fewer.

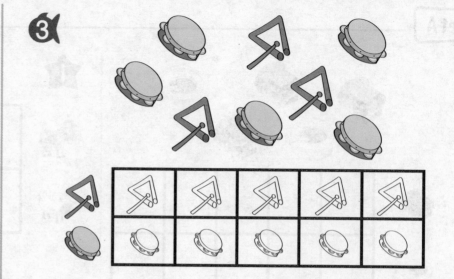

Set D

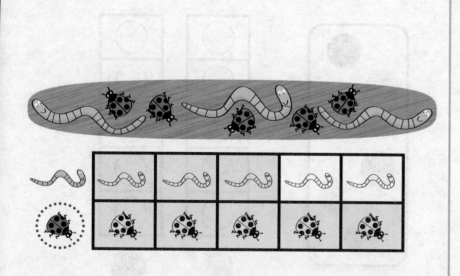

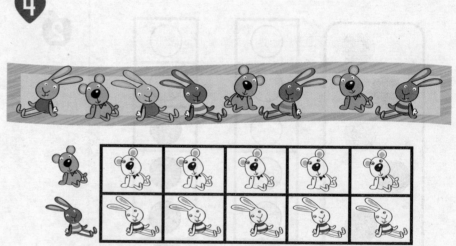

Directions Have students: ❸ look at the objects in the group above the graph, color a picture on the graph for each object, and then circle the object next to the row that shows which group has more; ❹ look at the picture above the graph, color the graph for each toy, and then circle the toy that answers the question. Ask: *Which toy is there more of?*

Name ______________________________

TOPIC 15

Test

1

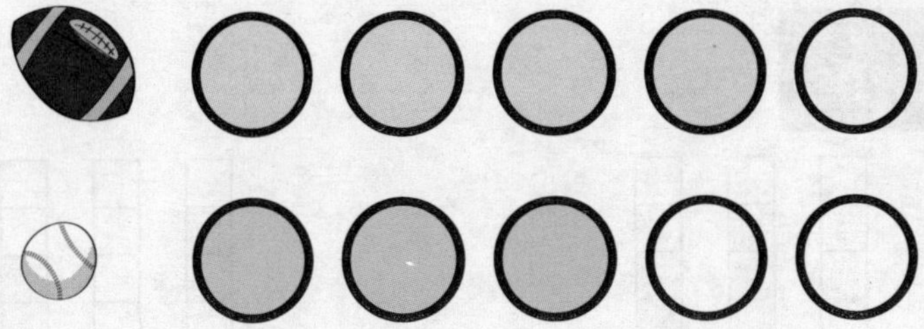

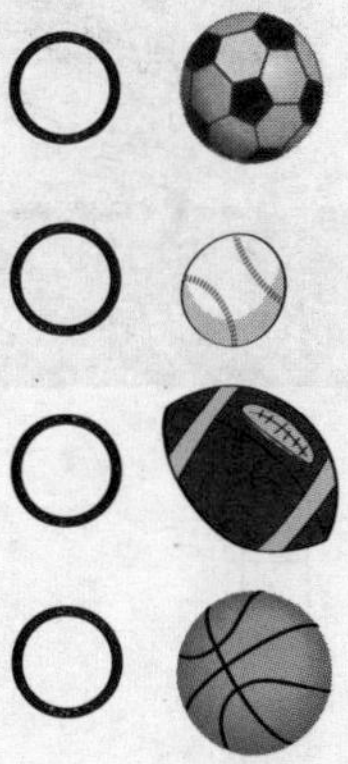

2

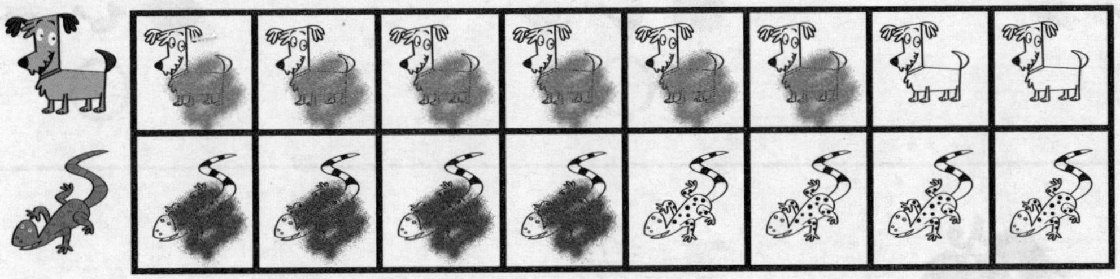

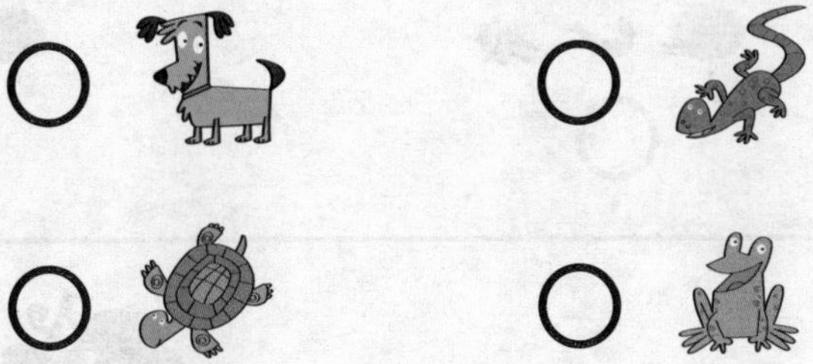

3

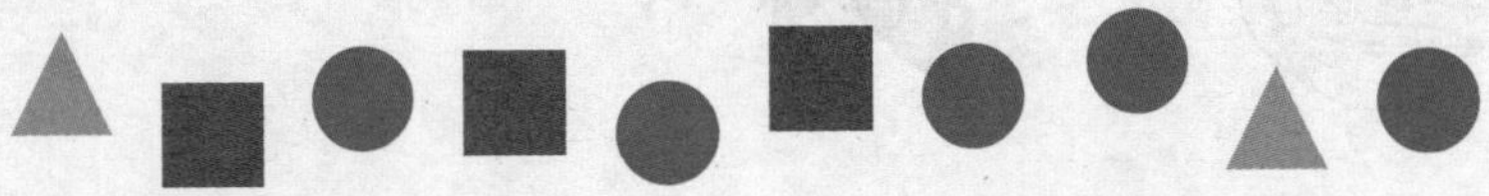

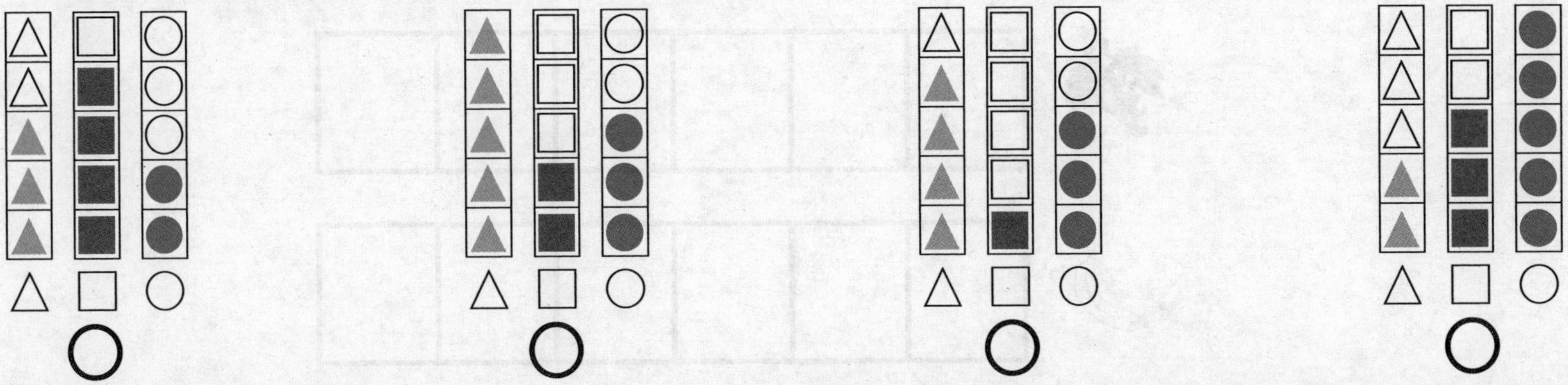

Directions Have students mark the best answer. 1 This graph shows which sport a class likes better. Which sport do more students like? 2 This graph shows which pet a class likes better. Which pet do more students like? 3 Which graph shows the correct number of each shape?

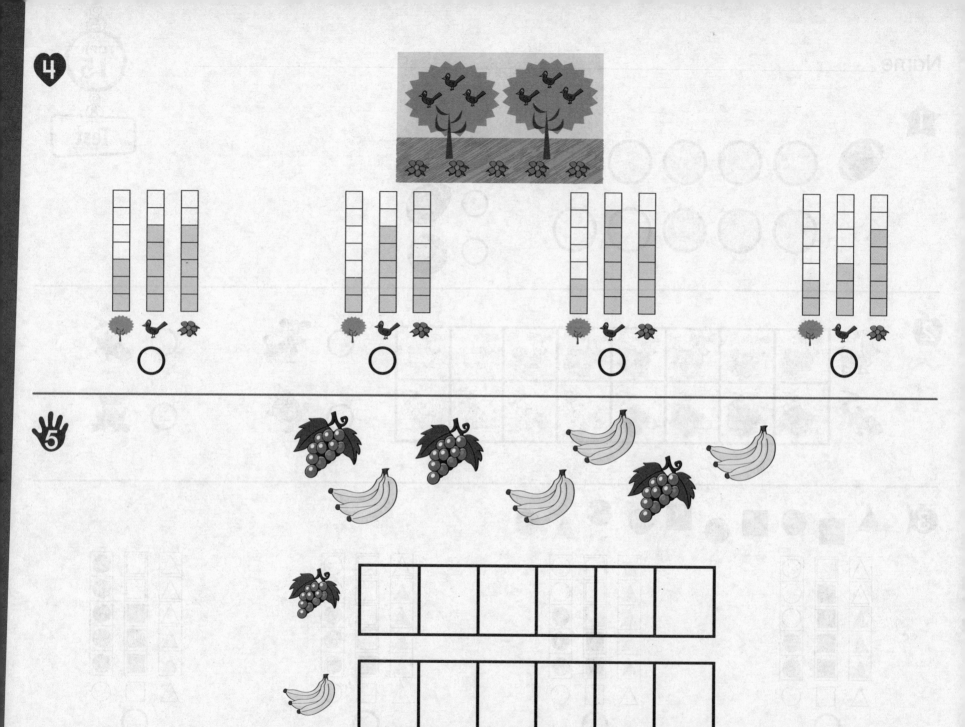

© Pearson Education, Inc. K

Directions Have students: ♥ mark the best answer. Which graph shows the correct number of each item in the picture? ✋ color a box on the graph for each fruit, and then circle the fruit next to the row that has more.

Personal Financial Literacy

Essential Question: How can understanding income, gifts, job skills, and wants and needs help you make decisions about money?

Math and Science Project: Animal Needs

Directions Read the character speech bubbles to students. **Find Out!** Have students find out about the basic needs of different organisms, such as food, water, nutrients, sunlight, space, and shelter. Say: *Different organisms need different things. Talk to friends and relatives about the different needs of plants, animals, and humans.* **Journal: Make a Poster** Then have students make a poster. Ask them to draw pictures of themselves, a puppy, and a flower. Then have them draw 3 needs of each and tell about how those needs are similar and different.

Name _____

Review What You Know

1  25¢

2

_____

- - - - - - - - - - -

_____ ¢

3

_____

- - - - - - - - - - -

_____ ¢

4  10¢

5  7¢

6  6¢

Directions Have students: **1** circle the cost of the bear; **2** write the value of a penny; **3** write the value of a nickel; **4**–**6** draw coins to show the price of each object.

Directions Have students cut out the vocabulary cards. Read the front of the card, and then ask them to explain what the word or phrase means.

earn

skill

gift

income

want

need

My Word Cards

Point to the gift.
Say: *Sometimes you get money for a special event. This is called a **gift**.*

Point to the coins.
Say: *Counting money is a **skill** you need when you earn money.*

Point to the lemonade stand.
Say: *You can **earn** money by working.*

Point to the groceries.
Say: *You **need** food to live.*

Point to the toys.
Say: *You do not need toys to live. Things you do not need to live are called **wants**.*

Point to the picture.
Say: *Money earned from doing work is called **income**.*

 Name _____

Directions Say: *Look at the pictures. Which pictures show ways to make money? Circle the ways to make money.*

⭐**TEKS K.9A** Identify ways to earn income. Also, K.9. Mathematical Process Standards K.1A, K.1D, K.1F.

Digital Resources at PearsonTexas.com

 Solve Learn Glossary Check   Tools   Games

Guided Practice

Directions Have students circle the student who is earning money.

Topic 16 | Lesson 1

2

3

_____

— — — — — — —

_____ ¢

_____

— — — — — — —

_____ ¢

Directions Have students: **2** circle the students who are earning money and draw Xs on the students who are **not** earning money; **3** find the value of the money that Daniel and Jada each earn, write the number of cents, and then circle who earns more money.

Directions Have students:  and circle the student who is earning money and draw an X on the student who is **not** earning money;  circle the set of coins that shows the 6 cents that Alex earns; draw a picture of a household chore they can do to earn money.

Topic 16 | Lesson 1

Name _____

Another Look

🏠 **HOME CONNECTION**
Your child learned about
different ways to earn money.

HOME ACTIVITY Discuss
with your child different
activities he or she can do to
earn money.

 1

2

_____

_ _ _ _ _ _ _ _

_____ ¢

Directions Say: *What are the students doing? Circle the student who is earning money and draw an X on the student who is **not** earning money.* Then have students: ★ circle the student who is earning money and draw an X on the student who is **not** earning money; 🍎 find the value of the money that Marta earns, and then write the number of cents.

4

5¢

5¢

◯ ＝

¢

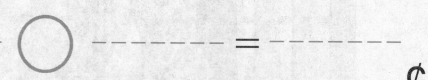

6

6¢

◯ ＝

¢

Directions Have students: **3** and **4** circle the student who is earning money and draw an X on the student who is **not** earning money; **5** listen to the story, and then write an addition sentence to match. Say: *Jada sells 2 bracelets. How much money does she make if she sells 2 bracelets?* **6** listen to the story, and then write a subtraction sentence to match. Say: *Jackson gives Alex 10¢ to pay for his bagel. How much money does Alex give back to Jackson?*

Topic 16 | Lesson 1

Solve & Share

Name _____

1, 2, 3, ...

Directions Say: *Emily has a job as a dog walker. Look at the pictures of things she may use to do her job. Circle 2 math skills she would use in her job: finding length, weighing, measuring, or counting. Explain why.*

★ **TEKS K9.C** List simple skills required for jobs. Also, K.9. **Mathematical Process Standards** K.1A, K.1D, K.1F, K.1G.

Digital Resources at PearsonTexas.com

Solve Learn Glossary Check Tools Games

I need these math skills.

Do I need these math skills?

measuring

1, 2, 3, ...

counting

+ −

adding or subtracting

weighing

counting money

finding length

Guided Practice

1

Directions Have students circle 2 math skills that can be used most when washing a car: weighing, measuring, counting money, or sorting. Then have them explain why.

Topic 16 | Lesson 2

Name _____

2

3

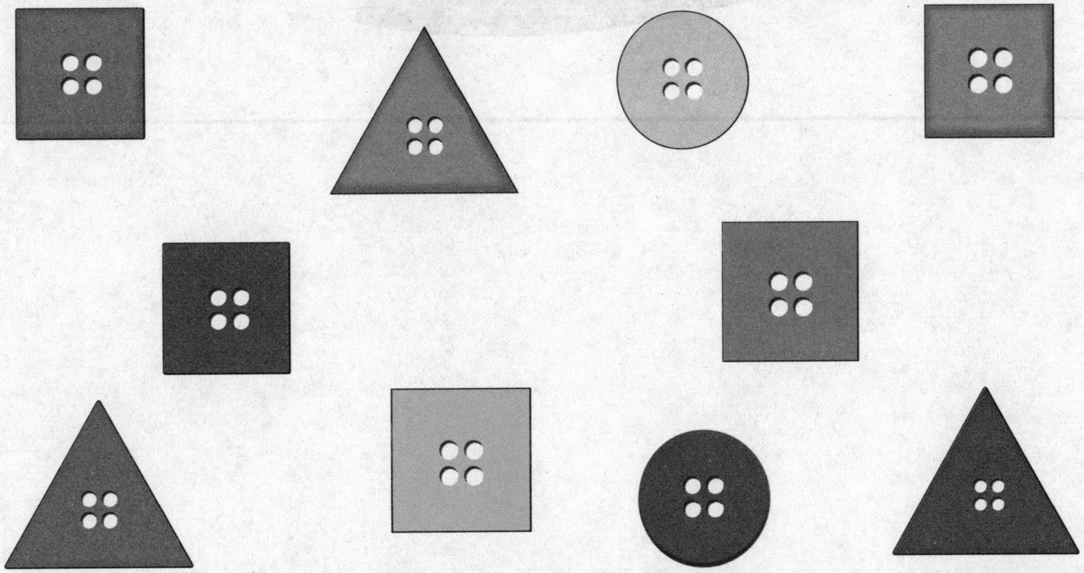

Directions Have students: **2** circle the jobs that can use the math skill of counting money, draw an X on the jobs that can use the math skill of sorting, and then underline the jobs that can use the math skill of measuring; **3** listen to the story. Say: *Tiffany is sewing square buttons on a sweater. Circle the buttons that belong on her sweater.*

Independent ☆ Practice

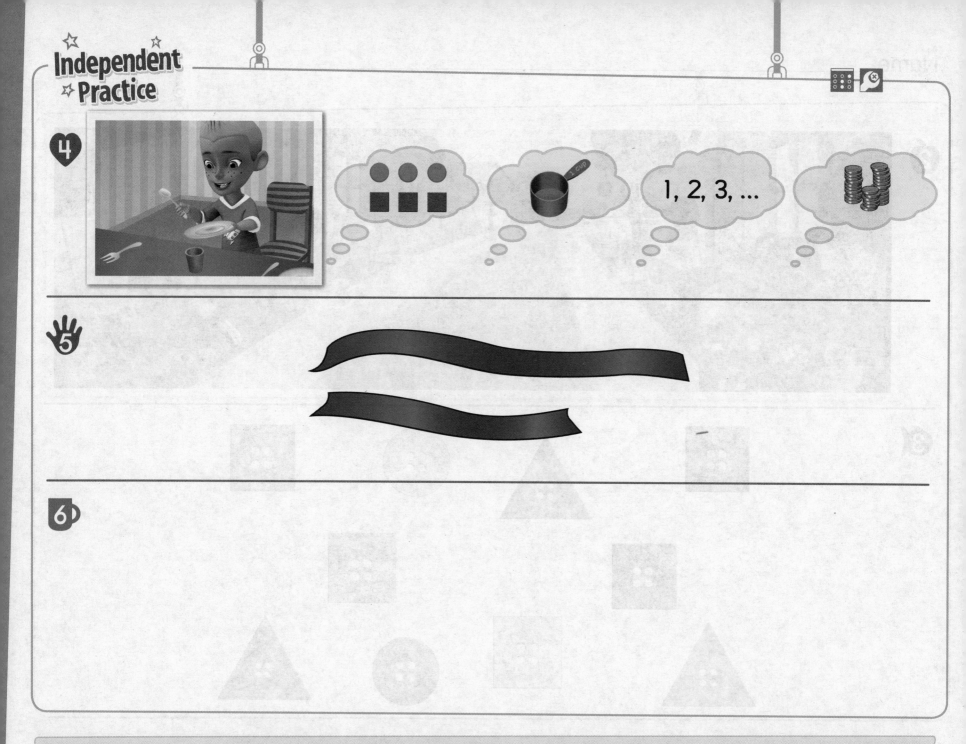

4

5 (hand icon)

6

Directions Have students: **4** circle 2 math skills that can be used most when setting the table: sorting, measuring, counting, or counting money, and then explain why; **5** listen to the story and solve the problem. Say: *Harriet uses ribbon to make bows to sell at a craft fair. Circle the longer ribbon.* **6** draw a job that involves sorting and counting money as job skills.

806 eight hundred six   © Pearson Education, Inc. K   **Topic 16 | Lesson 2**

Another Look

🏠 **HOME CONNECTION**
Your child learned about different job skills.

HOME ACTIVITY Act out different jobs with your child and discuss the skills used in each job.

1

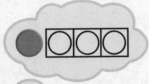

2

Directions Say: *Circle 2 math skills that can be used most at a yard sale: measuring, finding length, counting money, or sorting.* Then have students: ⭐ circle 2 math skills that can be used most at a bake sale: graphing, adding or subtracting, counting money, or finding length, and then explain why; 🍎 circle 2 math skills that can be used most when babysitting: measuring, counting money, adding or subtracting, or sorting, and then explain why.

_____ _____ _____

_ _ _ _ _ _ = _ _ _ _ _ + _ _ _ _ _

_____ _____ _____

Directions Have students: **3** circle the jobs that can use the math skill of sorting and draw an X on the jobs that can use the math skill of measuring; **4** draw a job that involves counting money and measuring as job skills; **5** draw 3 more plants in the garden, and then write an addition sentence that matches the picture.

Name _____

Directions Say: *Look at the pictures of Emily receiving money. How are the pictures the same? How are they different? Circle 2 of the pictures that are alike. Tell why.*

⭐ **TEKS K.9B** Differentiate between money received as income and money received as gifts. Also, **K.9.** **Mathematical Process Standards** K.1A, K.1B, K.1C, K.1F.

Digital Resources at PearsonTexas.com

 Solve   Learn   Glossary   Check Tools Games

☆ Guided ☆ Practice

 1

 **2**

Directions Have students circle the students that are receiving money as gifts and draw an X on the students who are doing activities to earn money.

❤️ 4

✋ 5

☕ 6

$$1 + \underline{\quad\quad} = 4$$

Directions Have students listen to the story and write the number that tells how many. ❤️ *Gina earns money by doing chores. She takes out the trash, sweeps the kitchen, and vacuums the carpet. How many chores does Gina do?* ✋ *Meg walks the dogs shown after school to earn money. How many dogs does she walk?* ☕ *Clark earns money by washing dishes. If he has already washed 1 dish and needs to wash 4 dishes in all, how many more dishes does he need to wash? Draw a picture and complete the number sentence to answer the question.*

Name _____

Another Look

🏠 **HOME CONNECTION**
Your child learned the difference between money received as a gift and money earned as income through work or chores.

HOME ACTIVITY Take turns with your child naming different ways a child could earn money, such as chores like taking out the trash.

⭐ 1

🍎 2

Directions Say: *Circle the picture that shows a way to earn money through work, and then draw an X on the picture that shows a way to receive money as a gift.* Then have students: ⭐ and 🍎 circle the picture that shows a way to earn money, and then draw an X on the picture that shows a way to receive money as a gift.

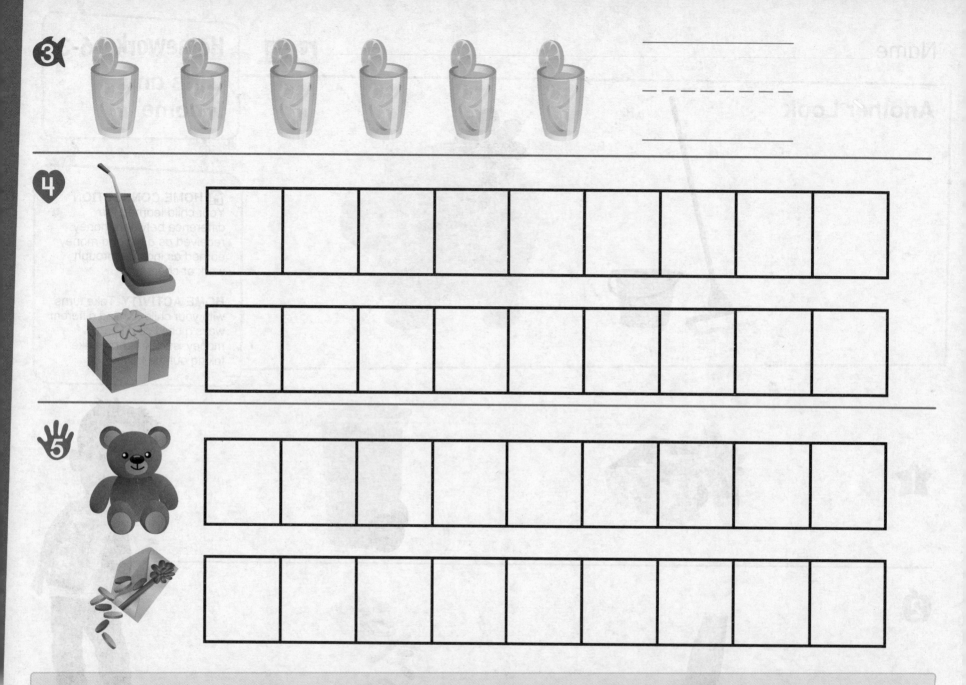

3

4

5

Directions Have students: **3** listen to the story and then write the number that tells how many. Say: *Lee sells the glasses of lemonade shown to earn money. How many glasses of lemonade does he sell?* **4** listen to the story, make a graph to help answer the question, and then circle the picture that shows more. Say: *Erica earns 4 pennies vacuuming the house and receives 3 pennies as a gift from her grandmother. Does Erica get more money from her work or her gift?* **5** listen to the story, make a graph to help answer the question, and then circle the picture that shows more. Say: *Betty sells a toy for 8 pennies and receives 6 pennies as a gift from her dad. Does Betty get more money as a gift or by selling the toy?*

© Pearson Education, Inc. K

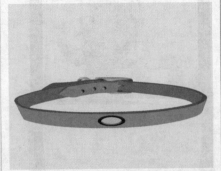

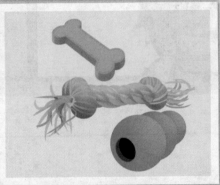

Directions Say: *Look at the pictures around the dog, Rocky. Circle the pictures of things that Rocky needs. Explain why you circled the pictures that you did.*

⭐ **TEKS K.9D** Distinguish between wants and needs and identify income as a source to meet one's wants and needs. Also, K.9. **Mathematical Process Standards** K.1A, K.1F, K.1G.

Digital Resources at PearsonTexas.com

 Solve   Learn   **A-Z** Glossary   Check   Tools   Games

Guided Practice

⭐1

2

Directions Have students: ⭐ circle the item that shows a need you can buy with the money shown; ❷ draw an X on the item that shows a want you can buy with the money shown.

© Pearson Education, Inc. K

Topic 16 | Lesson 4

Name _____

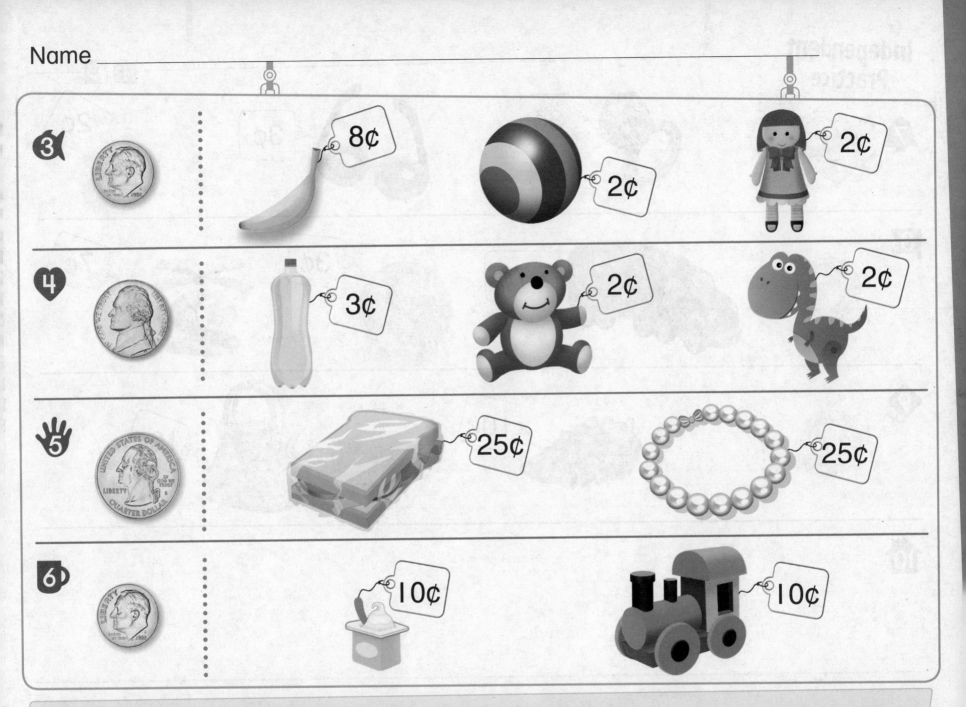

3 8¢ 2¢ 2¢

4 3¢ 2¢ 2¢

5 25¢ 25¢

6 10¢ 10¢

Directions Have students: **3** listen to the story and solve the problem. Say: *Sandy earns 10¢ sweeping the kitchen floor. She needs to buy food and wants to buy a toy. Circle the item she needs to buy and draw an X on the item she wants to buy with the 10¢ she earns.* **4** listen to the story and solve the problem. Say: *Taylor receives 5¢ as a gift. He needs to buy water and wants to buy a toy. Circle the item he needs to buy and draw an X on the item he wants to buy with the 5¢ he earns.* **5** draw an X on the item that shows a need you can buy with the money shown; **6** draw an X on the item that shows a want you can buy with the money shown.

7 | Ring **3¢** | Glasses **3¢** | Bomb **2¢**

8 | Truck **7¢** | Ball **3¢** | Helicopter **7¢**

9 | Grapes **10¢** | Purse **10¢**

10

Directions Have students: **7** listen to the story and solve the problem. Say: *Tricia makes 5¢ vacuuming the living room. She needs to buy food and wants to buy a toy. Circle the item she needs to buy and draw an X on the item she wants to buy with the 5¢ she earns.* **8** listen to the story and solve the problem. Say: *Andy receives 10¢ as a gift. He needs to buy food and wants to buy a toy. Circle the item he needs to buy and draw an X on the item he wants to buy with the 10¢ he earns.* **9** circle the item that shows a need you can buy with the money shown; **10** draw a picture that shows an item you need.

Topic 16 | Lesson 4

Name _____

Homework 16-4
Wants and Needs

Another Look

🏠 **HOME CONNECTION**
Your child learned the difference between wants and needs.

HOME ACTIVITY Have your child list different wants and needs and discuss how income can be used to meet the wants and needs.

 1

2

Directions Say: *Circle the item that shows a need you can buy with the money shown.* Then have students: 🔺 circle the item that shows a need you can buy with the money shown; **2** draw an X on the item that shows a want you can buy with the money shown.

Topic 16 | Lesson 4

Digital Resources at PearsonTexas.com

eight hundred nineteen **819**

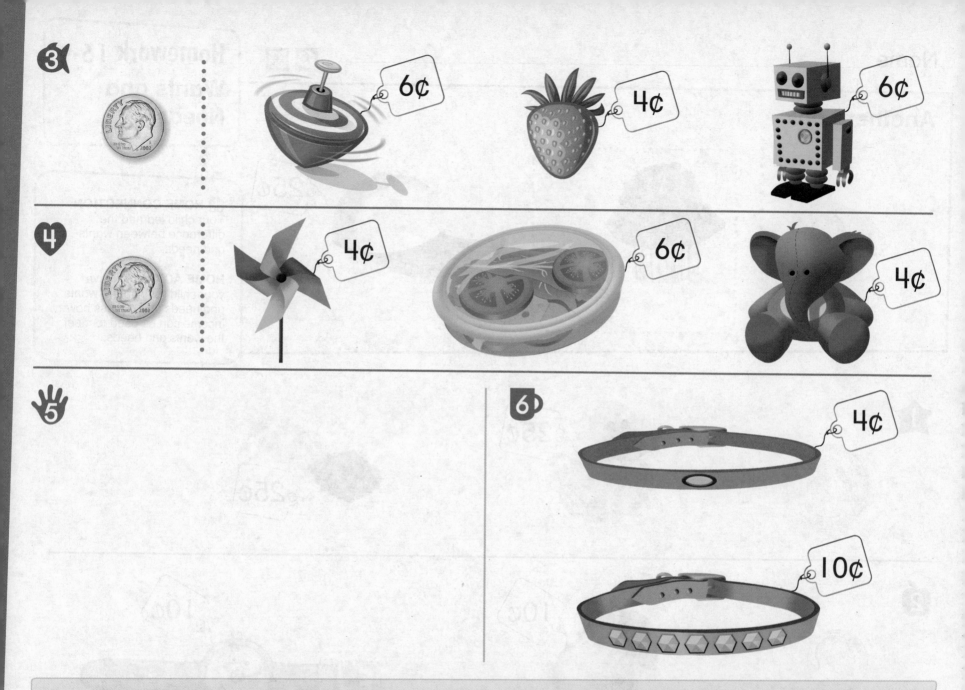

3 6¢   4¢   6¢

4 4¢   6¢   4¢

5

6 4¢

     10¢

Directions Have students: **3** listen to the story and solve the problem. Say: *Todd makes 10¢ raking the yard. He wants to buy a toy and needs to buy food. Circle the item he needs to buy and draw an X on the item he wants to buy with the 10¢ he earns.* **4** listen to the story and solve the problem. Say: *Marcus receives 10¢ as a gift. He needs to buy food and wants to buy a toy. Circle the item he needs to buy and draw an X on the item he wants to buy with the 10¢ he earns.* **5** draw an item that shows something you need; **6** listen to the story and solve the problem. Say: *Tyler needs to buy a collar for his cat. He has 10¢ to buy a collar. He also wants to buy a toy. Circle the collar that he should buy and explain why.*

© Pearson Education, Inc. K

Topic 16 | Lesson 4

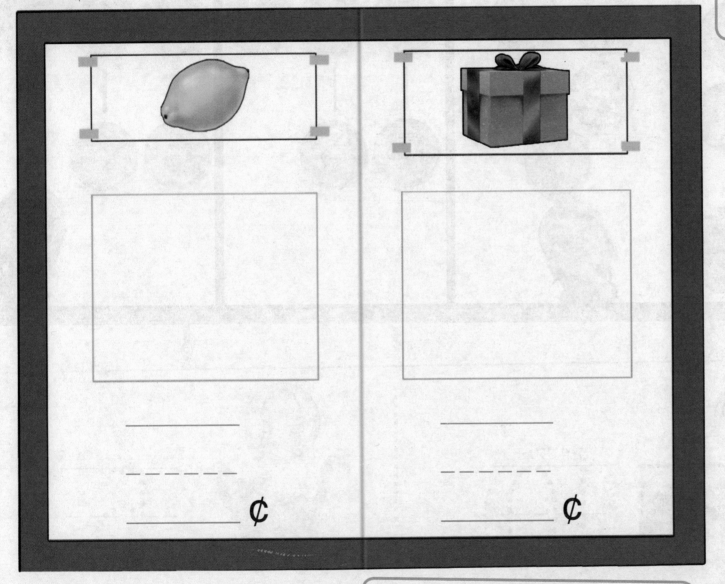

¢

¢

⊙ **TEKS K.1A** Apply mathematics to problems arising in everyday life, society, and the workplace.
TEKS K.1C Select tools, including real objects, manipulatives, paper and pencil, … and techniques, including mental math, … and number sense as appropriate, to solve problems. Also, K.9, K.9B. **Mathematical Process Standards** K.1B, K.1E, K.1F.

Directions Say: *Emily earns 10 cents working at a lemonade stand. She also receives 8 cents as a gift from her parents. How can you use coins to find out whether she makes more money working or as a gift?*

☆ Guided Practice

1

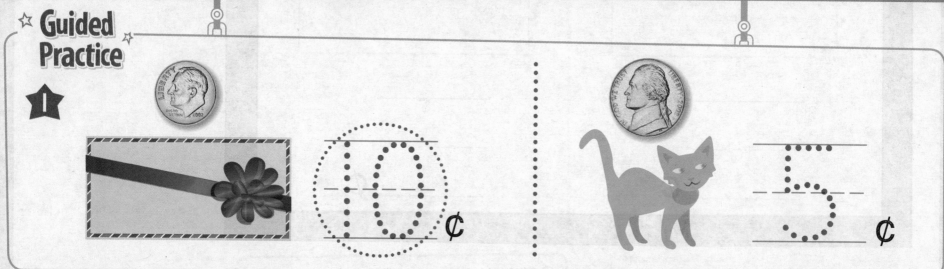

10 ¢   5 ¢

Directions Have students listen to the stories about getting money, find the value of the money, write how much was received as gifts and earned doing work, and then circle the greater number. **1** *Erica receives a gift of money and she earns money brushing a cat. Does she get more money working or as a gift?*

Name _____

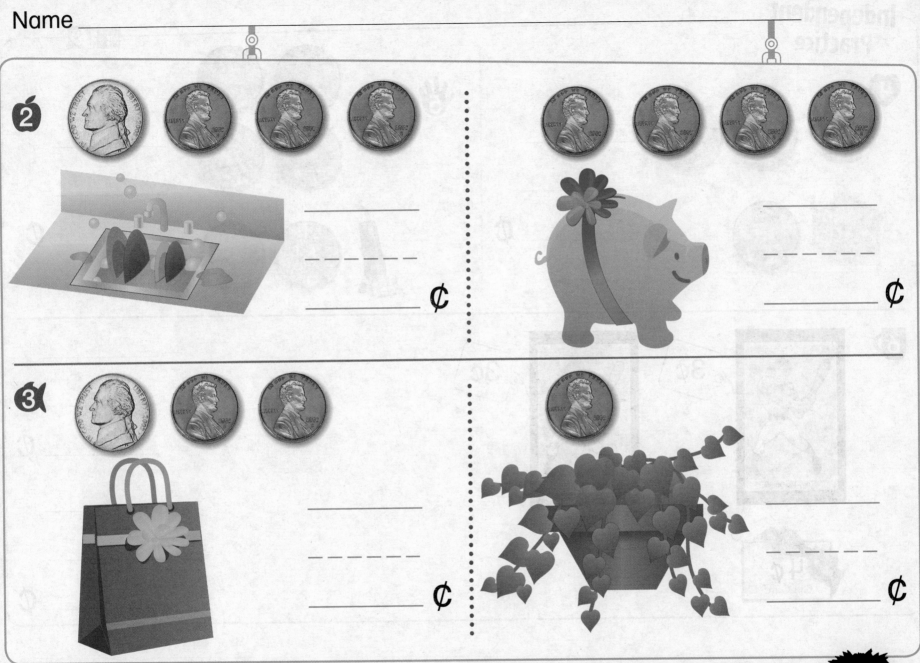

2

_ _ _ _ _ _

_____ ¢

_____

_ _ _ _ _ _

_____ ¢

3

_____

_ _ _ _ _ _

_____ ¢

_____

_ _ _ _ _ _

_____ ¢

Directions Have students listen to the stories about getting money, find the value of the money, write how much was received as gifts and earned doing work, and then circle the greater number. ❷ Marissa earns money washing dishes and receives money as a gift from her parents. Does she get more money doing chores or as a gift? ❸ Rhonda receives money as a gift from her sister and earns money watering plants. Does she get more money working or as a gift?

Independent Practice

4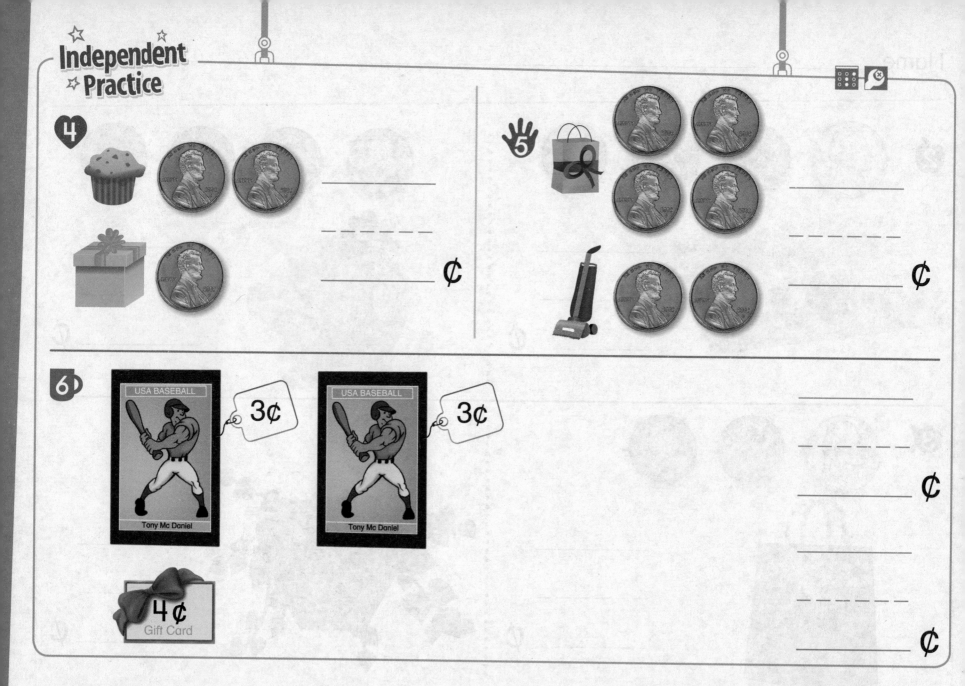

_____

- - - - - - - - -

_____ ¢

5

_____

- - - - - - - - -

_____ ¢

6

USA BASEBALL — Tony Mc Daniel — 3¢

USA BASEBALL — Tony Mc Daniel — 3¢

4¢ Gift Card

_____

- - - - - - - - -

_____ ¢

_____

- - - - - - - - -

_____ ¢

Directions Have students listen to the stories about getting money, compare the amounts, find the difference between the 2 amounts, and then write the number. **4** _Debbie earns 2 cents selling muffins and is given 1 cent as a gift._ **5** _Frank receives a gift of 4 cents and earns 2 cents vacuuming._ Then have students: **6** listen to the story, and then draw the coins to show the amounts. Say: _Oliver earns money selling baseball cards and is given a gift card with money on it. Does he get more money selling baseball cards or as a gift? Circle the picture that is worth more._

© Pearson Education, Inc. K

Topic 16 | Lesson 5

Another Look

4¢

2¢

2 ¢

🏠 **HOME CONNECTION**
Your child solved word problems that compared amounts of money received as gifts and money earned as income.

HOME ACTIVITY Use coins to tell your child a story comparing a gift of money and money earned from working. Have your child figure out the difference between the 2 amounts by either using coins, drawing, or by using mental math.

⭐1 Gift Card 5¢

7¢

_____
_____
¢

2 4¢

9¢

_____
_____
¢

Directions Say: *Wendy earns 4 cents selling lemonade and receives 2 cents as a gift. Draw the coins, and then draw a line from each coin in the top row to each coin in the bottom row to find the difference between the 2 amounts of money. Write that number.* Then have students listen to stories, draw coins to show the amounts, compare the amounts, find the difference between the 2 amounts, and then write the number. ⭐1 *Quinn receives 5 cents on a gift card and earns 7 cents washing windows.* 2 *Perry earns 4 cents walking dogs and receives 9 cents as a gift.*

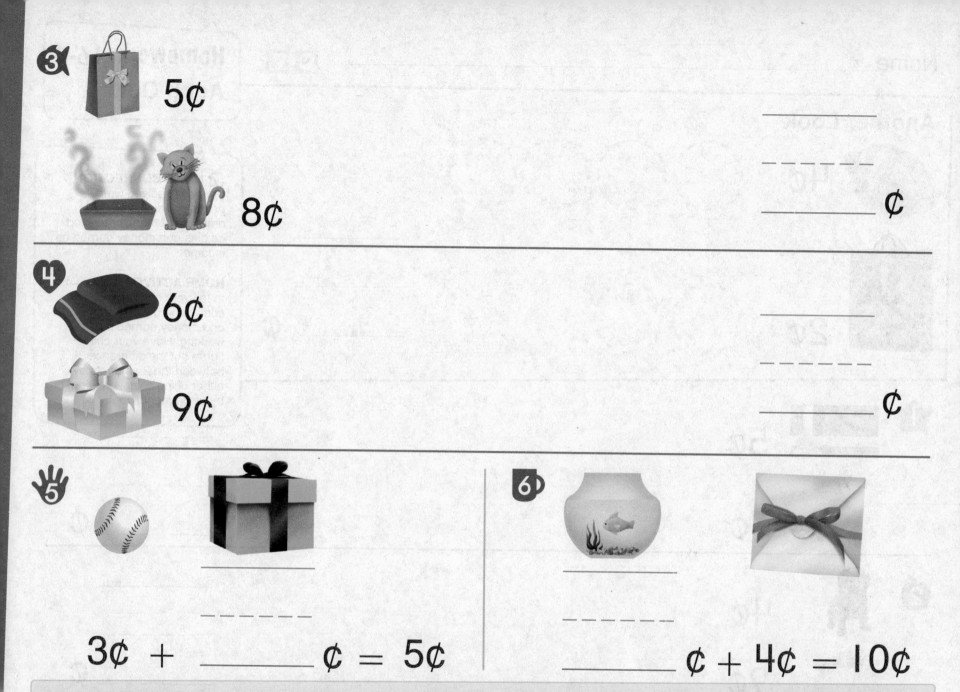

3 5¢

8¢

_____
- - - - - - -
_____ ¢

4 6¢

9¢

_____
- - - - - - -
_____ ¢

5

_____
- - - - - - -

3¢ + _____ ¢ = 5¢

6

_____
- - - - - - -

_____ ¢ + 4¢ = 10¢

Directions Have students listen to the stories about getting money, draw coins to show the amounts, compare the amounts, find the difference between the 2 amounts, and then write the number. **3** _Nick is given 5 cents as a gift and earns 8 cents cleaning the litter box._ **4** _Jimmy earns money folding towels and he also receives money as a gift from his grandparents._ Then have students: **5** listen to the story, and then complete the number sentence. Say: _Zac has a total of 5 cents. If he sold a baseball for 3 cents, how much money did he receive as a gift?_ **6** listen to the story, and then complete the number sentence. Say: _Carla has a total of 10 cents. If she received 4 cents as a gift, how much did she earn feeding fish?_

© Pearson Education, Inc. K

⭐ 1

1, 2, 3, ...

Directions Have students circle 2 math skills that can be used most in the job: counting, sorting, measuring, or weighing. Then explain why.

2

3

25¢ 25¢

4

10¢ 10¢

Directions Have students: **2** and **3** circle the picture that shows a way to earn money through work, and then draw an X on the picture that shows a way to receive money as a gift; **4** circle the item that shows a need you can buy with the money shown.

© Pearson Education, Inc. K

1

○   ○   ○   ○

2

BAKE SALE

BAKE SALE!

YARD SALE!

Lemonade

○   ○   ○   ○

3

○   ○   ○   ○

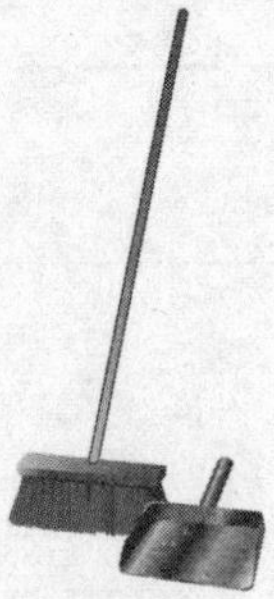

Directions   Have students mark the best answer. **1** Which activity shows a way to earn money? **2** Which shows a job that does **not** use counting money as a skill? **3** Which does **not** show an activity you could do to earn money?

Topic 16

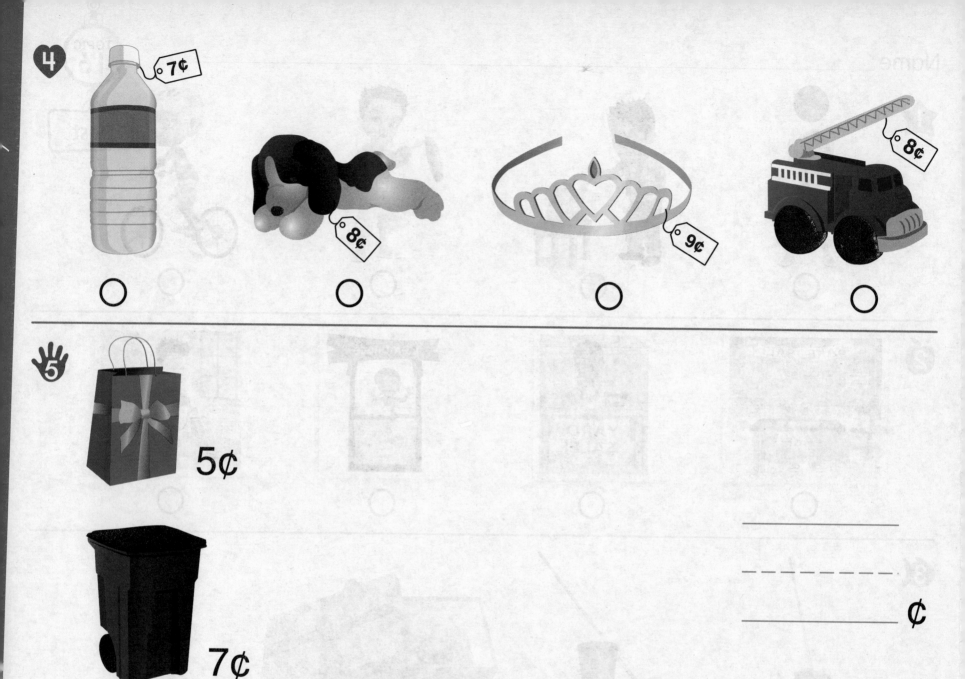

4

7¢   8¢   9¢   8¢

○   ○   ○   ○

5

5¢

7¢

_____

- - - - -

_____ ¢

Directions Have students: ❤ mark the best answer. Ask: *Which shows a need you can buy with 10 cents?* ✋ listen to the story about getting money, draw coins to show the amounts, compare the amounts, find the difference between the 2 amounts, and then write the number. Say: *Lisa is given 5¢ as a gift and earns 7¢ taking out the trash.*

Here's a preview of next year. These lessons help you step up to Grade 1.

Step Up to Grade 1

Lessons

TEKS 1.2B Use ... models to compose and decompose numbers up to 120 in more than one way as so many hundreds, so many tens, and so many ones.

TEKS 1.2E Use place value to compare whole numbers up to 120 using comparative language.

TEKS 1.3B Use objects and pictorial models to solve word problems involving joining, separating, and comparing sets within 20 and unknowns as any one of the terms in the problem ....

TEKS 1.5B Skip count by twos, fives, and tens to determine the total number of objects up to 120 in a set.

TEKS 1.6A Classify and sort regular and irregular two-dimensional shapes based on attributes using informal geometric language.

TEKS 1.6D Identify two-dimensional shapes, including circles, triangles, rectangles, and squares, as special rectangles, rhombuses, and hexagons ....

TEKS 1.6E Identify three-dimensional solids ... and describe their attributes using formal geometric language.

The following Grade 1 TEKS are introduced in the Step-Up Lessons.

Name _____

Solve & Share

For each problem, show a different way to cover each balloon with 1 blue or 1 red tile. Write the number of each tile. Does the number of blue or red tiles change the total number of balloons?

⭐ TEKS 1.3B Use objects and pictorial models to solve word problems involving joining, ... within 20 and unknowns as any one of the terms in the problem .... **Mathematical Process Standards 1.1A, 1.1C, 1.1D, 1.1E, 1.1F.**

Digital Resources at PearsonTexas.com

| Solve | Learn | Glossary | Tools | Games |

1. __5__ ▨ and __7__ ▨

2. _____ ▨ and _____ ▨

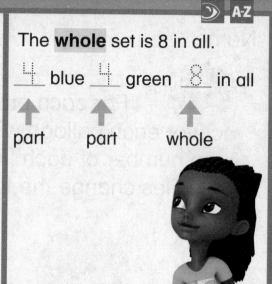

Kami has a set of 8 balloons in all.

Part of the set is blue.

4 are blue.

Part of the set is green.

4 are green.

The **whole** set is 8 in all.

4 blue 4 green 8 in all

↑ part   ↑ part   ↑ whole

Do You Understand?

Show Me! Is 4 and 5 another way to show 8? Explain.

☆ **Guided Practice** ☆ Write the numbers to show parts of 8.

1.

6  and 2

2.

____ and ____

3.

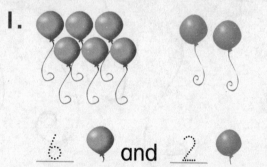

____ and ____

4.

____ and ____

© Pearson Education, Inc. K

Step Up | Lesson 1

☆ **Independent** ☆ **Practice**   Write the numbers to show parts of 9.

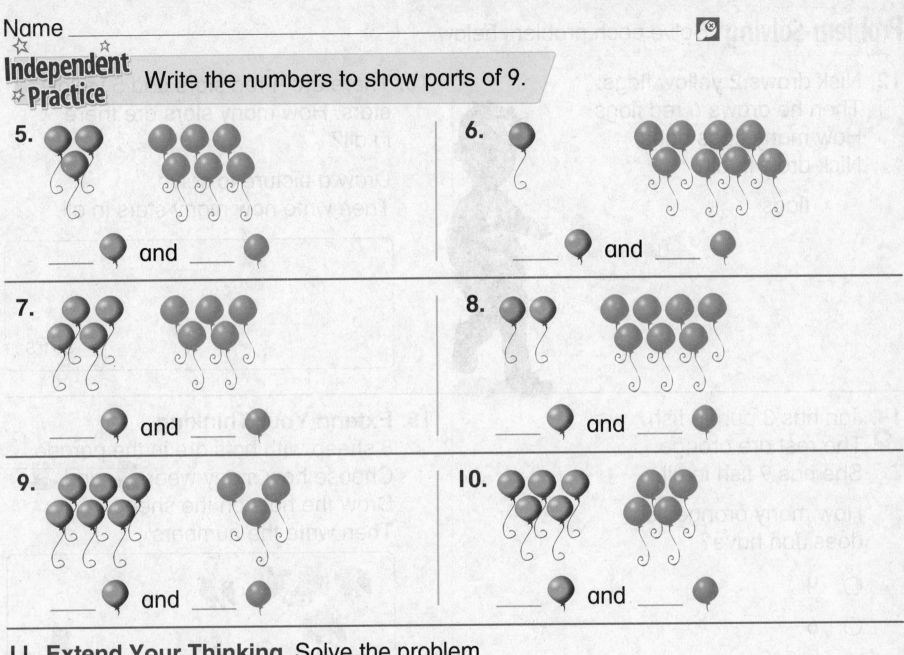

5. ____ 🎈 and ____ 🎈

6. ____ 🎈 and ____ 🎈

7. ____ 🎈 and ____ 🎈

8. ____ 🎈 and ____ 🎈

9. ____ 🎈 and ____ 🎈

10. ____ 🎈 and ____ 🎈

11. Extend Your Thinking Solve the problem.

There are 9 hats in all. 2 are red.
The rest are yellow. How many hats are yellow?   ____ yellow hats

Problem Solving Solve each problem below.

12. Nick draws 2 yellow flags.
Then he draws 6 red flags.
How many flags does
Nick draw in all?

_____ flags

Use counters to solve.

13. There are 4 red stars and 5 yellow stars. How many stars are there in all?

Draw a picture to solve.
Then write how many stars in all.

_____ stars

14. Jan has 3 purple fish.
☆ The rest are orange.
She has 9 fish in all.

How many orange fish
does Jan have?

○ 4

○ 6

○ 8

○ 10

15. Extend Your Thinking
8 sheep with hats are in the parade.
Choose how many wear 🎩 and 🎩.
Draw the hats on the sheep.
Then write the numbers.

_____

_____

_____ in all

Name _____

Solve & Share

Your bag has 2 different colors of connecting cubes. Take out a handful of cubes. Make sure to get some cubes of each color.

How can you use numbers to show how many cubes you picked in all? Show how.

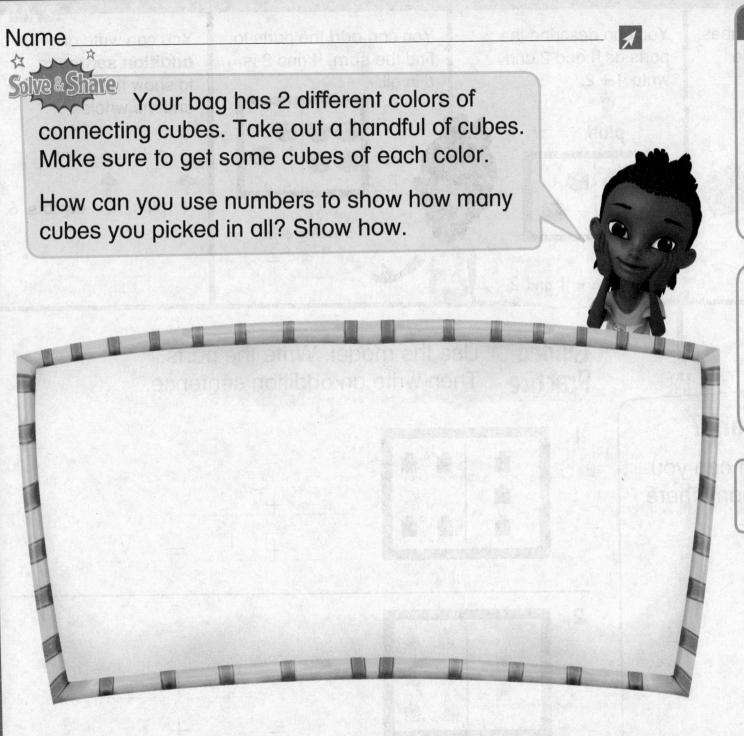

⭐ **TEKS 1.3B** Use objects and pictorial models to solve word problems involving joining, ... within 20 and unknowns as any one of the terms in the problem ... . Also, 1.5D, 1.5E. **Mathematical Process Standards** 1.1B, 1.1C, 1.1D, 1.1F, 1.1G.

Digital Resources at PearsonTexas.com

 Solve   Learn   A-Z Glossary   Tools   Games

Kenny picked 4 red cubes. Then he picked 2 blue cubes.

You can describe the parts as 4 and 2 and write 4 + 2.

plus

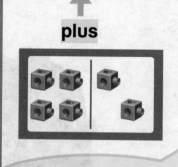

The parts are 4 and 2.

You can **add** the parts to find the **sum**. 4 and 2 is 6 in all.

6 is the sum of 4 and 2.

You can write an **addition sentence** to show the parts and the whole.

4 + 2 = 6

4 plus 2 **equals** 6.

Do You Understand?

Show Me! What can you do to find how many there are in all?

☆ **Guided Practice** ☆ Use the model. Write the parts. Then write an addition sentence.

1.

___3___ + ___4___

___3___ + ___4___ = ___7___

2.

___ + ___

___ = ___ + ___

Step Up | Lesson 2

Independent Practice

Use the model. Write the parts. Then write an addition sentence.

3.

___ + ___

___ + ___ = ___

4.

___ + ___

___ + ___ = ___

5.

___ + ___

___ = ___ + ___

6. **Extend Your Thinking** Jim picked up 9 rocks. He picked up 4 of them on his way to school. He picked up the rest on his way home. How many rocks did Jim pick up on his way home?

Draw a picture to solve.
Then write an addition sentence.

___ + ___ = ___

Problem Solving Solve each problem below.

7. Ben found 4 orange leaves.
Then he found 3 yellow leaves.
How many leaves did Ben
find in all?

Draw a picture to show the story.
Then write an addition sentence.

____ + ____ = ____

8. Ava drew 9 apples. 3 of them are
green. The others are red.
How many red apples did she draw?

Which addition sentence matches
this story?

○ 9 + 3 = 12

○ 4 + 5 = 9

○ 3 + 6 = 9

○ 3 + 3 = 6

9. **Extend Your Thinking** Draw a
picture to show an addition story
about red worms and brown worms.
Write an addition sentence to tell
how many worms there are in all.

____ = ____ + ____

© Pearson Education, Inc. K

Step Up | Lesson 2

Name _____

Solve & Share

Beth has 9 dogs. 5 are outside the doghouse. The rest are inside. How can you find out how many dogs are inside?

⊕ TEKS 1.3B Use objects and pictorial models to solve word problems involving ... separating, ... within 20 and unknowns as any one of the terms in the problem ... . **Mathematical Process Standards 1.1A, 1.1B, 1.1C, 1.1D.**

Digital Resources at PearsonTexas.com

Solve   Learn   Glossary   Tools   Games

There are 8 counters in all.

8

There are 6 counters in the part you know.

8

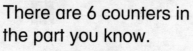

How many counters are in the missing part?

8

 I know that 6 and 2 are parts of 8.

8

6
part
I know

2
missing
part

Do You Understand?

Show Me! There are 8 counters. 3 are **not** covered. How can you find the number of covered counters?

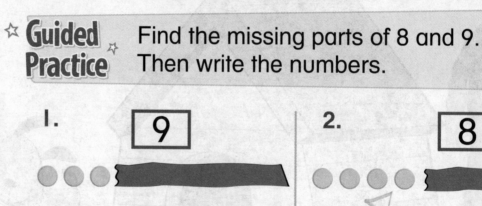 **Guided Practice** Find the missing parts of 8 and 9. Then write the numbers.

1. **9**

3
part I know

6
missing part

2. **8**

4
part I know

4
missing part

3. **8**

2
part I know

6
missing part

4. **9**

4
part I know

5
missing part

Name _____

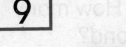
Find the missing parts of 8 and 9. Then write the numbers.

5. 9

●●●●●●● ▬▬▬

part I know   missing part

6. 8

●●●●● ▬▬▬

part I know   missing part

7. 9

●●●●●●●● ▬▬

part I know   missing part

Find the missing part. Complete the addition sentence.

8. Dave has 8 bagels. He toasts 3 of them. How many bagels are **not** toasted?

$3 + \underline{\quad} = 8$

9. Kathy has 9 eggs. 5 eggs hatched. How many eggs did **not** hatch?

$5 + \underline{\quad} = 9$

10. Extend Your Thinking There are 8 dogs. There are 4 more small dogs than big dogs. Draw a picture to find the missing part. Then write the numbers.

_____ small dogs and _____ big dogs

Problem Solving Use counters to solve each problem below.

11. Jan has 9 blocks. 3 blocks are green. The rest are pink. How many blocks are pink?

_____ blocks

12. Joey sees 8 frogs. Some of the frogs are in the pond. 6 frogs are on the grass. How many frogs are in the pond?

_____ frogs

13. There are 9 mice in all. 3 mice are on the cheese. The rest are not. How many mice are **not** on the cheese?

| 3 | 5 | 6 | 9 |
| O | O | O | O |

14. **Extend Your Thinking** There are 9 marbles in all. There is 1 inside the jar. The rest are outside. Draw a picture to match the story, and then write how many are inside and outside.

_____ inside _____ outside

Name _____

Solve & Share

Alex has 5 connecting cubes on the table. He hides some cubes. How can you use numbers to show how many cubes are hidden?

⊕ **TEKS 1.3B** Use objects and pictorial models to solve word problems involving ... separating, ... within 20 and unknowns as any one of the terms in the problem ... . Also, 1.5D, 1.5E. **Mathematical Process Standards 1.1B, 1.1C, 1.1E, 1.1F.**

Digital Resources at PearsonTexas.com

| Solve | Learn | Glossary | Tools | Games |

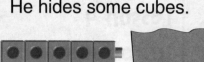 Mike has 8 cubes. He hides some cubes.

5 is the part you see. What is the hidden part?

You can describe the whole as 8 and one of the parts as 5. Find the hidden part by writing 8 − 5.

8

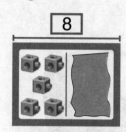

You can **subtract** to find the **difference**. 8 − 5 is 3.

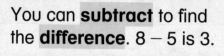
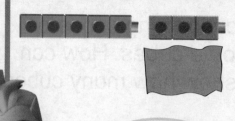

3 is the hidden part. It is the difference.

You can write a **subtraction sentence**.

$$8 - 5 = 3$$

8

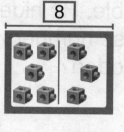

8 minus 5 equals 3.

Do You Understand?

Show Me! The whole is 9. One of the parts is 3. How can you find the difference?

☆ **Guided Practice** ☆ Complete the model. Write the parts. Then write a subtraction sentence.

1.

6

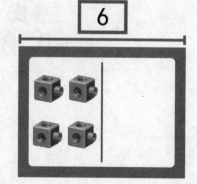

$$\underline{6} - \underline{4}$$

$$\underline{6} - \underline{4} = \underline{2}$$

2.

8

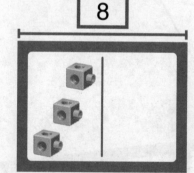

$$\underline{} - \underline{}$$

$$\underline{} = \underline{} - \underline{}$$

© Pearson Education, Inc. K

Name _____

Complete the model. Write the parts.
Then write a subtraction sentence.

3.

| 7 |

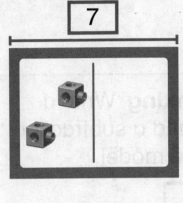

___ − ___

___ − ___ = ___

4.

| 9 |

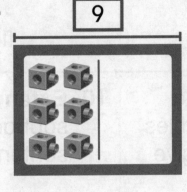

___ − ___

___ − ___ = ___

5.

| 6 |

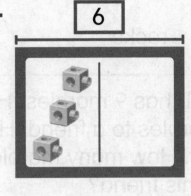

___ − ___

6. **Extend Your Thinking** There are
7 kittens in all. 1 is inside a basket.
The rest are outside. How many
kittens are outside the basket?

Draw a picture to show the story.
Then write the missing part.

7 − ____ = 1

Problem Solving Use cubes to solve each problem below.

7. Lena has 8 rocks.
She drops 4 of the rocks into a pond.
How many rocks does Lena have now?

_____ rocks

8. Tony picks 7 flowers.
He gives 4 flowers to his sister.
How many flowers does Tony still have?

_____ flowers

9. Rob has 9 marbles. He gave some marbles to a friend. He has 2 marbles left. How many marbles did Rob give to his friend?

Choose the subtraction sentence that matches the story.

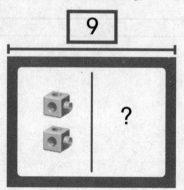

○ $9 - 3 = 3$

○ $9 - 2 = 7$

○ $7 - 3 = 4$

○ $7 - 2 = 5$

10. Extend Your Thinking Write a subtraction story and a subtraction sentence about the model.

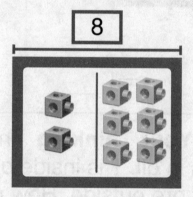

_____ − _____ = _____

Name _____

⭐ **Solve & Share**

Guess how many cubes are in your bag. Then empty the bag in the space below. Without counting each cube, guess how many cubes there are. Write each guess.

Now count the cubes and write the total number of cubes.

 TEKS 1.2B Use ... models to compose and decompose numbers up to 120 in more than one way as so many hundreds, so many tens, and so many ones. Also, 1.2C. **Mathematical Process Standards** 1.1C, 1.1D, 1.1E.

Digital Resources at PearsonTexas.com

Solve Learn Glossary Tools Games

Guess 1: _____ cubes

Guess 2: _____ cubes

Actual number:

_____ cubes

35 stands for 3 tens and 5 ones.

The 3 in 35 is the tens digit. The 5 in 35 is the ones digit.

35 has 2 digits.

Tens	Ones
3 tens	5 ones

Tens	Ones
3	5

35

You can use a model to show the tens and ones.

The tens digit goes on the left. The ones digit goes on the right.

Do You Understand?

Show Me! How are these numbers alike? How are they different?

46 **64**

☆ Guided Practice ☆

Count the tens and ones. Then write the numbers.

1.

Tens	Ones

→

Tens	Ones
2	5

25

2.

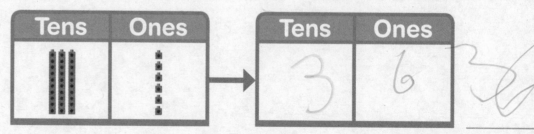

Tens	Ones

→

Tens	Ones
3	6

36

850 eight hundred fifty

Step Up | Lesson 5

Name _____

☆ **Independent**
☆ **Practice**

Count the tens and ones. Then write the numbers.

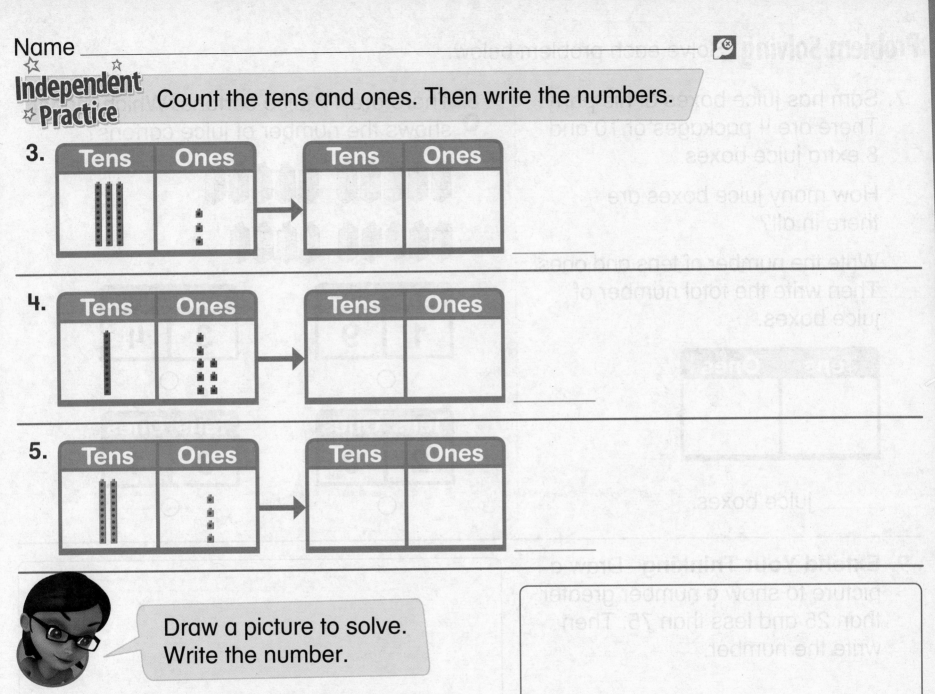

3.

Tens	Ones

Tens	Ones

4.

Tens	Ones

Tens	Ones

5.

Tens	Ones

Tens	Ones

Draw a picture to solve.
Write the number.

6. **Extend Your Thinking** Mary has a number. It has the same number of tens and ones. What could Mary's number be?

7. Sam has juice boxes at his party. There are 4 packages of 10 and 8 extra juice boxes.

How many juice boxes are there in all?

Write the number of tens and ones. Then write the total number of juice boxes.

Tens	Ones

_____ juice boxes

8. There are 19 juice cartons. Which model shows the number of juice cartons?

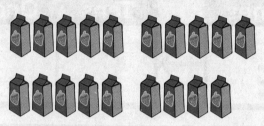

Tens	Ones
1	9

○

Tens	Ones
3	4

○

Tens	Ones
2	9

○

Tens	Ones
9	1

○

9. **Extend Your Thinking** Draw a picture to show a number greater than 25 and less than 75. Then write the number.

My number is _____.

Name ______________________________

Step Up to Grade 1

Lesson 6

Making 120 with Tens

Solve & Share

Alex put counters on some ten-frames. What is an easy way to count how many counters there are in all? Count how many and write the number.

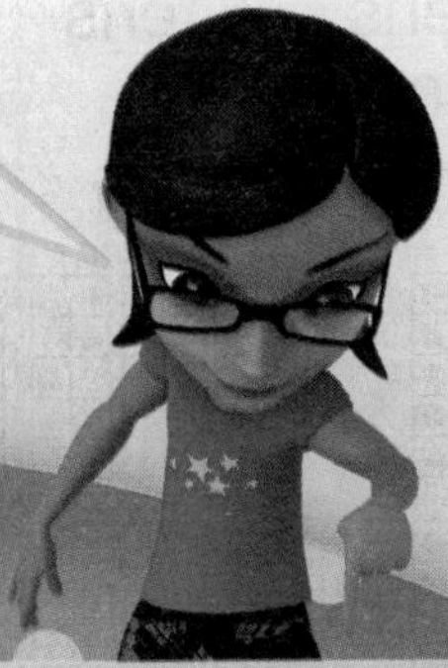

TEKS 1.5B Skip count by twos, fives, and tens to determine the total number of objects up to 120 in a set. Also, 1.2C, 1.5C. **Mathematical Process Standards** 1.1B, 1.1C, 1.1D.

Digital Resources at PearsonTexas.com

Solve | Learn | Glossary | Tools | Games

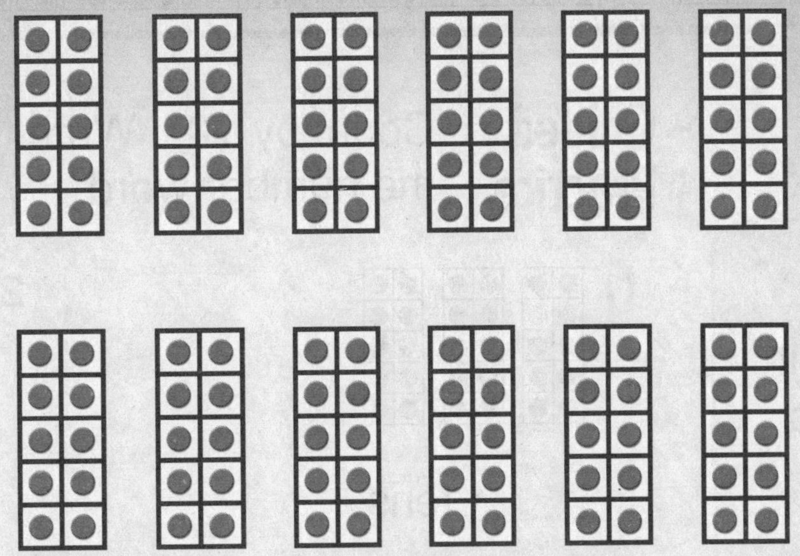

_____ counters in all.

Let's count by 10s.

1 ten	2 tens	3 tens	4 tens	5 tens	6 tens	7 tens	8 tens	9 tens	10 tens
10	20	30	40	50	60	70	80	90	100
ten	twenty	thirty	forty	fifty	sixty	seventy	eighty	ninety	one hundred

11 tens is 110. One hundred ten.

12 tens is 120. One hundred twenty.

Do You Understand?

Show Me! When might it be better to count by 10s instead of by 1s?

⭐ **Guided Practice** ⭐ Count by 10s. Write the numbers and the number word.

1.

___3___ tens

__30__

thirty

2.

_____ tens

_____

_____

© Pearson Education, Inc. K

Independent Practice

Count by 10s. Write the numbers and the number word.

3.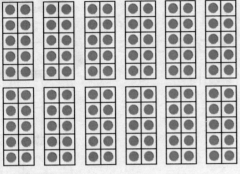

_____ tens

_____

_____

4.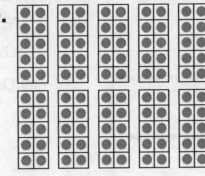

_____ tens

_____

_____

5.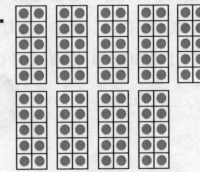

_____ tens

_____

_____

Write the missing numbers.

6. **Extend Your Thinking**

Mike writes a pattern.

He forgets to write some numbers.
What numbers did Mike forget to write?

What is Mike's pattern?

10, 20, 30, _____, _____, 60, 70, _____, 90, _____, 110, 120

Problem Solving

Draw counters in the ten-frames to solve each problem below. Then write the numbers and the number word.

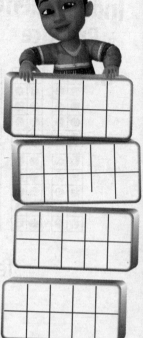

7. Miguel has 4 boxes. 10 books are in each box. How many books does Miguel have in all?

_____ tens

_____

8. Max has 6 boxes. There are 10 books in each box. How many books does Max have in all?

_____ tens

_____

9. Tanya has some books. She puts them in piles of 10. Which number does **not** show how many books Tanya could have?

○ 30

○ 40

○ 45

○ 50

10. Extend Your Thinking Tod counts by 5s to 50. Alex counts by 10s to 50. Write the numbers Tod says.

5, _____, _____, _____, _____,

_____, _____, _____, 50

Write the numbers Alex says.

10, _____, _____, _____, 50

What numbers do both boys say?

_____, _____, _____, _____, _____

Name _____

Solve & Share

How can place-value blocks help you decide which number is larger? Circle the number that is larger.

37   73

⊕ TEKS 1.2E Use place value to compare whole numbers up to 120 using comparative language. Also, 1.2. Mathematical Process Standards 1.1C, 1.1F, 1.1G.

Digital Resources at PearsonTexas.com

| Solve | Learn | Glossary | Tools | Games |

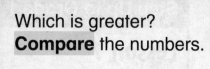

Which is greater?
Compare the numbers.

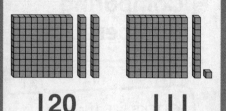

120   111

First, compare the hundreds.

The hundreds are the same.
So, compare the tens.

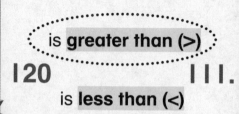

is **greater than (>)**

120   111.

is **less than (<)**

120 has more
tens than 111.

Now compare
these numbers.

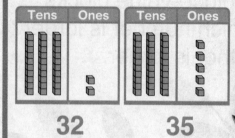

32   35

The tens are the same.
So, compare the ones.

is greater than

32   35.

is less than

32 has fewer ones
than 35.

Do You Understand?

Show Me! Which number
is greater, 38 or 26? How
do you know?

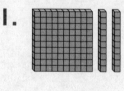

☆ **Guided Practice** ☆   Write a number to match each model.
Then circle **is greater than** or **is less than**.

1.

120   is greater than

is less than   113.

2.

is greater than

_____   is less than   _____.

Name _____

Write a number to match each model.
Then circle **is greater than** or **is less than**.

3.

_____ is greater than

_____ is less than _____ .

4.

_____ is greater than

_____ is less than _____ .

5.

_____ is greater than

_____ is less than _____ .

6.

_____ is greater than

_____ is less than _____ .

7.

_____ is greater than

_____ is less than _____ .

8.

_____ is greater than

_____ is less than _____ .

9. Extend Your Thinking Read the clues
to find the mystery number.

The number is greater than 40. It has 5
1s. It is less than 49. What is the mystery
number?

Draw a picture to show the number.
Then write the number.

The mystery number is _____ .

Problem Solving — Solve each problem below. Then complete each sentence.

10. Maya sees 26 girls at the park. She sees 34 boys at the park.

Does Maya see more girls or more boys?

She sees more _____.

_____ is less than _____.

11. Kyle counts 119 pennies. He counts 113 dimes.

Does Kyle count more pennies or more dimes?

He counts more _____.

_____ is greater than _____.

12. Tina has 36 shells. Chris has fewer shells than Tina.

How many shells could Chris have?

| 33 | 36 | 39 | 42 |
| ○ | ○ | ○ | ○ |

13. **Extend Your Thinking** Choose 2 numbers between 100 and 120. Write a sentence that compares the numbers.

My numbers are _____ and _____.

I can draw a picture to show a number as hundreds, tens, and ones.

Name _____

Solve & Share

Circle 2 shapes that are the same in some way. Tell what's the same about them in the red box.

Put an *X* on 2 shapes that are different. Tell what's different about them in the yellow box.

⊕ **TEKS 1.6A** Classify and sort regular and irregular two-dimensional shapes based on attributes using informal geometric language. Also, 1.6. **Mathematical Process Standards** 1.1D, 1.1E, 1.1F, 1.1G.

A B C D

E F G H

Digital Resources at PearsonTexas.com

Solve	Learn	Glossary	Tools	Games

Same

_____

_____

_____

Different

_____

_____

_____

Look at how the **plane shapes** below are alike and different.

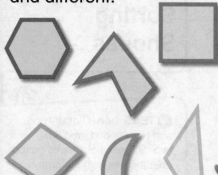

You can **sort** plane shapes by how they look.

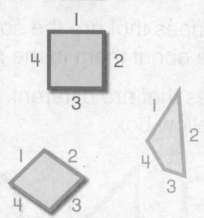

I am going to sort and find shapes that have 4 sides.

All 3 of these shapes have 4 **sides**.

```
    1
 4 □ 2
    3

   1
  2
 4  3

 1  2
  ◇
 4  3
```

These shapes do not have 4 sides.

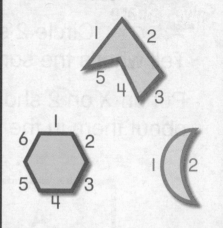

Do You Understand?

Show Me! Which 2 shapes would you put in the same group? Tell why.

☆ **Guided Practice** ☆ Solve each problem below.

1. Circle the shapes that have 5 straight sides.

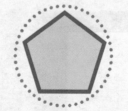 

---

2. Circle the shapes that have fewer than 5 straight sides.

862 eight hundred sixty-two

Name _____

Solve each problem below.

3. Circle the shapes that have more than 3 straight sides.

4. Circle the shapes that have 4 straight sides.

5. Circle the shapes that have straight sides.

6. Circle the shapes that have curved sides.

7. Extend Your Thinking Draw 2 different shapes with straight sides.

8. Extend Your Thinking Karla draws 2 shapes. The shapes do **not** have straight sides. Draw the 2 shapes Karla could have drawn.

Problem Solving Solve each problem below.

9. Ron collects pictures of things that have curved sides. He found a picture of the sun and a picture of a table.

Circle the picture Ron will put in his collection.

10. Fay draws a picture of a door. Eysha draws a picture of a basketball. Circle the picture that does **not** have curved sides.

---

11. Which plane shape has 4 sides?

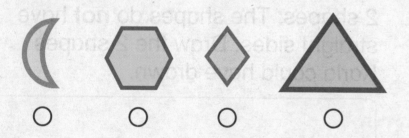

○   ○   ○   ○

12. Extend Your Thinking Circle 2 shapes. Tell how they are the same. Then tell how they are different.

Same	Different

© Pearson Education, Inc. K

Step Up | Lesson 8

Name ____________________

Step Up to Grade 1

Lesson 9

Identifying Plane Shapes

Solve & Share Draw an object from your classroom that matches each shape below.

How do you know that the shape you drew is the same as the one on the page?

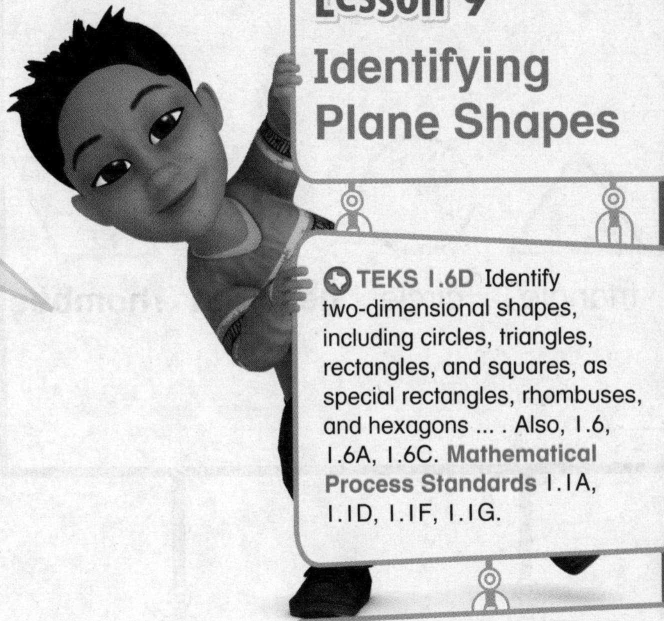

TEKS 1.6D Identify two-dimensional shapes, including circles, triangles, rectangles, and squares, as special rectangles, rhombuses, and hexagons ... . Also, 1.6, 1.6A, 1.6C. **Mathematical Process Standards** 1.1A, 1.1D, 1.1F, 1.1G.

Digital Resources at PearsonTexas.com

Solve Learn Glossary Tools Games

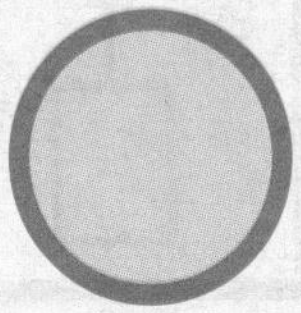

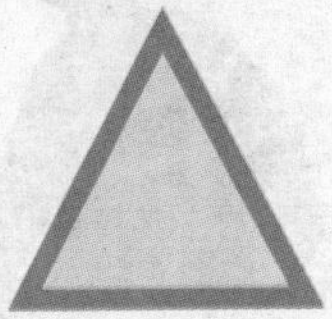

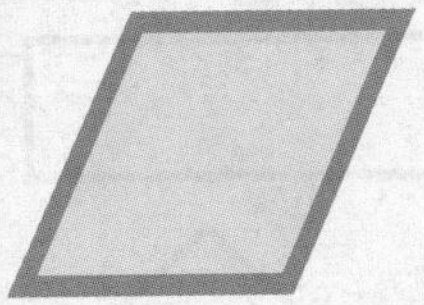

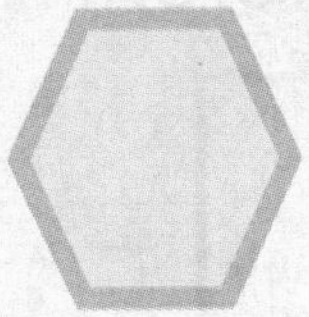

2-D shapes are plane shapes.
Plane shapes are flat shapes.

triangle   circle   **hexagon**   **rhombus**

rectangle   square

A square is a special rectangle.

You can see plane shapes in solid objects.

JUICE

B

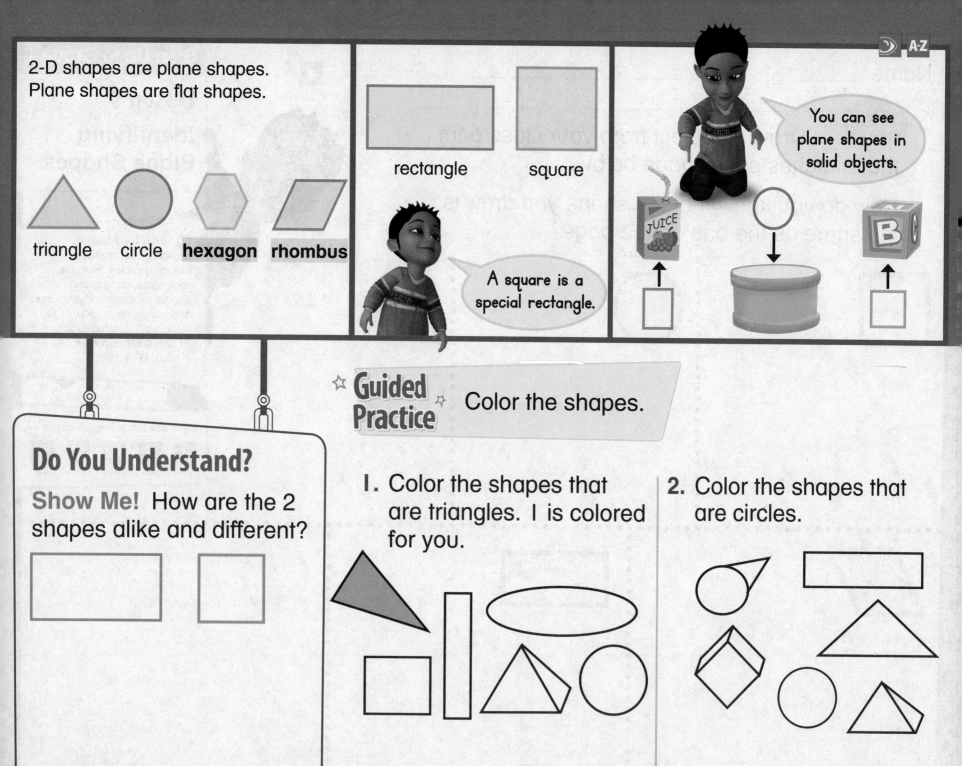

Do You Understand?

Show Me! How are the 2 shapes alike and different?

☆ **Guided Practice** ☆ Color the shapes.

1. Color the shapes that are triangles. 1 is colored for you.

2. Color the shapes that are circles.

© Pearson Education, Inc. K

Step Up | Lesson 9

Name _____

Draw each shape.

3. Draw a circle.

4. Draw a triangle.

5. Draw a square.

6. Draw a rectangle.

7. Draw a hexagon.

8. Draw a rhombus.

9. Extend Your Thinking Name the plane shape that you see in each object.

_____

_____

_____

_____

10. Vana sees a plane shape.
It looks like a round button.
It also looks like a dime.
What shape does Vana see?

11. Peter draws a plane shape.
It has 4 sides. The sides are the same length. The sides are straight lines.
What shape does Peter draw?

12. I am a plane shape.
I look like a coin.
Which shape am I?

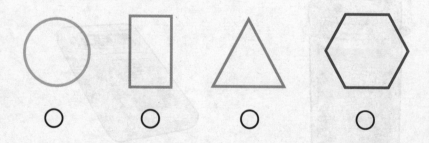

13. Extend Your Thinking Draw pictures of objects in your classroom. Write the names of the shapes in the objects you draw.

Name ______________________________

Solve & Share

Can you find objects in the classroom that are shaped like the objects below? Write the name of the object you find.

Step Up to Grade 1

Lesson 10
Identifying Solid Figures

TEKS 1.6E Identify three-dimensional solids ... and describe their attributes using formal geometric language. Also, 1.6. **Mathematical Process Standards** 1.1A, 1.1C, 1.1D, 1.1F.

Digital Resources at PearsonTexas.com

Solve | Learn | Glossary | Tools | Games

____

____

____

____

____

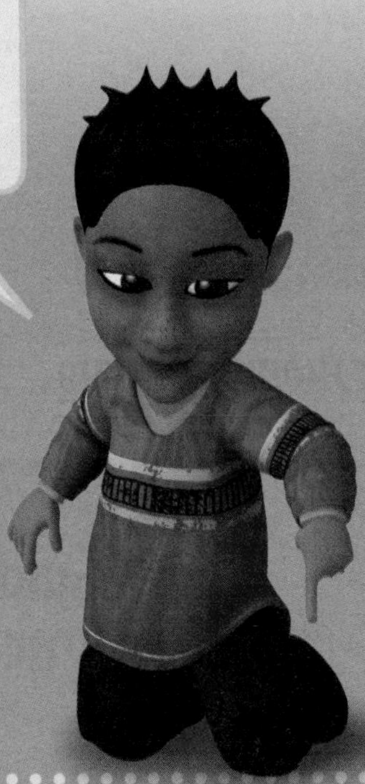

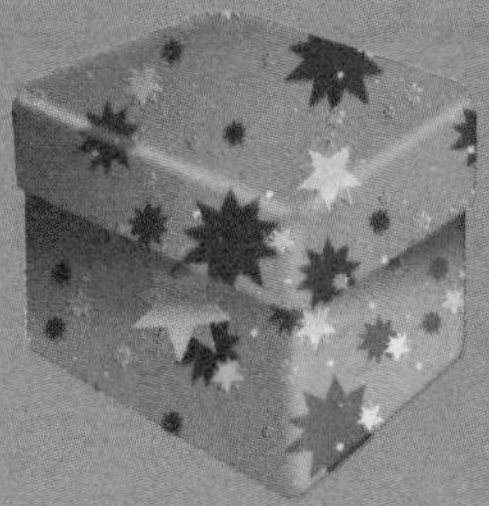

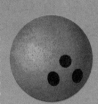

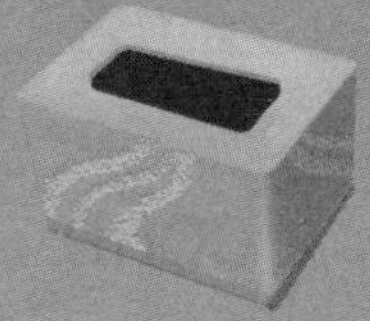

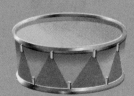

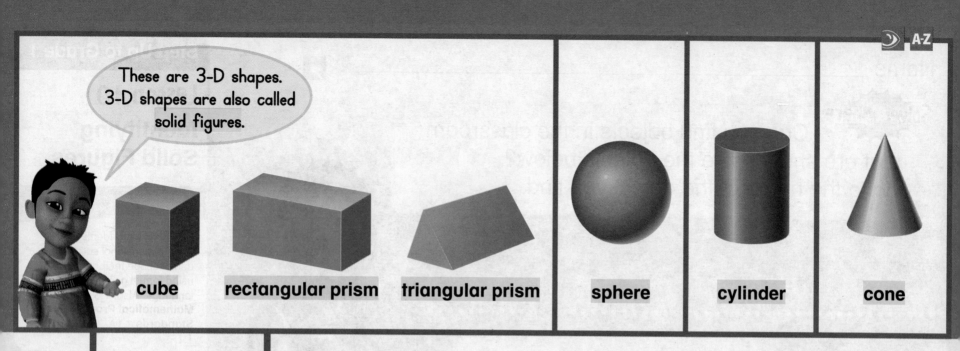

These are 3-D shapes. 3-D shapes are also called solid figures.

cube **rectangular prism** **triangular prism** **sphere** **cylinder** **cone**

Do You Understand?

Show Me! How are solid figures different from plane shapes?

 Guided Practice
Look at the solid figure. Then circle the objects that have almost the same shape.

1.

cone

2.

sphere

© Pearson Education, Inc. K

Name _____

Look at the solid figure. Then circle the objects that have the same shape.

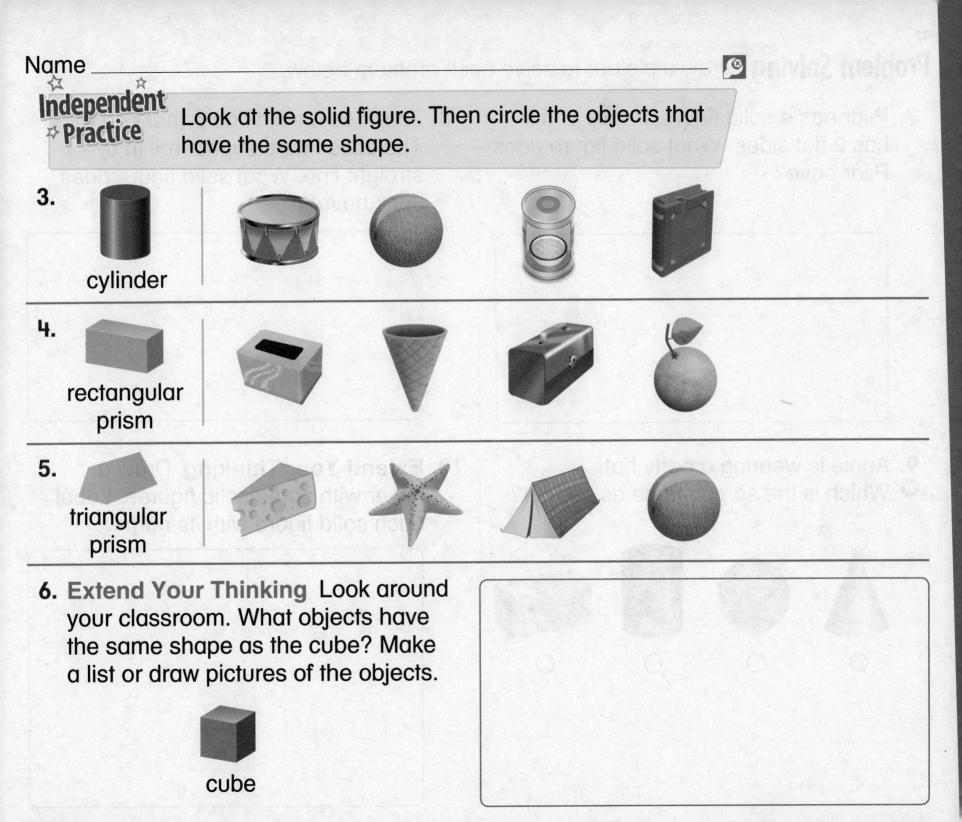

3. cylinder

4. rectangular prism

5. triangular prism

6. Extend Your Thinking Look around your classroom. What objects have the same shape as the cube? Make a list or draw pictures of the objects.

cube

7. Pilar has a solid figure. It rolls and it has 2 flat sides. What solid figure does Pilar have?

8. Jack has a solid figure that can roll. The solid figure cannot roll in a straight line. What solid figure does Jack have?

9. Annie is wearing a party hat. Which is the same shape as her hat?

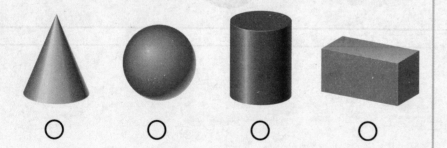

○   ○   ○   ○

10. Extend Your Thinking Draw a tower with some solid figures. Label each solid figure with its name.

Glossary

1 fewer

1 more

2 fewer

2 more

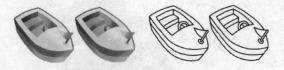

about the same

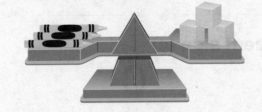

above

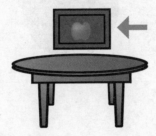

add

$$3 + 2 = 5$$

addition sentence

$$4 + 1 = 5$$

after

after

25   26

as long as
(same length as)

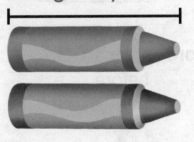

as short as

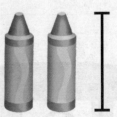

as tall as

balance scale

before

before

↓

25 26

below

cent

I cent (¢)

cent sign (¢)

circle

coin

column

1	2	3	4	5
11	12	13	14	15
21	22	23	24	25
31	32	33	34	35

compare

more

fewer

cone

corner

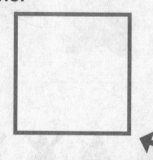

cost

3¢

count

1   2   3

count by 2s

count by 10s

cube

cylinder

difference

$$8 - 3 = 5$$

different

dime

10 cents (10¢)

does not belong

double ten-frame

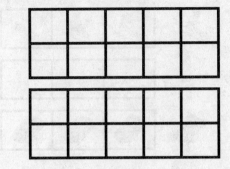

earn

equal sign (=)

$$4 + 3 = 7$$

fewer (than)

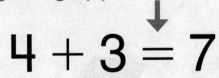

fewest

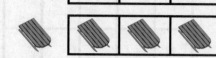

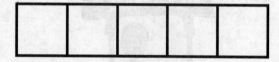

five-frame

flat surface

gift

graph

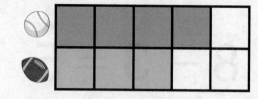

greater (than)

9   **6**

heavier

height

holds

hundred chart

column

1	2	3	4	5	6	7	8	9	10
11	12	13	14	15	16	17	18	19	20
21	22	23	24	25	26	27	28	29	30
31	32	33	34	35	36	37	38	39	40
41	42	43	44	45	46	47	48	49	50
51	52	53	54	55	56	57	58	59	60
61	62	63	64	65	66	67	68	69	70
71	72	73	74	75	76	77	78	79	80
81	82	83	84	85	86	87	88	89	90
91	92	93	94	95	96	97	98	99	100

row

in all

© Pearson Education, Inc. K

income

join

left

length

less (than)

lighter

longer

minus sign (−)

$$8 - 3 = 5$$

model

more (than)

most

need

nickel

5 cents (5¢)

none

0

number story

1 and 3 is 4.

numbers

zero 0

one 1

two 2

three 3

four 4

five 5

six 6

seven 7

eight 8

nine 9

ten 10

order

0 → 1 → 2 → 3 → 4 → 5

part

pattern

10 20 30 40 50

penny

1 cent (¢)

picture graph

plus sign (+)

↓

3 + 1 = 4

Glossary

quarter

25 cents (25¢)

real graph

rectangle

related fact

 $1 + 3 = 4$

 $4 - 3 = 1$

roll

row

1	2	3	4	5
11	12	13	14	15
21	22	23	24	25
31	32	33	34	35

same (alike)

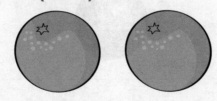

same number as

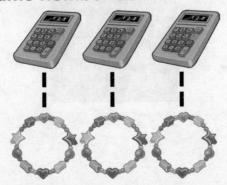

same shape

same size

separate

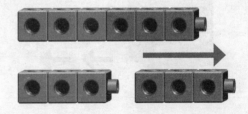

set

shorter

side

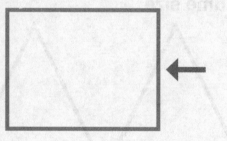

slide

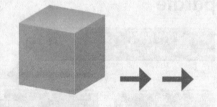

skill

5...　6...　7...　7¢

solid figure

sort

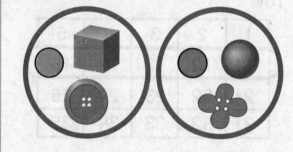

sphere

square

stack

subtract

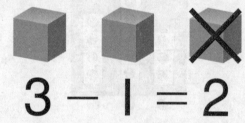

$3 - 1 = 2$

subtraction sentence

$3 - 1 = 2$

sum

$2 + 7 = 9$

survey

take away

taller

ten-frame

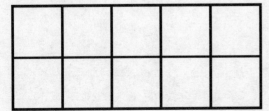

thirty

30

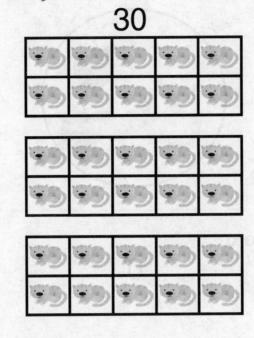

triangle

twenty

20

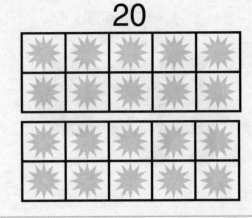

value

1¢   5¢

10¢   25¢

vertex (vertices)

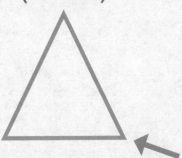

want

weighs

weight

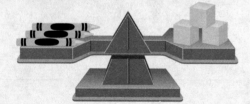

whole

zero

0

Photographs

Every effort has been made to secure permission and provide appropriate credit for photographic material. The publisher deeply regrets any omission and pledges to correct errors called to its attention in subsequent editions.

Unless otherwise acknowledged, all photographs are the property of Pearson Education, Inc.

Photo locators denoted as follows: Top (T), Center (C), Bottom (B), Left (L), Right (R), Background (Bkgd)

001 Artcphotos/Shutterstock;**075** Patryssia/Fotolia;**115** Christopher Elwell/Shutterstock;**189** Jorge Salcedo/Shutterstock;**233** Erik Lam/Shutterstock;**307** Remik44992/Shutterstock;**307** Remik44992/Shutterstock;**353** Tankist276/Shutterstock

469 Winai Tepsuttinun/Shutterstock;**515** Alon Othnay/Shutterstock;**565** Andrey Pavlov/Shutterstock;**603** Defpicture/Shutterstock;**665** Michael Flippo/Fotolia;**705** Michaela Stejskalova/Shutterstock;**755** Okeanas/Shutterstock;**793** WithGod/Shutterstock